The End of the Present World
and the
Mysteries of the Future Life

The End of the Present World

and the

Mysteries of the Future Life

by Father Charles Arminjon

Translated by
Susan Conroy and Peter McEnerny

SOPHIA INSTITUTE PRESS®
Manchester, New Hampshire

The End of the Present World and the Mysteries of the Future Life was originally published in 1881 in French under the title *Fin du Monde Présent et Mystères de la Vie Future*.

For the English translation of Sacred Scripture, we used the New American Bible, Saint Joseph Edition. In some instances, the Douay-Rheims edition more closely matched the Latin phrases interspersed throughout the original French text; these latter cases are footnoted accordingly.

Printed in the United States of America

Cover design by Ted Schluenderfritz

Cover painting: *Apocalypse* (1831), by Ludwig Ferdinand Schnorr von Carolsfeld (1788-1853); © Private Collection / The Bridgeman Art Library.

Sophia Institute Press®
Box 5284, Manchester, NH 03108
1-800-888-9344
www.sophiainstitute.com

Library of Congress Cataloging-in-Publication Data

Arminjon, Charles, 1824-1885.
    [Fin du monde présent et mystères de la vie future. English]
    The end of the present world and the mysteries of the future
life / by Charles Arminjon ; translated by Susan Conroy and Peter
McEnerny.
       p. cm.
    Includes bibliographical references.
    ISBN 978-1-933184-38-8 (pbk. : alk. paper) 1. Eschatology.
I. Title.
    BT821.3.A7613 2008
    236 — dc22

                       2008037585

Reading this was one of the greatest graces of my life. I read it at the window of my study, and the impression I received from it is too intimate and too sweet for me to express . . .
All the great truths of religion, the mysteries of eternity, plunged my soul into a happiness not of this earth . . .

St. Thérèse of Lisieux

Contents

Preface

St. Thérèse of Lisieux, "the Little Flower," gave us the most impressive endorsement of this book, *The End of the Present World and the Mysteries of the Future Life*:

> Reading this was one of the greatest graces of my life. I read
> it at the window of my study, and the impression I received
> from it is too intimate and too sweet for me to express . . .
> All the great truths of religion, the mysteries of eternity,
> plunged my soul into a happiness not of this earth . . . I ex-
> perienced already what God reserves for those who love
> Him (not with the eye of man, but with that of the heart),
> and seeing that the eternal rewards had no proportion to
> the light sacrifices of life, I wanted *to love, to love* Jesus with
> *passion*, to give Him a thousand proofs of love while I still
> could. I copied out several passages on perfect love, on the
> reception that the good God will give His elect at the mo-
> ment when *He Himself* becomes their great and eternal re-
> ward, and I kept repeating unceasingly the words of love
> burning in my heart."[1]

In spite of the *enormous* influence this book had on the life and heart of the greatest saint of modern times, who *in turn* has inspired millions of lives throughout the world for more than a *century*, no one had ever translated it into English and published it in America. I personally felt called — *compelled* — to bring back to life again this book that inspired in Thérèse "an irresistible impulse toward God," in the hope that it may have a similar influence on souls of our time.

The author, Father Charles Arminjon, was a highly esteemed preacher in France. His book consists of nine conferences that he preached at the Chambéry Cathedral and then published in 1881 under the title *Fin du Monde Présent et Mystères de la Vie Future*. He delivered these conferences with the express purpose of combating "the fatal error and great plague of our century," which he described as "the absence of the sense of the supernatural, and the profound neglect of the great truths of the future life."

St. Thérèse first read this book in May of 1887, when she was only fourteen years old. She told us that it immersed her in a happiness not of this world. It gave her a presentiment of what God reserves eternally for those who love Him. It taught her that our sacrifices in this life are almost as nothing compared with the rewards that await us in everlasting life.[2] It inspired her to love our Lord Jesus even more ardently — to love Him "with *passion*." And it reminded her that life on earth passes by very quickly, and so we should love and serve Him now, while we still can.

Very shortly after reading this book, with her heart aflame with the desire to give everything to God, Thérèse requested and obtained her father's permission to enter the cloistered Carmelite Monastery in Lisieux. According to Monsignor Andre Combes in *The Spirituality of Saint Thérèse*, Father Arminjon's writings had nourished in Thérèse an "impatience for the joys of Heaven and a paramount esteem for a life wholly consecrated to Divine Love." Thus, Father Arminjon deserves "not only a title to fame" for preaching and publishing these conferences, "but also a right to the *gratitude* of all devoted followers of St. Thérèse, and so of the whole Church."

And to that, I say, *Amen!*

⌒

On June 4 and 5 in the year 1887, St. Thérèse copied out the following extract from Father Arminjon's seventh conference, on "Eternal Beatitude and the Supernatural Vision of God":

As no mother ever loved her dearest son, so the Lord loves His predestinate. He is jealous of His dignity and could not permit Himself to be outdone by His creature on the score of fidelity and generosity. Oh! The Lord cannot forget that the saints, when they once lived on earth, paid homage to Him by the total donation of their repose, their happiness and their whole being; that they would have liked to have had an inexhaustible flow of blood in their veins, in order to shed it as a living and imperishable pledge of their faith; that they would have desired a thousand hearts in their breasts, so as to consume them in the unquenchable fires of their love; and to possess a thousand bodies, in order that they might deliver them to martyrdom, like victims unceasingly renewed. And the grateful God cries out: *Now, my turn!* The saints have given me the gift of themselves: can I respond other than by giving myself, without restriction and without measure? If I place in their hands the scepter of creation, if I surround them with the torrents of my light, that is a great deal; it is going beyond their highest hopes and aspirations, but it is not the utmost endeavor of my Heart. I owe them more than Paradise, more than the treasures of my knowledge; I owe them my life, my nature, my eternal and infinite substance. If I bring my servants and friends into my house, if I console them and make them thrill with joy by enfolding them in the embrace of my charity, this satisfies their thirst and their desires super-abundantly, and is more than the perfect repose of their hearts requires; but it is not enough for the gratification of my divine Heart, for the repletion and perfect satisfaction of my Love. I must be the soul of their souls, I must pene-trate and imbue them with my divinity, as fire penetrates iron; by showing myself to their spirits, undisguised, un-veiled, without the intervention of the senses, I must unite myself to them *in an eternal face-to-face*, so that my glory il-luminates them, exudes and radiates through all the pores of their being, so that, "knowing me as I know them, they may become Gods themselves."

St. Thérèse repeatedly referred to the phrases she had read from Father Arminjon's pen "as a guarantee to us that, at a certain time, she really did make it the guiding theme of her interior life, the foundation of her hope and the stimulus for all her sacrifices."

As soon as I had read St. Thérèse's enthusiastic endorsement of this book, I sought to find a copy of it. I searched for *years*. I even wrote a letter to the cloistered Carmelite nuns in Lisieux, France — at the very same convent where St. Thérèse lived for the last nine years of her life. The Sisters sent a handwritten letter back to me, in French, saying that they were unable to send me Father Arminjon's book because it was no longer published. At first, I was discouraged by their reply, but something inside me would not let me abandon my search. If this book had such an enormous influ-ence on the life of St. Thérèse, and if reading this was truly "one of the greatest graces" of her life, as she herself said it was, then there must be value in it, and it should not be dismissed so easily.

Finally, after approximately seven years of searching, I discovered *one single copy* of this book, written in its original French language and owned by a Carmelite priest, Father Donald Kinney. As I held this book in my hands, I felt as if I were holding a "lost treasure!" My heart has been on fire to share this treasure with others. Since 1987, I have dreamed of making this book available for English-speaking readers here in America. You are now holding my dream in your hands!

☞

It is very profitable for us to keep in mind what is traditionally referred to as "the four last things": death, judgment, heaven and hell — and Father Arminjon's conferences are a powerful aid in bringing these four last things to mind in a very unforgettable way! This book encourages us to live in this world with our hearts set on *the life to come* — with our "eye on the prize," so to speak. It inspires us to prepare our souls for God, to strive more earnestly to attain everlasting life with Christ, and to help save souls who will love Him eternally. It encourages us to avoid the pitfall of being overly preoccupied with the many distractions, anxieties, pleasures, and pursuits of this fleeting life on earth. "Vanity of vanities, and all is vanity, except to love God and to serve Him alone."[3]

Let me share with you another passage that clearly meant a great deal to the Little Flower. She copied it out by hand, dated it May 30, 1887, and kept in her *Manuel du Chrétien* at the Carmelite Monastery. It is a beautiful quotation from St. John Chrysostom about the effects of Divine Love when it takes hold of a soul, and it was taken from Father Arminjon's fifth conference, on purgatory:

The man who is inflamed with the fire of divine love is as indifferent to glory and ignominy as if he were alone and unseen on this earth. He spurns all temptations. He is no more troubled by pincers, gridirons, or racks than if these sufferings were endured in a body other than his own. What is full of sweetness for the world has no attraction for him, no taste; he is no more liable to be captivated by some evil attachment than is gold, seven times tested, liable to be tarnished by rust. Such are, even on this earth, the effects of divine love when it firmly takes hold of a soul.

Just before little Thérèse was called home to God in 1897, she wrote, "I feel that my mission is about to begin — my mission to make God loved as I love Him." I pray that St. Thérèse and Father Arminjon will intercede for us earnestly, that by opening our minds and hearts to the mysteries of the future life, we may be inspired to love and serve God more generously in this life — with a love as pure and ardent as that of the saints. And may we be so blessed as to hear Him say to us in heaven, "Now, my turn!"

Susan Conroy
Feast of Our Lady of Mount Carmel
July 16, 2008

Notes

1 Translated from *Histoire d'une Âme* (*Story of a Soul*), the autobiography of St. Thérèse of Lisieux.

2 Cf. Rom. 8:18.

3 Thomas à Kempis, *Imitation of Christ*; Eccles. 1:2.

Acknowledgments

I would like to express my sincere appreciation to all those who played such a marvelous role in bringing this book to life again. This English edition is the fruit of many years of work and a true "labor of love" on the part of *several* individuals. *Fr. Donald Kinney* showed stunning generosity in sending his rare French edition to me after I had been searching for a copy of it for seven years. I began translating it in the mid-1990s. Ten years into the project, I discovered that there were individuals in Ireland undertaking the same project. We agreed to collaborate in bringing this treasure to you. I am happy to acknowledge Mr. *Peter McEnerny* for his excellent work of translation, and Mr. *N. Martin Gwynne* of Britons Catholic Library for his enthusiastic participation in our efforts to share this book with English-speaking readers. Closer to home, Mr. *Paul Lerley* meticulously reviewed all of my own translation work throughout all nine chapters of this book. *Fr. John Heisler* and *Dr. Michael Rombeiro* graciously and generously assisted in translating the Latin into English.

Foreword

by Father Charles Arminjon

Dear Reader,

It has seemed to us that one of the saddest fruits of rationalism, the fatal error and great plague of our century, the pestilential source from which our revolutions and social disasters arise, is the absence of the sense of the supernatural and the profound neglect of the great truths of the future life. *The earth is afflicted with a dreadful desolation*, because the majority of men, fascinated by the lure of fleeting pleasures, and absorbed in their worldly interests and the care of their material affairs, no longer fix their thoughts on the principal considerations of the Faith, and stubbornly refuse to *recollect within themselves*. It may be said of our present generation what the prophet Daniel said, in his time, of the two old men of Babylon: "They suppressed their consciences; they would not allow their eyes to look to heaven, and did not keep in mind God's just judgments."[1]

The two causes of this terrifying indifference and profound universal lethargy are, obviously, ignorance and the unrestrained love of sensual pleasures that, by darkening the interior eye of the human soul, bring all its aspirations down to the narrow level of the present life, and cut it off from the vision of the beauties and rewards to come. Now, since wise men have found at all times that contradictions are overcome with their *opposites,* it seemed to us that the most efficacious remedy with which to fight confidently against the inveterate evil of *naturalism* was a lucid, clear, and exact exposition, without diminution, of the essential truths dealing with the future life and the inevitable termination of human destinies.

Perhaps we shall be accused of expressing this or that assertion of ours too crudely and starkly, and of broaching the most serious and formidable points of Christian doctrine, without, at the same time, modifying and softening them so as to adapt them to the prejudices or apathy of certain souls, unacquainted with such grave considerations — like a physician who carefully allows only a limited amount of light to a sick friend, in order not to hurt his painful eyes by excessive glare. However, in the religious and supernatural order, the phenomena and effects wrought upon the soul are often the reverse of those that occur in the physical and material order. In the visible world, an excessive amount of light dazzles: it leads to dimness of vision and causes blindness.

On the other hand, as soon as the mind enters the intellectual realm, and is transported into the vast sphere of invisible and uncreated matter, excess is no longer to be feared. Jesus Christ is the great luminary of our intellects, the food and life of our hearts: He is never better understood, or more loved, than when He manifests Himself liberally in the integrity of His doctrine and the most eminent splendors of His divine personality. The example of the Apostles, announcing the gospel amidst the twilight of paganism, and boldly preaching *Jesus Christ crucified* before the Roman Senate and amidst the philosophers of the Areopagus, is enough to tell us that truth is attractive to souls *naturally Christian,* and that it enlightens and convinces them only insofar as it is presented to them in all its strength and all its clarity.

Our trial is limited in its duration to the period of the present life. If, as the rationalists maintain, this life is only a link in the chain of our destiny, and if the course of time wherein man is subject to strife, temptation, and the blandishments of the senses and of creatures should continue indefinitely, then Jesus Christ will never be king, virtue brings no hope, and evil will remain eternally triumphant. Thus, it is quite certain that the scene being played here below will, sooner or later, reach its climax and end. Mankind will then enter upon a new phase of existence, and all that we cherish, all that we search after in this present life, will be less than a shadow, and vain smoke. This is a certain fact, which all our discoveries and the marvels of our genius will not be able to anticipate.

Now, the moral value of life is determined by the end to which it tends, just as the utility of a road is estimated by the traveler only insofar as it helps to bring him more surely and directly to the final point of the journey he has undertaken. Accordingly, to deal with the future life and the last ends is really to expound the science and philosophy of human life, setting out the fundamental principles on which the whole of perfection and morality is based.

The volume of our conferences that we are publishing is a continuation of the one we brought out on the *Reign of God*. The reign of God is inaugurated, grows, and comes to its completion in the course of time; it will not be perfect and consummated until the age to come. So, instead of giving our book the title *The End of the Present World and the Mysteries of the Future Life*, we could, with equal justice, have called it *The Triumph of Jesus Christ and His Church in the Future Life*.

Our arguments and maxims on the vanity of the *face of this passing world*, the futility of all undertakings conceived outside the perspective of the Faith and not having the final end as their aim, the irremediable misfortune reserved for the wicked, and our other subjects — the advent and reign of the Antichrist and the temple of immortality, the rewards destined for the just, the restoration of fallen man through the law of sacrifice and the purifying crucible of suffering — seemed useful to us in order to shed the salve of consolation upon wounded and embittered hearts, to lift up disheartened and dejected souls, and, in the calamitous and troubled days through which we are living, to help Christians become men of *Sursum*, by inspiring them with resignation and patience; in order, furthermore, to strengthen them amidst the present sorrows, by raising up their hopes and desires toward a better fatherland.

By drawing upon the pure founts of Tradition and the Fathers and instructing ourselves by the light of Holy Scripture, we have sought to satisfy the anxious and troubled souls of our time, and to offer them the true solution to the mysteries of life as taught to us by Christianity. May we contribute to making Jesus Christ and His Church loved, and to inculcating more and more in those who read our work this cardinal truth: "To serve God and keep His Commandments is the whole of man!"

Chambéry
May 8, 1881

---

[1] Dan. 13:9.

The End of the Present World
and the
Mysteries of the Future Life

First Conference

‿

The End of the World

The Signs That Will Precede It and the Circumstances That Will Accompany It

Veniet dies Domini sicut fur,
in quo coeli magno impetu transient.

‿

The day of the Lord will come like a thief,
and on that day the heavens will
pass away with great violence.

Cf. 2 Peter 3:10

St. Paul teaches us that the present world is an immense laboratory where all of nature is in great unrest and in labor until the day
when, freed from all bondage and corruption, it will blossom out
into a radiant and renewed order.[1]

Man himself, in his course here below, is no more than a traveler, sailing across the fluctuating, tempestuous sea of time, and
the earth that bears him is but the boat destined to guide him toward the land of immortal and unending life. Nations, too, like individuals, are destined one day to disappear.

The story of mankind would be no more than an inexplicable
drama, a series of confused, aimless, isolated facts, if, sooner or
later, it did not have its appointed time and climax. In the present
natural order, everything with a beginning is destined to end; a
continuous chain must have a link at both ends, not just one. The
present world, precisely because it was created, necessarily tends
toward its conclusion and end.

How will that great transformation be effected? What will be
the conditions and the new form of our earth when, after it has
been destroyed and completely transfigured by fire, it will no longer be watered by the sweat of man, and will have ceased to be the
troubled, blood-stained arena of our strife and passions? We shall
speak of this shortly.

In this first talk, our aim will be to recall the testimony of Holy
Scripture and particularly that of today's Gospel [it appears that

this "conference," or lecture, was originally delivered on the last Sunday after Pentecost when the Gospel was Matthew 24:15-35], which assure us that after a long period of centuries, the visible order of things on earth will give way to a new and permanent order, and the changing era of time will be replaced by the era of stability and repose.

As we broach this delicate and difficult subject, one of the most important that can be treated in Christian preaching, since it touches upon the present and future circumstances of our country and our destinies, it seems right to us to point out that we shall steer clear of every perilous opinion, relying neither upon dubious revelations nor upon apocryphal prophecies, and making no assertion that is not justified by the doctrine of the Sacred Books, or permitted by authentic teaching of the Fathers and of Tradition.

In these conferences, we shall recall in turn: first, what the premonitory signs and indications of the end of time are to be; secondly, what will be the marks and nature of the persecution by this man of sin, announced by the apostle Paul as the precursor of the final coming of the Son of God; thirdly, what will be the circumstances of the resurrection and judgment; finally, what will be the place of immortal life and the state of the world after the resurrection.

In our commentary on Sacred Scripture, and, particularly, on the twenty-fourth chapter of St. Matthew, we shall seek to resolve these three fundamental questions:

- Is the doctrine of the end of time an indubitable doctrine, founded on reason and in harmony with the facts of present-day science?

- May we deduce from the words of Christ whether the end of time is near or far?

• By what means will this final cataclysm, this great crowning change, come about?

In the face of these formidable problems that defy the light and grasp of human understanding, our voice is hesitant, and can only stammer. May your blessing, my Lord Bishop, strengthen it.[2] May the Spirit of God enlighten our mind, and place on our lips words of truth, strength, wisdom, and discretion!

⁀

The materialistic, atheistic science of our century, the sort that is propagated in magazines, taught from most official rostrums, and given credence by the mainstream of present-day anti-Christian opinion, persists in regarding the order and perfection of the universe merely as the result of chance. It affirms that matter is eternal . . . Denying creation, it could not logically admit that the world can have an end. According to this false science, the present universe will always subsist, or, if it becomes progressively better, this will be solely through the effect of man's genius, the increasing impulse given to the arts and industrial achievements, the varied combination and play of fluids and elements, decomposing and reconstituting themselves to give birth to new forms — in short, by the application and activation of the innumerable and still unknown forces that nature conceals in her bosom; forces that, by themselves, are capable of surging forward into limitless and indefinite growth; and, just as the worm, in perfecting itself, turned into a quadruped, from quadruped to two-footed creature, from two-footed creature to man, in the same way, man, with the aid of science, will one day attain the pinnacle of his sovereignty. He will conquer time and space, make himself wings in order to propel himself toward the stars, and explore the wonders of the constellations. In the eyes of the atheistic science, paradise and eternal life, as conceived by Christians, are an allegory and a myth. Progress is the last end, the law and foundation of the life of man, the final point and aim where all his thoughts and aspirations should converge. Let man courageously cast aside the bonds and darkness of superstition and of oppressive outdated beliefs; let him have faith in himself alone, and, in a more or less proximate future, he will be invested with an unlimited, unrestrained kingship over the elements and creation.

Nature, completely subdued by his genius, will then open like the horn of plenty upon a new humanity, pouring forth the fullness of desirable goods; and if the present generations fail to attain this ideal of bliss, they may take comfort from the prospect that it will be found by some more distant descendants, and all the more glorious for these, in that they will have acquired them independently, and without the assistance of God, and will be solely the result of their own perseverance, efforts, and ingenuity.

Need I say that these fantasies, these crass, nonsensical theories, are contradicted by reason and the common assent of all nations?

They are contradicted by Christian reason. If, in fact, as our Christian faith and conviction tell us, temporal life had its principle and beginning in God, it must also have in God its consummation and destiny. Man was created to know, love, and serve God; and, if he did not succeed one day in possessing Him and being irrevocably united with Him, the Creator's plan, devoid of any rational end, would be no more than a monstrosity and an aberration. Mankind, thwarted in its love, its tendencies and aspirations, would become another Sisyphus, or a sort of roulette ball, dancing in the air and condemned to spin forever on the wheel of fate's blind necessity. What place would there be for justice, morality, the security of families and of public authority, in a system where everything was in a state of disorder and contradiction, where the ideal never became reality, good was never separated from evil, and no standard existed by which to decide the importance of moral living and the true assessment of human acts?

"History," a skeptical author of our time has said, "is the judge of peoples, and her judgment, which continues throughout the ages, renders the Last Judgment pointless and superfluous."

Our reply will be that the judgment of history is not a public judgment, whereas evil is public and rises up with an arrogance that is a scandal to men and a constant outrage against God. The judgment of history remains incomplete, because every good or bad act is a mainspring of good or evil, a seed of life or death, all the fruits and results of which its author could neither feel nor foresee. That is why, if the universal judgment had not been foretold to us, it would be our duty to demand it, to insist on it as a necessary consequence, as the final enactment of that Divine Providence which guides the movement of history throughout the ages, and as a final measure to complete His work and place His seal on it.

This universal judgment is but the last scene of the universal drama: the general fulfillment of all the partial judgments emanating from God's justice. It is only on this understanding that history becomes clear and comprehensible, that we shall see it, not as the confused mind and eyes of man imagine it to be, but as it really is, like a book open to every eye.

A great orator of our time has said, "History is not over; it will begin in the valley of Josaphat."

Christian reason and the common assent of all nations thus bear witness that the world must end and that there will be a new order. This truth is also in conformity with science and observed facts.

It is a recognized principle, and a general law of nature, that everything subject to movement or decomposition, everything consumed by time or limited in extent, is liable to wear out and age, and, in the end, disappears and perishes. Science teaches us that no vital force, or created agent, has the power to deploy its energy beyond a limited duration, and that, by virtue of the creative law, the field of its activity is restricted within a given sphere, whose boundary cannot be crossed. The most perfect and soundly built organisms could not be made to function indefinitely.

Not only living beings, such as animals and plants, but even minerals are subject to opposing forces of affinity or repulsion, and tend continuously to separate in order to form new groupings. Thus, the hardest rocks and granite undergo corrosion and weathering that, sooner or later, will bring them tumbling down. Stars are seen to extinguish and vanish in the firmament. Every movement, even that of the heavens, tends to become slower. Eminent astronomers have detected, in the sun and the stars, losses of heat and light, admittedly imperceptible, that nevertheless will not fail, after the passage of many centuries, to have a disastrous effect on our climate and seasons.

Be that as it may, it is certain that our earth no longer possesses the same fecundity or vegetative strength it had in the first ages of the human race. Just as the world had its youth, so there will come a time when the world will have its twilight, when it will hasten toward its evening and decline.

These are truths of observation and common sense that reason grasps easily, but Christianity alone has succeeded in demonstrating their certainty and excellence. "It is in this respect," a Protestant thinker has said, "that Christian doctrine is quite distinct from philosophical doctrines. It affirms that a new existence awaits man after this life. An absolute requirement for the fulfillment of that existence is that nature, which has become obscure and impenetrable to man, should be explained and clarified in some future state, which will prove the harmony between visible and invisible things, the transient and the everlasting, matter and spirit. Only in that future, only with such an end to human existence, can the conscience of man find repose. For this hope we are indebted to Christ, *whose promise permits us to expect, after the final crisis*, a new earth *and new heavens*."[3]

⌒

So, the world will have an end; but is this end remote or near? That is a serious, exciting question, no less worthy of reflection by Christian souls.

Holy Scripture on this point does not leave us completely in the dark. Certainly, speaking of the exact date, Jesus Christ says: "As for the exact day or hour, no one knows it, neither the angels in heaven nor the Son, but the Father only."[4] On the other hand, He consented to give definite signs and indications, intended to let us know that the fulfillment of the prophecies is close, and that the world is nearing its end.

Jesus Christ has proceeded in the same way with mankind considered as a whole, as with individuals: thus, our death is certain, but the hour is unknown to us. None of us can say whether he will be living a week or a day from now, and I who am speaking to you do not know whether I shall complete the talk I have begun. But, if we can be taken by surprise at any time, there are, nevertheless, signs that attest that our final hour is imminent, and that we would be laboring under a crass illusion if we imagined that we had a long stretch of life still awaiting us here below.

The End of the Present World

Our Lord tells us, "From the fig tree learn a lesson. When its branch grows tender and sprouts leaves, you realize that summer is near. Likewise, when you see all these things happening [that is to say, wars, famines, earthquakes], you will know that the Son of Man is at your door."[5] As a matter of fact, these public calamities and disturbances, and the changes in the elements and in the normal course of the seasons, that will mark the final coming of the Son of God, are vague, indefinite signs . . . They have appeared, with greater or lesser intensity, in every ill-fated period of human history, and in all periods of crisis and religious disorder.

At the time of the Maccabees, signs were already seen in the sky. For forty days, the whole city of Jerusalem observed men on horseback in the air, clad in gold brocade and armed with lances, like cavalry units. The horses, drawn up in squadrons, charged one another. The men seemed to be armed with javelins and drawn swords; their weapons were made of gold, and their helmets and breastplates were dazzling. The terror-stricken people prayed fervently to God, in order that these omens might turn to their deliverance, and not to their confusion and ruin.[6]

During the siege of Jerusalem, under Titus, the Holy of Holies and the Temple were shaken by mysterious movements; strange noises were heard coming from them, and voices from invisible beings cried out, "Let us depart hence, let us depart hence." A Grand Rabbi, dumbfounded by these terrifying, supernatural manifestations, exclaimed, "O Temple, why are you troubled, and why do you frighten yourself?"

Accordingly, in order not to give rise to any misunderstanding or false interpretation, Christ tells us that the afflictions and prodigies of nature, which will mark the latter ages of mankind, are only the prelude and beginning of still greater sorrows: *These are the early stages of the birth pangs.*[7]

Thus, one cannot draw any final conclusions on the end of time based on the present disasters and revolutions, the moral disorders, the great religious and social cataclysms of which Europe and the world are currently the scene. The signs today are the same signs that occurred in ancient times, and experience shows that they are insufficient to prove the proximity of the judgment.

It is important, though, to consider that Christ, in His prophecy, combines in a single scene the signs relating to the end of the world and those relating to the destruction of Jerusalem. He does so, first, because of the analogy between the two events . . . Secondly, because in God there is no distinction or succession in time. The impending events and those more remote are clearly present to His mind, and He sees them as if they had occurred at the same moment . . . Moreover, our Lord Jesus Christ knew that the Apostles, before they were enlightened by the Holy Spirit, were imbued with illusions and all the Jewish prejudices; in their eyes, Jerusalem was the whole universe, and its ruin meant, for them, the collapse of the world. As a result of this narrow, exaggerated patriotism that dominated them, the Apostles continued in their vigilant and unceasing anticipation until the ruin of Jerusalem. Such were the dispositions that Christ endeavored to arouse, seeking to instruct them and lead them away from gross earthly hopes, rather than excite their curiosity by disclosing to them the hidden secrets of the future.

Hence, in His prophecy, He shows them, as it were, two perspectives and two horizons, having analogous features and alike in relief, pattern, and coloring. In St. Matthew and St. Mark, the two events — the destruction of Jerusalem and the end of the world — seem rather to be merged. In St. Luke, the two occurrences are very clearly distinguished: there are features that refer solely to the end of the world, such as these:

There will be signs in the sun, the moon, and the stars. On the earth, nations will be in anguish, distraught at the roaring of the sea and the waves. Men will die of fright in anticipation of what is coming upon the earth. The powers in the heavens will be shaken. After that, men will see the Son of Man coming on a cloud with great power and glory.[8]

⟜

Will the world last another hundred years? Will it end with our present millennium? Will mankind, under the Christian law of grace, go through a span of years corresponding to the period passed under the law of nature or the Mosaic law?

These are questions upon which no hypothesis or conjecture may be ventured. All the calculations and inquiries in which learned interpreters have indulged are idle quests, lacking any purpose other than the satisfaction of vain curiosity. Providence has ordained that this day should not be known, and that nobody shall succeed in discovering it until it actually arrives: *"De die illa nemo scit."*[9]

And let no one object that, if we cannot assign the day, we can at least determine the period or the year. No, for St. Augustine remarks that the word *day*, in Sacred Scripture, is to be understood in the sense of any length of time. The testimony of the holy Doctor concurs with that of the prophet Malachi, who tells us, "Yes, He is coming, says the Lord of hosts. But who will endure the day of His coming? And who can stand when He appears?"[10] Zechariah is still more precise and explicit: "On that day there shall no longer be cold or frost. There shall be one continuous day, known to the Lord, not day and night, for in the evening time there shall be light."[11]

The reason is that the end of the world will not simply be the effect of some natural cause, but depends above all on the will of God, which has not been revealed to us.

It is a matter of faith that human destinies will be brought to a close when the measure of saints shall have been filled up, and the number of the elect consummated. Now, no man, whether from reasons that are certain, or even on the strength of probable conjecture, can know the number of the predestinate, still less the time that will elapse before this number is complete. Who, for example, would dare to assert whether more or fewer men will be saved in the centuries to come than were saved in the preceding centuries? And irrespective of whether the number of future saints is greater or less than the number of past saints, how is it possible to predict the length of time in which their number will be consummated? Is it not an established fact in the life of the Church that there are periods of sterility when saints are rare, and periods of fecundity when they abound? That is why, considering the original cause of the world, which is none other than the hidden mystery of predestination, no one can conclude whether the end of the world is near or distant.[12]

However, if Christ teaches us that this final great day is a secret that God, in the designs of His sovereignty, has kept to Himself — *tempora et momenta quae Pater posuit in sua potestate*[13] — and that will defy all our calculations until the very hour of its fulfillment, nevertheless, in order to forewarn us against negligence and a false sense of security, He unceasingly reminds men: first, that the end of the world is certain; secondly, that it is relatively proximate; thirdly, that it will not occur until there have come to pass, not ordinary, habitual signs, such as have happened at all times, but the particular, distinctive signs He has clearly indicated to us. These signs are not just calamities and revolutions in the stars, but events of a public character, pertaining to both the religious and the social order, which mankind cannot fail to perceive.

⌒

The first of the events foreshadowing the end of time is the one to which the Savior refers in Matthew 24:14, when He says, "This good news of the Kingdom will be proclaimed throughout the world as a witness to all the nations. Only after that will the end come." The second of these signs will be the appearance of the man of sin, the Antichrist.[14] The third: the conversion of the Jewish people, who will adore the Lord Jesus and recognize Him as the promised Messiah.[15] Until then, says St. Paul, "Let no man deceive you by any means . . . as if the day of the Lord were at hand."[16]

It is evident that the last two events, which St. Paul declares are to mark the approach of the great tribulation, have not so far been fulfilled. The Antichrist has not yet appeared, as we shall show in the next discourse. The Jews, as a nation, have not yet cast off the thick veil that prevents them from acclaiming as God Him whom they crucified. It remains to be ascertained whether, at the present time, the gospel has been preached all over the earth, and given for a testimony to the totality of nations.

On this point the Fathers and Doctors are divided. Some say that the words of Christ are to be interpreted morally, and should be understood in the sense of a partial, summary preaching: for them to be fulfilled, it is enough that missionaries should have enlightened a certain number of individual minds in the various parts of the inhabited earth, and that, on each deserted and remote hillside, the Cross should have been raised at least once. Others, more numerous, like St. Jerome and Bede,[17] insist that the words of the Son of God should be understood in the most strict and literal sense.

Cornelius à Lapide, the most learned of the interpreters of the Sacred Books, expresses the opinion that the end of time will not come until Christianity has been not only proclaimed and propagated, but established and organized, and has subsisted at the level of a public institution, among men of every race and nationality in such a way that, before the centuries have run their course, there will not be a single barbarian shore, not one island lost in the ocean or any place, at present unknown, in the two hemispheres, where the gospel has not shone in all its splendor, where the Church has not made herself manifest in her legislation, her solemnities and hierarchy, including the bishops and lower clergy — in a word, where the great prophecy "There will be one fold and one shepherd" has not been completely fulfilled.[18]

We incline to this latter opinion. It is more in harmony with the testimony of Holy Scripture. It is more in accord with the wisdom and mercy of God, who makes no distinction between the civilized and the barbarian, Greeks and Jews, but, desiring the salvation of all men, does not exclude any of them from the light and gift of Redemption. Finally, it accords better with the ways of Providence, which shows an equal solicitude for all peoples, and calls them in turn to the knowledge of its law, in the time appointed by its immutable decrees.

One need only glance at a map to recognize that the gospel law is far from having been promulgated to all peoples, and that innumerable multitudes at the present time remain sunk in darkness, and do not possess the slightest shadow of revealed truth.

Thus, Central Asia and the mountains of Tibet have so far defied the endeavors of our most intrepid missionaries. No one has yet been able to give us an exact account of the social and religious customs of the peoples of Equatorial Africa, in spite of the recent discovery of great lakes and high tableland where, formerly, there was held to be nothing but sand and desert. Britain and other nations have established colonial outposts on the shores of Oceania (the South Sea islands), but the interior of these vast continents has yet to be explored.

Clearly, the gospel has not yet been preached as a witness to all nations! Can we even say that it has been preached with sufficient luster, and in such a way as to leave with no excuse those who have refused to obey it? On each page of the annals of the Propagation of the Faith, we find this sorrowful strain, welling up from the hearts of apostles: "Therefore ask the harvest-master to send workers to his harvest."[19]

Now, it is written that, at the end of time, the gospel will have been given as a witness to all the nations. David cries out, "All peoples, to the ends of the earth, will remember the Lord and return to Him, because dominion belongs to Him and He governs the nations."[20]

Further on, David continues, "May He rule from sea to sea, and from the River to the ends of the earth. His foes shall bow before Him, and His enemies shall lick the dust. The kings of Tarshish and the Isles shall offer gifts; the kings of Arabia and Sheba shall bring tribute."[21]

The Lord then speaks to the Church through Isaiah: "Enlarge the space of your tent, spread out your tent cloths unsparingly; lengthen your ropes and make firm your stakes. For you shall spread abroad to the right and to the left; your descendants shall dispossess the nations and shall people the desolate cities."[22]

These texts are explicit and precise. It is clear from their testimony that there will come a time when all heresies and schisms will be overcome, and when the true religion will be known and practiced in all places illuminated by the sun.

This unity will assuredly not be achieved easily; mankind will not reach this golden age along paths strewn with roses: the foundations of the Church were built up with the blood of martyrs, mingled with the sweat of the Apostles.

So we must expect strife and bitter resistance. Blood will be shed; the spirit of darkness will once more throw up its seductions and wiles in abundance; we may count on there being more terrible persecutions of the Church than those she has sustained hitherto.

On the other hand, we must learn to scrutinize the thoughts of God, and to read from the decrees of His power. All the admirable inventions of modern times have their divinely appointed end. Would God in our days have given man a glimpse of the secrets and hidden treasures of creation? Would He have put into his hands all those marvelous instruments such as steam, magnetism, and electricity for the sole purpose of providing a new spur to his pride, of being the docile slave of his selfishness and greed? Such was not the thought He expressed by the voice of the prophet, when He said, "I will give wings to my Word, harness fire to my chariots, seize my apostles as if in a whirlwind, and transport them in the twinkling of an eye amidst the barbarian nations."

Thus, the time is near when Christ will gain complete triumph, when in very truth, He can be called Lord of the earth: *Deus omnis terrae vocabitur.*[23]

At present many signs point to a great victory for Christianity. Do not our enemies have a presentiment of it? Does not a secret instinct warn them that the days of their power are numbered, and that the time when it is given to them to prevail cannot be of long duration? This is why they enlist in the war they wage against the

Church all the hateful corruption, all the hypocrisies anxious to drop their masks, all the hostile sciences, all the shady and godless politics. The revolution boldly raises its standard against religion, property, and the family; saps the foundations of the social structure; and mounts its attacks against us simultaneously, and on every front. The press, freed from every restraint, disseminates the most subversive doctrines and the deadliest poisons in a thousand organs.

We can understand that, in such a situation, the mighty should feel irresolute in their counsels, and their courage and constancy seem to falter. We can understand that, beyond the clouds and troubled horizons, they discern somber prospects, and predict a renewed outbreak of crime, wars, and frightful upheavals. Yet it is precisely the incredible audacity, the continually renascent fury of our enemies, that gives us hope of a glorious new era for the Church. Christianity, in our day, is being attacked everywhere: in the arts and sciences, in Church and state, in Europe as well as Asia, in the old and new world: a sure sign that it will triumph everywhere. When will this be? God knows, but the fact is certain. The blood of martyrs becomes the seed of Christians. The Church has immutable promises. As she comes out of the Red Sea, she enters the Promised Land. The hour of darkness gives way to that of light and triumph. Following the outrages of Golgotha, she hears resounding around her the blessings and hosannas of the deliverance.

So let us not lose heart. Let us welcome the future in the making; and if, at the present time, our country is a prey to convulsions and torn by discord; if her fortune and political influence have become a prize, fought over by unsatiated ambitions and vulgar nonentities, like the Prodigal Son of the Gospel, it will not be long before the memory of the peace and honor of the centuries of her youth return to her mind; she will cast off her chains and the mask of her ignominy.

Yet, even if the end of the world were to be deferred for many centuries, what are centuries compared with the years of eternity? They are a second, an instant, more fleeting than lightning. When the Son of God was raised up to heaven, seated upon a cloud, the Apostles could not take their eyes from the place in the sky where He had vanished. Suddenly, two angels in white garments appeared to them, and said, "Men of Galilee, why do you stand here looking up at the skies? This Jesus who has been taken from you will return, just as you saw Him go up into the heavens."[24]

Elsewhere, Christ says, "Within a short time, you will lose sight of me, but soon after that you shall see me again, because I go to the Father."[25]

⁓

Although Christ wanted to leave us ignorant of the exact time of the end of the world, He deemed it fitting to give us detailed information on the manner and circumstances of this great event.

The end of the world, He says, will happen instantaneously and unexpectedly: "The day of the Lord will come like a thief."[26]

It will come at a time when the human race, sunk in the uttermost depths of indifference, will be far from thinking about punishment and justice. Divine Mercy will have exhausted all its resources and means of action. The Antichrist will have appeared. Men over the whole surface of the earth will have been called to the knowledge of the truth. The Catholic Church will have blossomed out into the fullness of her life and fecundity for the last time.

Nevertheless, all these superabundant favors and prodigies will, once more, vanish from the hearts and memory of man. By a criminal abuse of graces, mankind will have returned to its vomit. Concentrating their affections and all their aspirations on the goods and gross pleasures of this world, they will, as the Sacred Books tell us, have turned their backs on God so far as to be unable to look up to heaven, and remember its just judgments.[27] All faith will be extinguished in hearts. All flesh will have corrupted its ways. Divine Providence will judge that it is beyond remedy.

As Christ says, it will be as in the days of Noah.[28] At that time, men lived without a care, made plantations, built luxurious houses, poked fun at the old fellow Noah as he set himself up as a carpenter and worked day and night, building his ark. "Madman! Dreamer!" they would say. This went on until the day when the Flood came and engulfed the whole earth: "The flood came and destroyed them all."[29]

Thus, the final catastrophe will take place when the world is at its most secure: civilization will be at its zenith, markets will be overflowing with money, and government stocks will never have been higher. There will be national celebrations, great exhibitions, and mankind, wallowing in an unprecedented material prosperity, will have ceased to hope for heaven. Crudely attached to the basest pleasures of life, men, like the miser in the Gospel, will say, "My soul, you possess goods to last for many years. Eat, drink and be merry."[30]

But suddenly, in the middle of the night, *in media nocte* — for it will be amidst the darkness, and at that fateful midnight hour, when the Lord once appeared in His lowliness, that He will appear again — men, startled out of their sleep, will hear a great clamor and noise, and a voice will be heard saying, "Behold, the groom is here! Come out and greet Him!"[31]

In the annals of Savoy, the memory and tradition is preserved of an appalling catastrophe that presents us with the image and outline of what will happen when God abandons the human race, and His patience is finally exhausted.

It was hundreds of years ago, on November 24, 1248, the eve of the day when the Church celebrates the feast of St. Catherine. That evening, the season was mild, the air calm, and the stars twinkled in the sky. The whole valley where the present town of Chambéry is situated lay quiet and secure.

An evil, irreligious man then ruled tyrannically over a town, now gone forever, but which at that time stood next to the city of my story.[32]

This man had gathered together a large number of merry companions. With banquets and drunken revelry, he was celebrating the sacrilegious plunder of a monastery that he had turned to profane use, after mercilessly expelling the monks and holy inmates who were the legitimate owners. Probably, as in Balthazar's time,[33] it was a sumptuous meal, and the wine and liqueurs, mingled with blasphemies and sardonic laughter, flowed in abundance. Suddenly, in an instant, in the middle of the night, the earth was shaken by a tremendous shock. Sky and ground seemed to be shaken by horrible whirlwinds, voices, and howling of storms, which you would have thought came from the caverns of hell; and, before the guests could rise to their feet, before they could utter a cry for help, they were buried alive beneath the collapsing mass of a gigantic mountain: one town, five hamlets, and a whole region of six thousand inhabitants were engulfed in chasms, the traces of which are written in indelible characters on the fragments of our souls, and remain as an ineffaceable and living memory of mingled legend and horror in the minds of our people.

This image, borrowed from one of the most memorable and dreadful events that have occurred in our history is, in one sense, more vivid and striking than that of Noah and the Flood: for, at least at the time of Noah and the Flood, men had time to collect their thoughts, and obtain the grace of repentance before they perished, and the disaster struck only gradually. If all did not succeed in saving themselves for the present life, St. Peter tells us explicitly that the greater number returned to God, and saved themselves for the life to come.[34]

In St. Peter's first letter, he says that, when the holy soul of Jesus Christ had been separated from His body, "it was in the spirit also that He went to preach to the spirits in prison; they had disobeyed as long ago as Noah's day, while God patiently waited until the ark was built."[35]

On the day of judgment, however, it will be as described in the preceding story: it will all happen with unparalleled promptness and violence: *Coeli magno impetu transient*.[36]

Christ tells us: "If a man is on the roof terrace, he must not come down to get anything out of his house. If a man is in the field, he must not turn back to pick up his cloak. It will be hard on pregnant or nursing mothers in those days ... If anyone tells you, 'Look, the Messiah is here' or 'He is there,' do not believe it . . . for as the lightning from the east flashes to the west, so will the coming of the Son of Man be."[37]

⌒

By what means will this great destruction take place? What will be the efficient cause, the principal agent, the direct, immediate instrument?

Holy Scripture did not intend to omit any of the circumstances concerning this event, the gravest and most decisive of all that have succeeded one another since the creation. It teaches that the world will not perish by inundation as at the Flood, will not collapse by virtue of an earthquake, and will not be buried under ashes and lava as were Hurculaneum and Pompeii in the region of Titus, but will be set ablaze and destroyed by fire: *Terra autem et quae in ipsâ sunt opera exurentur.*[38] Such was already the ancient belief, common among the Egyptians and Persian philosophers. Cicero said that the world would end by fire.

The remarkable thing is that present-day science concurs with the Sacred Books, in showing that fire will be the great architect of God's justice, and of the renovation that will follow when this has been manifested.

Thus, science, like the Bible, has revealed that fire was the first created force to have developed its energy and displayed its activity. It was by fire that nature was made fruitful, and the elements set to work; thence came, also, the great transformations of the primitive world, the erection of mountains, the making of the stars, and, finally, the emergence of the universe, with all the order and variety it presents to our admiring gaze.

Genesis 1:2 says, "The earth was a formless wasteland, and darkness covered the abyss." In other words, as the experts and commentators explain, matter was volatilized, and in the state of vapor. Before the Creator had bestowed its properties and diverse forms, by dividing and coordinating it in the six days' labor, all these constituents were jumbled, disunited, and in a chaotic state. Earth, sun, and stars presented a picture of a vast liquescent or gaseous sea, scattered around the immensity of space. This sea was motionless and inert. It bubbled on its surface and in its innermost depths and was set in motion under the quickening breath of an eternal, all-powerful agent, which was none other than the Spirit of God: "The Spirit of God moved over the waters."[39]

The Holy Spirit subjected the material substance to a sort of incubation. Under the action and by the effects of this sovereign heat of immeasurable intensity, the elements underwent a casting and recasting, perfected themselves, acquired their power and energy, and shed their dross, like gold, which is refined and separated from its rust, in the crucible where it is cast. When, thus transformed by the blast of this furnace of the Holy Spirit, they were rendered capable of hearing the Word of God, the Creator called them in turn and said:

"Let there be light." And there was light; and, after He had made night and day and laid out the sky, He separated the solid matter from the vaporous mass surrounding it, and said, "Let the dry land appear," and the land was consolidated. He spoke also to the waters, leaving, on our globe, out of the liquid part, only what was necessary to irrigate it and fill the basins of the seas, and sent away the remainder, in the state of vapor or ether, to fill the vast expanses above all the spheres and skies: "God made the dome, and it separated the water above the dome from the water below it."[40]

It was a grand, sublime scene, which would give rise to long and magnificent developments. Who would not feel his spirits rise, and his heart quiver, at the sight of the creative act, that masterpiece of divine wisdom and power, throwing up streams of light and beauty from the shapeless, shadowy ocean, implanting movement and action in all the inert beings, which the divine Spirit had invested with His character, penetrating them with His fire and radiance?

"By the Word of the Lord the heavens were made; by the breath of His mouth all their host."[41] Today, however, we cannot speak of these admirable works except in passing, and insofar as they bear upon our chosen subject.

Now, this same Spirit of God, who has strewn treasures of harmony and perfection throughout the universe, will act in the same way, when it comes to ordaining new heavens and building that palace which shall serve eternally as a dwelling-place for glorified man.

Here, we are not fantasizing, and our voice is not our own, but that of all the prophets who have spoken, and of all the evangelists who have written: "Fire goes before Him and consumes His foes round about . . . The mountains melt like wax before the Lord."[42] Under the effect of its brilliance, the sun will darken and the moon will no longer give its light, and the stars will fall. That is, having been dissolved for the second time, they will vanish like droplets in the air.[43]

That fire will be the one which will devour the wicked like straw, penetrate their bones to the marrow, and consume them forever.

It will be the final trial for the just who will be living in the last days. For them, it will take the place of purgatory, the cleansing flames of which, at the moment of the resurrection, will be extinguished, never to be lit up again. It will be the crucible wherein they will cast off the remains of their earthly rust, so that no stain may darken the whiteness of their garments, when they appear before the throne of God.

We may be quite certain that all these events will take place. They are certain, with absolute certitude, as God is Himself, as is His Spirit of Truth, which is not subject to any error or change.

As a matter of fact, we can state that every one of us here will have left this lower world, before being witnesses of this great scene of desolation and ruin. Nonetheless, Jesus Christ has judged it fitting that we should be instructed concerning it, because these great truths are not of speculative order, but are intended to bring about practical and immediate effects in the conduct of our lives.

The End of the Present World

⌒

In truth, if the earth and all it contains must one day disappear by fire, the goods of this world are no more to be esteemed than wood and straw. What point is there, then, in making them the object of our desires and cares? Why seek to build and leave marks of our genius and power where we have no permanent abode, and where the form of this world will be removed, like a tent that has no travelers to shelter?

It may be said that it will be a thousand years before this frightening cataclysm takes place; but Christ has said that a thousand years are but an instant compared with eternity, and when the moment comes — when, from the land of the future life, we are the witnesses and actors in that supreme drama — the whole span of humanity will seem so short to us that we shall scarcely consider it to have lasted a single day.

The great prophet St. Paul, for whom time had no bounds and space no size, believed that he had already been transported there. In his cave at Bethlehem, St. Jerome could hear the trumpet of doom awakening the dead, and his hair stood on end, out of fear, and his flesh and bones quivered with an indescribable shudder. Lastly, Christ tells us to meditate upon these great teachings, for it is certain that we shall be taken by surprise, and that the time will come sooner than we think.

At the end of the fourteenth century, an extraordinary personage appeared from the depths of Spain. His name was Vincent Ferrer.[44] A prophet and wonder-worker since his youth, he grew up amidst universal astonishment. The Spirit of God lay upon him, took possession of his heart, and inflamed him with a zeal unknown since St. Paul. It ruled his body, which he sustained, despite his extreme weakness, amidst the most crushing labors, and the harshest austerities. The power to work miracles was granted him — in short, he uttered the most prodigiously powerful words that mankind had ever heard since St. Paul.

A superhuman being, although he was a man, he constantly refused the honors the Pope urged him to accept. His life was one of continuous prayer, fasting, and preaching. For twenty years, he traveled through Europe, and, for twenty years, Europe trembled beneath the ardor and fire of his inspired voice.

The last judgment was the favorite subject of his preaching. He himself declared to all that he had been specially sent by the Sovereign Judge to proclaim the approach of the last days.

One day, at Salamanca, a city renowned for its theologians and scholars, a countless throng crowded around to hear the messenger from heaven. Suddenly, raising his voice in the middle of the multitude, he said, "I am the angel of the Apocalypse whom St. John saw flying through the midst of heaven, crying aloud: Ye nations, fear the Lord and render Him glory, for the day of judgment is near."

At these strange words, an indescribable murmur broke out amidst the assembly. There were shouts of "Madness!" "Bragging!" "Impiety!"

The messenger of God paused, gazing at the sky in a kind of rapture or ecstasy; then, he continued and, raising his voice, cried out again, "I am the angel of the Apocalypse, the angel of the judgment." The agitation and murmuring reached its height. "Calm yourselves," said the saint. "Do not take scandal at my words. You will see with your own eyes that I am what I say. Go to the gate of St. Paul, at the end of the city, and you will find a dead woman. Bring her to me, and I shall raise her to life, as proof of what St. John said of me."

Once more, shouts and an even greater protest greeted this proposal. Nevertheless, a few men decided to go to the gate indicated.

There, they did indeed find a dead woman, took her up, and laid her amidst the assembly.

The apostle, who did not for a moment leave the elevated spot from which he was preaching, said, "Woman, in the name of God, I command you to rise." The dead woman immediately rose, wrapped in her shroud, cast off the winding-sheet that covered her face, and showed herself full of life, in the middle of the assembly. Vincent then added, "For the honor of God and the salvation of all these people, say, now that you can speak, whether I am really the angel of the Apocalypse, entrusted with proclaiming to all the approach of the last judgment."

"You are that angel," replied the woman, "truly you are."

In order to place this marvelous testimony between two miracles, the saint spoke to her again, "Do you prefer to remain alive, or do you wish to die once more?"

"I should willingly live," said the woman.

"Live then."

In fact, she lived many years longer, a living witness, says one historian, of an astounding prodigy, and of the highest mission ever entrusted to man.

We shall not discuss the authenticity of this story. It has raised doubts among certain hagiographers, and the circumstances surrounding it have given rise to criticism and debate. In defense of our opinion, it suffices to say that the Church has not condemned it, since, in the bull of canonization of the saint, it is said, "He had the words of the eternal gospel to proclaim, as the angel flying through the midst of heaven, the kingdom of God, to every tongue, tribe, and nation, and to show the proximity of the last judgment."

However, it is more than five hundred years since this event happened, and the last judgment announced by the wonder-worker of the fourteenth century has not taken place. Are we to conclude that the saint was misled, and that the miracle of this resurrection, attested by serious, trustworthy witnesses, recalled and handed down in sculpture and painting, must be assigned to the realm of legend, and held to be an allegory, a mere invention?

St. Vincent Ferrer spoke in the same way as holy Doctors had done before him, and as the majority of great apostolic men have done after him. Thus, as a matter of fact, St. Jerome censured a certain Juda, the famous author of an *Ecclesiastical History*, for having asserted that the violence of the persecution portended the end of the world, which would occur in a short time; yet, the same St. Jerome, in one of his letters,[45] brilliantly depicting the calamities and disasters he had witnessed, himself expressed almost the same opinion. St. Cyprian[46] (Epistle 58) wrote these words: "You must be convinced and hold for certain that the day of the final desolation has begun to dawn upon you, and that the time of the Antichrist is near . . ."

In the eulogy of his brother Satyrus, St. Ambrose exclaims, "He was removed from life, that he might not be a witness of the end of the world, and the complete destruction of the universe."[47] St. Gregory the Great and St. Bernard expressed the same sentiments, in their books and discourses.[48] These illustrious Doctors and great saints spoke in this way, either because they saw faith becoming scarce and the calamities of their age increasing every day in alarming proportions, or because they were gripped by fear at the thought of that great day, and wanted to plant that salutary fear in men who had gone astray in order to bring them back to the knowledge of God and good living. Yet, we cannot say that they strayed from the truth; they spoke in accordance with Scripture, which, by emphasizing this fundamental truth, unceasingly shows the prospect of the advent of the divine Judge as imminent: *Prope est iam Dominus.*[49]

The End of the Present World

In this, the Apostles and inspired writers have not deceived us, inasmuch as time is nothing to those who have crossed over the frontiers of earthly life. The whole span of the centuries, says the Holy Spirit, is no more than the fleeting day: "*tamquam dies hesterna quae praeteriit.*"[50] Just as, in the firmament, there are stars separated by myriads of miles which, on account of their distance, appear to merge, so as to form one single point, when observed from this earth: in the same way, from the heights of the life of God, where we shall one day be immersed, time will be such as if it did not exist. A year — a hundred thousand years — millions of years, contemplated from the bosom of eternity, will not seem to us any more than mere points. We shall consider these lengths of time as so microscopic, so fractional, that, in a sense, there will not be any difference between those which our mind can discern.

Consequently, these words of St. John the Evangelist may with perfect truthfulness be applied to the general resurrection, as well as to the partial resurrections performed by Jesus Christ: "An hour is coming in which all those in their tombs shall hear the voice of the Son of God and come forth unto the resurrection of life."[51]

Moreover, our eternal destiny will be settled irrevocably at death, and the particular judgment that must follow will soon determine the circumstances in which we shall appear at the tribunal of divine justice, and the place that will there be assigned to us.

Compared with this inevitable ending of human destinies, our political controversies are nothing but idle noise. Revolutions, which cause the disappearance of peoples and bring down republics and empires, are less than a change of scene or decoration in the theater. All those colossal enterprises and marvelous works to which men devote their minds, and which they bring to perfection at the cost of the greatest sacrifices and the most hazardous efforts, appear like a mere wisp of smoke, and are more fragile works than the web spun by a spider, and most often last less than a day.

There will then be no other distinction between men than that of merit and virtue. All vain and ambitious thoughts will have vanished. Politics will have ceased. Science itself will be destroyed: *scientia destruetur.*[52]

Happy those who have heard the divine Word, and kept it faithfully in their hearts. Happy those who, awakening from their sleep, shall have walked honestly and openly, following the apostle's recommendation. Happy those who, like the wise virgins, shall have carefully conserved the oil of their lamp, and formed their sheaf for the day of the dazzling, solemn harvest.

These shall be called the predestinate, because, as St. John says, their names are written in the book of life of the Lamb who was slain from the beginning of the world. May that destiny be ours. Amen.

Notes

[1] Rom. 8:21-22.

[2] Monsignor Pichenot, Archbishop of Chambéry.

[3] Schelling, *Philosophie de la Révélation*.

[4] Matt. 24:36.

[5] Matt. 24:32-33.

[6] 2 Macc. 3:22-30.

[7] Cf. Matt. 24:8.

[8] Luke 21:25-27.

[9] Matt. 24:36.

[10] Mal. 3:1-2.

[11] Zech. 14:6-7.

[12] St. Augustine teaches that the angels know the number of predestinate, but it does not follow that they know how long the world will last, as they cannot know in what space of time the number of the predestinate will be complete.

[13] Cf. Acts 1:7: "The exact time is not yours to know. The Father has reserved that to Himself."

[14] Cf. 2 Thess. 2:2-4.

[15] Cf. Rom. 11:14-17.

[16] 2 Thess. 2:2.

[17] St. Jerome (c. 342-420), Doctor who translated the Bible into Latin; St. Bede (673-735), English monk, scholar, and Doctor.

[18] Cornelius à Lapide, *Commentary on Matthew*.

[19] Luke 10:2.

[20] Cf. Ps. 22:28, 29.

[21] Cf. Ps. 72:8-10.

[22] Isa. 54:2-3.

[23] Cf. Isa. 54:5.

[24] Acts 1:10-11.

[25] John 16:16.

[26] 2 Pet. 3:10.

[27] Dan. 13:9: "They suppressed their consciences; they would not allow their eyes to look to heaven, and did not keep in mind just judgments."

[28] Matt. 24:37-38.

[29] Luke 17:27.

[30] Luke 12:19.

[31] Matt. 25:6.

[32] The town of Saint-André, which in the thirteenth century thrived some four and a half miles from Chambéry.

[33] Dan. 5.

[34] Note by the publishers of the English edition: It is true that St. Jerome and other Catholic interpreters have held the view that some of those who had initially mocked Noah when he was building the ark repented

when the flood arrived and were saved after a period of expiation in purgatory. That these were "the greater number," however, is a view peculiar to Father Arminjon.

[35] 1 Pet. 3:19-20.

[36] Cf. 2 Pet. 3:10: "The heavens will pass away with great violence."

[37] Matt. 24:17-19, 26-27.

[38] 2 Pet. 3:10: "The elements will be destroyed by fire, and the earth and all its deeds will be made manifest." Although apocryphal, the book of Enoch seems to contain the principal beliefs prevailing in Judea in the time of Christ. It is said that, when men shall have filled up the measure of their iniquities toward God and Israel, then shall come the great cataclysm, of which the Flood was only the prelude and, as it were, the warning. This time, divine justice will go the whole way; evil will be conquered forever; the earth will be purified by fire, not by water. Beneath new heavens and upon a new earth will begin the reign without end of the elect, a reign of justice, truth, and peace, the true reign of God, wherein Israel will be the royal people.

[39] Gen. 1:2.

[40] Gen. 1:1-7.

[41] Ps. 33:6.

[42] Ps. 97:3, 5.

[43] In accordance with the Gospel texts that tell us plainly that the powers of heaven will be moved — *virtutes Dei commovebuntur* — and that the stars in the sky will fall, it must be acknowledged that it will not be only our earth, but the stars or, at the very least, the whole of our planetary system, that will be dissolved, thrown into disorder, and set ablaze. He who has created the heavens and directed their movements with such perfect and admirable harmony and order can, in an instant, and without any miracle, undo His work. By a secret cause, unknown to man, He can produce a confusion or change in the celestial movements that will, instantaneously and utterly, overturn them and, in the planets and the motion of their satellites, neutralize and suspend the forces and laws of attraction, which our experts consider invariable and eternal. We know that these things will take place, as the eternal Truth has formally foretold that the ruin and disruption of the heavens will come at the end of time; and this ruin is

certain, as it is written: "The heavens and the earth will pass away, but my words will not pass" (Matt. 24:35).

44 St. Vincent Ferrer (1350-1419), Dominican mission preacher who helped to mend the Great Schism of the West.

45 Second Letter to Ageruchia de Monogamia.

46 St. Cyprian (c. 200-258), Bishop of Carthage and martyr.

47 St. Ambrose (c. 340-397), Bishop of Milan and Doctor.

48 St. Gregory the Great (d. 604), Pope from 590, writer, and Doctor; St. Bernard of Clairvaux (1090-1153), abbot and Doctor.

49 Cf. Phil. 4:5: "The Lord is near."

50 Cf. Ps. 90:4: "For a thousand years in Your sight are as yesterday, now that it is past."

51 John 5:28.

52 1 Cor. 13:8: "Prophecies will cease, tongues will be silent, knowledge will pass away."

Second Conference

❧

The Persecution by the Antichrist and the Conversion of the Jews

Et tunc revelabitur ille iniquus,
quem Dominus Jesus interficiet spiritu oris sui,
et destruet illustratione adventus sui.

❧

And then that wicked one shall be revealed,
whom the Lord Jesus shall kill
with the spirit of His mouth
and shall destroy with the
brightness of His coming.

Cf. 2 Thessalonians 2:8

The world will have an end. This is a truth we have established, and which faith and reason alike prove.

The end of the world, and the subsequent final coming of the Son of God, will happen unexpectedly, with the rapidity of lightning, rending the clouds as it darts from east to west.

However, precisely when that day will come is a secret, hidden in the depths of the divine intelligence. We know neither the day nor the hour, and Jesus Christ, the ambassador of the Divinity on earth, tells us that He has been explicitly commanded not to disclose them to us.

Accordingly, all the opinions that learned and pious personages at different periods have permitted themselves to express on this question are no more than personal, private sentiments, assertions resting on mere conjecture, the error and futility of which has been demonstrated more than once by events.

St. Cyprian and Tertullian,[1] considering the fury of the persecutors and the violence of the war of extermination waged to the utmost against the Christians, designated these calamities and all these horrors as signs of the proximity of the last judgment.

"The end of the world is not far off," said St. John Chrysostom.[2] "The earthquakes and the chilling of charity are, as it were, the forerunners and omens of that terrible event."

We all know that, at the time of the fall of the Roman Empire and the social dissolution that accompanied that great cataclysm and, subsequently, at the beginning of the year 1000 of the Christian era, people believed they were close to the period foretold, and thought they were seeing the prelude of the final destruction in the public disasters and collapse of institutions.

Earlier, in the time of St. Paul, the same terror had gripped people's minds. Visionaries and leaders of factions interpreted the words of St. Matthew's Gospel in a grossly literal sense. Convinced that the destruction of the world would follow closely upon the destruction of Jerusalem, they indulged in a rash of extravagant predictions, filling people's imagination with horror. They drew men away from the fulfillment of their civil and religious duties, invited them not to marry, not to build, but to abandon themselves to a mind-softening inertia, while awaiting the catastrophe that was to strike them.

St. Paul felt obliged to correct these beguiled and erring souls, and said to them, "We beg you, brothers, not to be so easily agitated or terrified . . . into believing that the day of the Lord is here . . . since the mass apostasy has not yet occurred nor the man of lawlessness been revealed — that son of perdition and adversary who exalts himself above every so-called god proposed for worship, he who seats himself in God's temple and even declares himself to be God."[3]

Here, then, is a definite fact, given by the Holy Spirit and clearly announced by St. Paul, in order to dispel the fears to which some were abandoning themselves, and to help faithful Christians guard against false systems and uncertain, hazardous predictions.

What is clear and undeniable from the passage we have just quoted is that, before the end of the world, there will appear on earth a profoundly evil man, invested with a quasi-superhuman power, who, challenging Christ, will wage an impious and foolish war against Him. Through the fear this man will inspire, and, particularly, by his stratagems and seductive genius, he will succeed in conquering almost the entire universe; he will have altars erected to himself and will compel all peoples to adore him.

Will this strange man, unique in his evil, be one of our race? Will his face have the features of man, and will the same blood as ours flow in the veins of this ringleader of error and corruption? Or, as some have understood, will he be an incarnation of Satan, a demon thrown up from hell, and disguised in human form?

Or again, as other Doctors have maintained, is this wicked creature just a myth, an allegorical personage, in whom Holy Scripture and the Fathers intended to portray, in a single image, the totality of tyrants and persecutors — to set out prominently the collective image of all the wicked and all the heretics who have fought against Christ and His Church, since the beginning of time?

These various interpretations cannot be reconciled with the definite, precise text of the Sacred Books. Almost all the Doctors and Fathers, St. Augustine, St. Jerome, and St. Thomas,[4] clearly maintain that this terrifying malefactor, this monster of impiety and depravity, will be a human person. The learned Bellarmine shows that it is impossible to give any other meaning to the words of St. Paul and those of Daniel 11:36-37.[5] St. Paul designates this great adversary by a noun, calling him a man: *"the man of sin, the son of perdition."*

Daniel informs us that the Antichrist will attack all that is holy and worthy of respect, exalt himself boldly against the God of gods and consider as nothing the God of his Fathers: *"Is Deum patrum suorum non reputabit."*[6] The apostle Paul adds that Christ will kill him. All these various aspects and characteristics evidently cannot be applied to an ideal, abstract being; they can fit only an individual of flesh and blood — a real, definite personage.

The Fathers and Doctors endeavored to ascertain the origin of the Antichrist, and to discover from what parents and race he will come. They unanimously express the opinion that he will be born of Jewish parents, and some declare that he will be of the tribe of Dan. Such is the interpretation they give of the passage of Genesis, "Let Dan be a snake in the way, a serpent in the path";[7] and of this other one from Jeremiah: "The snorting of his horses was heard from Dan."[8] They also surmise that St. John, in Revelation, failed to mention the tribe of Dan through hatred of the Antichrist.

But all these suppositions are uncertain. What seems beyond doubt is that the Antichrist will be of Jewish birth. St. Ambrose, in his commentaries on the letter to the Thessalonians, says that he will be circumcised. Sulpicius Severus, in book II of his *Dialogues*, says that he will compel all his subjects to submit to circumcision.

Moreover, all concur in saying that at the beginning of his reign he will succeed, by means of his trickery and fame, in making the Jews believe that he is the Messiah whom they have unceasingly awaited, and they, in their blindness, will hasten to receive him and honor him as such. That is how Suarez and most of the commentators interpret this saying of our Lord Jesus Christ, in St. John, 5:43: "I have come in my Father's name, and yet you do not accept me; but let someone come in his own name and him you will accept."[9]

The same meaning must be given to these other words of St. Paul to the Thessalonians: "because they have not opened their hearts to the truth in order to be saved. Therefore God is sending upon them a perverse spirit which leads them to give credence to

The actions of the Antichrist

falsehood."[10] Now, is it likely that the Jews would acclaim as Messiah a man who did not belong to their race, and had not been circumcised? The Antichrist, then, will be a Jew.

Will he be born of an illegitimate union? The theologian Suarez tells us that it is uncertain. Nevertheless, it may be presumed that a man so utterly evil, so opposed to Christ in his life and morals, will have an infamous origin; and, just as Jesus Christ had the Immaculate Virgin as His mother, so we may conclude, by analogy and induction, that His avowed adversary will be born of an impure union, and will be the offspring of an unchaste woman. "He will be a child of fornication," says St. John Damascene, "and his birth will be saturated with the breath and spirit of Satan."[11]

∽

What may be safely asserted of this man of iniquity is that, right from his most tender years, he will be completely possessed by the spirit and genius of the Devil. The lion of the abyss, which, in the last ages of mankind, God will unleash in His inscrutable justice in order to punish the infidelity of men, will unite himself with him in a certain way, infusing him with the fullness of his evil. No doubt he will not be deprived of the assistance of his guardian angel, nor of the necessary help of sufficient grace, which God bestows in this life upon every single man;[12] but his hatred of God will be so violent, his aversion for every good work so invincible, and his association and commerce with the spirit of darkness so close and continual that, from his cradle to his last breath, he will remain immutably hostile to all divine invitations, and grace from above will never penetrate his heart.

St. Thomas tells us that, in his person and his works, he will reveal himself as the reverse of the Son of God, and will parody His miracles and works.

Since his origin, the evil spirit has ever pursued one single goal: to usurp the place of the Omnipotent God, to form a kingdom for himself here below, in compensation for the kingdom of heaven from which he is excluded by his rebellion; and, says Tertullian, the more surely to attain this goal, he is in the habit of making himself the *ape of God*, counterfeiting all His works.

The adversary of the last times, then, will not only set himself up as the avowed, personal enemy of Jesus Christ: he will aim openly to dethrone Him, to replace Him in the homage and veneration of men and have directed to himself the worship and glory that are due to the Creator alone. He will declare, says St. Thomas, that he is the supreme, eternal being, and, by virtue of this, he will ordain that honors and a cult of worship shall be accorded him. Thus, he will have priests, he will have sacrifices offered to him, he will demand that his name should be invoked in oaths, and that men should use it to guarantee the security of treaties: *Ita ut ostendens se tanquam sit Deus.*[13]

In order to lend greater credence to this belief, he will counter divine revelation with false revelations; in opposition to the ceremonies of divine worship, he will set up his own impious rites; and, against the eternal Church founded by Christ, he will constitute an abominable society, of which he will be the leader and pontiff. St. Thomas adds that, just as the fullness of the Divinity dwells corporally in the Incarnate Word, so the fullness of all evil will dwell in this terrible man, whose mission and works will be but an imitation in reverse, and an execrable counterfeit, of the mission and works of Christ.

Through him Satan will put the seal on his wickedness. He will make this living figure the quintessence, as it were, of all the sinister schemes he has formed against mankind, and will not cease to arouse in him the burning, implacable hatred of God that moves him; and the Lord of heaven, in His hidden counsels, will allow this firebrand from hell to prevail for a time.

St. Thomas characterizes this delegate of Satan by calling him "*caput omnium malorum*":[14] the prince and instigator of all the covetousness of the flesh and all the aberrations of the mind — so much so that the masters of lies and architects of evil who have followed one another in the course of the ages will seem, by comparison with this man, mere pygmies beside a giant. Thus, he will repeat the infamous deeds of Nero; he will be filled with the hatred and violence of Diocletian; he will have the cunning and duplicity of Julian the Apostate; he will resort to intimidation and will bend the earth beneath his scepter like Mohammed; he will be a learned man, a philosopher, a skillful orator, outstanding in the arts and in the manufacturing sciences; he will handle mockery and ridicule like Voltaire. Lastly, he will work wonders, and rise into the air like Simon Magus.[15]

If you ask why Divine Providence will allow him to exercise such power and seduction, St. Paul the Apostle gives us the reason: "Because they have not opened their hearts to the truth in order to be saved. In punishment, God is sending upon them a perverse spirit which leads them to give credence to falsehood, so that all who have not believed the truth but have delighted in iniquity will be condemned."[16] Suarez says that God will permit the coming of the Antichrist particularly in order to punish the incredulity of the Jews. The latter, not having wished to worship the true Messiah, nor to be convinced by His doctrine and miracles, God will permit, for their punishment, to be attached to a false Messiah, accord credence to his impious deeds and doctrine, and follow him in his dissolute life.

At that time, the peril for souls will be great, and the scandal of the contagion universal. Nevertheless, in order that those who are taken by surprise may not attribute their misfortune to anyone but themselves, the Holy Spirit has sought to give us an outline in advance of the principal stages of that terrible, decisive trial, the climax of all those that mankind has undergone.

First of all, in order to make us understand the violence and ferocity of the man of sin, and the skill with which he will conduct the war he has undertaken against the saints, St. John the apostle depicts him in Revelation 13 under the figure of a monstrous beast, having ten heads or diadems on his horns and, written on each of these diadems, the name of a blasphemy. According to interpreters, these ten heads and ten diadems signify ten dependent kings who will be his lieutenants and will act as the executors of his trickery and cruelty.

Moreover, St. John tells us that he will be invested with absolute sovereignty, and that his power will extend over all tribes and peoples, over men of every nation and language.[17]

As he succeeds in overcoming the saints by a persecution carried to the extreme limit, he will simultaneously give free rein to all kinds of licentiousness, and there will be no freedom except for evil.

Lastly, he will be a master in the occult sciences and in the art of magic, and, through the agency of demons, he will perform wonderful deeds, which deluded men will take for true miracles.

The first of these miracles mentioned by St. John will be an apparent resurrection. In one of the wars where the Antichrist will appear as if mounted on a chariot of light and fire, he will be mortally wounded in the head. For a time he will be seen lifeless, apparently dead. Then, suddenly, he will rise, and his wound will be instantaneously healed. At the sight of this, the deluded men, the unbelievers and free-thinkers of that time who, like those of our own day, lacking any faith in the supernatural and in revealed truth, will spurn miracles as implacably condemned by science and reason — these men, I say, will reinforce faith in the hoax. They will exclaim, with enthusiasm and admiration, "Who is like unto the beast? Who shall be able to fight and conquer the beast?"

Secondly, the man of sin will make fire come down from heaven, in order to create the belief that he is the master of nature, the ruler of seasons, and that he has dominion over the sky and the stars.[18]

Thirdly, he will make a statue speak; demons will use a tree or a lifeless piece of wood as an instrument, with whose aid they will utter their fabrications and false oracles. Pieces of furniture will also be seen to move and run around of themselves, mountains will change their position in an instant, and demons, transformed into angels of light, will appear in the air.

Then, by an incomprehensible judgment of God, the free-thinkers and the great skeptics of the last times will take these impostures and conjuring tricks seriously. Duped by their own presumption and credulity, they will plunge headlong into all the follies of necromancy and divination, thus vindicating, in the face of the world, the oracle of the Sacred Books: "The Spirit distinctly says that in later times some will turn away from the faith and will heed deceitful spirits and things taught by demons."[19]

Lastly, it is written that the pride of the man of sin will be boundless. He will open his mouth in blasphemy against God, to blaspheme His Name, His tabernacle, and the saints in heaven. Daniel says that he will think himself entitled to abolish the customs of the times and the laws.[20] That is, he will suppress feast days and Sunday observance, alter the order of months and the length and division of weeks, and remove Christian names from the calendar, replacing them with the emblems of the lowest animals. In a word, this counterfeit of Christ will be an *atheist* in the full sense of the term. He will make away with the Cross and every religious symbol; as Daniel again declares, he will substitute abominable rites for the Christian sacrifice in every church. Pulpits will be silent; teaching and education will be lay, compulsory, and godless. Jesus Christ will be banished from the child's cradle, from the altar where spouses are united, from the bedside of the dying. Over the whole surface of the earth, worship of any god other than this christ of Satan will not be tolerated.

In His impenetrable designs, God will allow men to undergo this supreme, terrible trial in order to teach them how great the power of the Devil is, and how immense their own weakness; He desired to announce it to us so that we might prepare ourselves even now to sustain it, by having recourse to Him through prayer, and by providing ourselves with the spiritual weapons of charity and faith. In addition, the Antichrist is destined to bring out, in its splendor, the fidelity and constancy of those whose names are written in the Book of Life, those whom all his violence and wiles will not succeed in daunting.

On the other hand, it is certain that the duration and bitterness of this persecution will make it the ultimate criterion for discerning the elect from the reprobate since it will also be the ruin of many whose perseverance will fail; thus, it will be a test "destined to be the downfall and the rise of many . . . so that the thoughts of many hearts may be laid bare."[21]

Apostasies will be numerous, and courage will become rare. It is written that the powers of the heavens will be shaken, and the stars of the firmament will fall. In other words, the leaders of peoples will be seen to bend the knee before the reigning idol, and, what is still more lamentable, among the dispensers of science, the

luminaries of theology, and the golden tongues of sacred eloquence, a large number will abandon the truth and let themselves
be carried along with the current of depravity.

Again, St. John speaks of a strange, mysterious character that
all, "both small and great, rich and poor, slave and freemen,"[22] will
be forced to have on their right hand or on their forehead; this
mark will be a sign of apostasy, attesting that all those who bear it,
whether to please the master, or to escape his wrath, have re-
nounced the true Christ and enlisted forever under the banner of
His enemy.

Those who bear this degrading mark will enjoy the advantages
of fortune in abundance; they will have the high salaries, the
public offices, and a multiplicity of pleasures and of all desirable
possessions; but those who refuse to clothe themselves with this
abominable seal will be outlawed. It is written that "no man might
buy or sell anything unless he was first marked with the name of
the beast or with the number that stood for its name." All those
who do not have this mark will be forbidden to draw water from
the public fountains, and will even be unworthy to open their eyes
to the light of day and breathe the pure air of the heavens.

"Those days will be more filled with anguish than any from the
beginning of the world until now or in all ages to come."[23] The just
will be dishonored and despised; they will be called fools and dis-
turbers of the peace; they will be accused of trampling upon honor
and patriotism, by refusing to acclaim the greatest man ever to have
appeared in the world, the incomparable genius who has raised
human civilization to the zenith of perfection and progress.

If the just were not to be sustained by a special assistance from
God, there would not be a single one who could withstand the violence of such temptation: *Ita ut in errorem inducantur (si fieri
potest) etiam electi.*[24]

The End of the Present World

In the dreadful days of the great French Revolution, there were still some havens, places of safety open to convicts and outlaws. The countryside was sane; there were impenetrable forests and hidden, isolated paths. However, in the period we are engaged in describing, science and human discoveries will have reached their zenith. Every mountain will have been bored. There will be no more rocks or caves, islands or deserts, where freedom can expect a refuge. The home itself will no longer be safe: for it is said that "brother will hand over brother for execution and likewise the father his child."[25]

It is not usual for the Sacred Books, when they reveal the future to us, to go into such precise, minute detail. The prophets speak to us only enigmatically, and in abbreviated form. In general, they limit themselves to marking out the main lines of future events. However, so far as the final combat waged against the saints is concerned, the inspired Apostles have followed the maxim *mala proevisa minus feriunt* ("evils foreseen do less harm"); and they have neglected nothing that might strengthen the just during those days of trial and great calamity.

Thus, they teach us that, at that time, the East will once more become the focal point of politics and human affairs, and that the impostor, possessed with the blind, maniacal passion to desecrate the holiest places (those that have been the scene of the labors and suffering of the God-Man), will establish his royalty at Jerusalem. For our consolation, they tell us that God will shorten the duration of his power, limiting it to forty-two months, or three and a half years.[26]

The number given in the Sacred Books probably does not express the length of time the man of sin will need in order to conquer the earth and reach the zenith of his omnipotence. It is not reasonable to suppose that, even with the aid of the superhuman and satanic powers that will be at his disposal, he will be able to become master of the earth in a single day. It is to be supposed that he will attain the fullness of his sovereignty only gradually, and will require a long period to subdue the nations and envelop the whole world in the murky web of his trickery and seduction. All we know from St. John and Daniel is that his dominion over men "of every race, tribe, and language" will subsist "*usque ad tempus, et tempora, et dimidium temporis*" — that is, one year, two more years, and half a year. Daniel tells us, "From the time when the perpetual sacrifice shall be taken away and the abomination of desolation shall reign in the holy place, a thousand two hundred ninety days will have elapsed."[27] Hence, it follows that the point when Christ will no longer be present on our altars, offering Himself as a victim to His Father's justice in order to offset men's crimes, is to be reckoned from the day when the Antichrist has obtained universal dominion: only then will the unbloody Sacrifice of the Altar cease to be celebrated; but, until that day, and during the time taken by the Antichrist to achieve his kingship, the Sacrifice of the Mass will continue to subsist.

St. John indicates the name of the Antichrist; but he deems it proper to tell us only in the form of numerals. We know that in various languages, numbers can be translated into letters of the alphabet and, conversely, the letters of the alphabet into numbers. So, St. John tells us that, in a language he does not make known to us, the name of the beast is expressed by the number 666.

The Fathers and Doctors have labored to discover the key to this mysterious number and to ascertain the name hidden beneath it, but their investigations have come to nothing. It is possible to imagine a vast number of names whose letters, according to the way they are put together, express the number indicated by St. John. We cannot go beyond the view of St. Irenaeus,[28] who assures us that the Holy Spirit presented the name of the Antichrist in the form of this enigmatic number, because He wanted its true meaning to remain unknown until the fulfillment of His prophecy, the day when it would be in the interest of men for the Antichrist to be revealed to them. Then, says St. John, "he that hath understanding, let him count the number of the beast."[29]

St. Paul tells us that God is faithful, for He has made a pact with temptation and does not permit man to be tested beyond his strength. Here, the temptation will exceed the normal conditions and laws of mankind. It befits the mercy of God that the remedy should be proportionate to the extent of the evil. Now, the means of succor foretold is the most superhuman and extraordinary, the most alien to the rules of history and the ordinary workings of Providence, of all those that heaven has sent man since the Incarnation.

Just when the tempest is at its most violent, when the Church is leaderless, when the unbloody Sacrifice has everywhere ceased and everything seems humanly lost, two witnesses, St. John tells us, will be seen to arise.

These two witnesses will be two strange men, appearing suddenly amidst the world, without anyone being able to say of what birth or origin they are, nor from what place or family they have come. This is how St. John speaks of them in the eleventh chapter of Revelation:

> I will commission my two witnesses to prophesy for those twelve hundred and sixty days, dressed in sackcloth. These are the two olive trees and the two lampstands that stand in the presence of the Lord of the earth.

No tongue can express the sheer amazement that will grip mankind at the sight of these two men, strangers to our passions and affairs, one of them having lived six thousand years, the other thirty centuries, in some ethereal region or other, beneath firmaments and upon spheres inaccessible to our senses and understanding. Yet, neither of these witnesses is alien to the human family. One of these candlesticks and olive trees is Enoch, the great-great-grandfather of Noah, the direct ancestor of the whole human race. The other is the prophet Elijah, who, as the Savior has said, is destined to restore all things.[30] He will come a second time to stem the tide of wickedness, more reckless and unrestrained than it was in the days of Ahab. It will also be the hour of the redemption of Israel. The great prophet will convince the posterity of Abraham that the Messiah has come, and will remove the veil of ignorance and darkness that has lain heavy upon their eyes for nineteen centuries.

What sort of appearance and bearing will these strangers from another age present? What venerable majesty will shine forth from their persons? What inspired language will flow from their lips? Holy Scripture does not tell us. It teaches us that they will prophesy for 1,260 days, clothed in sackcloth, their garments and features bearing the marks of humility and penance. According to Daniel, the persecution under the Antichrist will last for 1,290 days; so the preaching of Enoch and Elijah will be thirty days shorter. Hence, it follows that they will appear in the period when the persecution is unleashed with the greatest violence.

How, within the space of time set for their mission, will they manage to give their testimony in all inhabited places, and cover the whole extent of the earth? We answer that it will not be necessary for them to visit every town; it will be enough for them to appear in the principal ones, and for their preaching to be heard in the capitals and main centers of population where the Antichrist has been present and has exercised his most powerful fascination. Furthermore, it is unlikely that Enoch and Elijah will be constantly together; it is more probable that they will preach separately, until, by a command from God, or following a providential inspiration, they suddenly come together for the supreme battle.

At first, no doubt, incredulous men will refuse to admit their identity. They will seek to lay hold of them, and punish them as tricksters and sham visionaries; public opinion will shower them with satirical barbs and mockery, and the organs of publicity will persist in ignoring them, and pretend not to know of them. The persecutor, foaming with rage, will try to have them put to death; but, as long as their mission lasts, they will be guarded by a superior force. Here is what St. John says:

> And if anyone tries to harm them, fire will come out of the mouths of these two witnesses to devour their enemies. Anyone attempting to harm them will surely be slain in this way. These witnesses have power to close up the sky so that no rain will fall during the time of their mission. They also have power to turn water into blood and to afflict the earth at will with any kind of plague.[31]

The Gospel is not so specific about the result and efficacy of the mission of these two great witnesses; but it may be taken as certain that they will undeceive a large mass of the deluded, and bring back most of those whom fear or ambition had enticed from worship of the true God. Indeed their preaching will need to have a power that no other words since those of the Gospel have ever had, since it will overcome the obstinacy of the Jews, who, bowing to the luster of the marvels and the evidence of the facts, will return beneath the staff of the Shepherd of shepherds, to form with the Christians one flock and one fold.[32]

However, God gives His graces with due proportion. When the light has been given, when men have had all the time they need to distinguish truth from error, God, in His wisdom, will then suspend the miracle. That is how Providence invariably acts. So it was of old with Samson when, once the Philistines had been humbled and defeated, God took away from him His spirit and the stupendous strength with which He had endowed him. Heaven proceeded again in the same way with Joan of Arc: once her mission had been fulfilled, when she had routed the English and placed the crown back upon the head of Charles VII, her genius and military talent seemed to pale; she was taken prisoner and reverted to the normal circumstances of human life.

So shall it be in the case of Enoch and Elijah. Besides, the miracle, if prolonged, would have no other effect than to confirm in their obduracy those stubborn men who had refused to receive their words with a submissive ear and heart. In short, the two witnesses are not dead, although one of them is six thousand and the other three thousand years old, and it is necessary that they should seal their testimony by the shedding of their blood, and be subjected to the law of human nature from which Christ Himself did not desire to be spared.

Here, then, is what will take place, says St. John, in the chapter already quoted:

And when they shall have finished their testimony, the beast that ascends out of the abyss shall make war against them and shall overcome them and kill them. And their bodies shall lie in the streets of the great city which is called spiritually Sodom; where their Lord also was crucified. And men, tribes, and people shall see their bodies for three days and a half; and they shall not suffer their bodies to be laid in sepulchers. And they that dwell upon the earth shall rejoice over them and make merry; and shall send gifts one to another, because these two prophets tormented them that dwelt upon the earth. And after three days and a half, the spirit of life from God entered into them; and they stood upon their feet; and great fear fell upon them that saw them ... And at that hour there was made a great earthquake; and the tenth part of the city fell. And there were slain in the earthquake, names of men, seven thousand; and the rest were cast into a fear and gave glory to the God of heaven.[33]

St. John does not tell us what the fate of the Antichrist will be, but St. Paul teaches that "the Lord Jesus will destroy him with the breath of His mouth and annihilate him by manifesting His own presence."[34]

Some have concluded from this passage that Christ is to come down in person to strike His great adversary, and that this will be the day when He will appear in His glory and majesty. This interpretation is incorrect. St. Thomas and St. John Chrysostom explain the words *quem Dominus Jesus destruet illustratione adventus sui* ("whom the Lord Jesus will destroy with the brightness of His coming") in the sense that Christ will strike the Antichrist by dazzling him with a brightness that will be like an omen and sign of His Second Coming. St. Paul does not at all say that Christ will kill him with His own hands, but by His breath, *spiritu oris sui* ("with the spirit of His mouth") — that is, as St. Thomas explains, by virtue of His power, as a result of His command; whether, as some believe, executing it through the cooperation of St. Michael the Archangel, or having some other agent, visible or invisible, spiritual or inanimate, intervene. What is certain is that Satan will be hurled back into the darkness of the abyss, the reign of the man of evil will be utterly destroyed, and his power, which aspired to extend up to the heavens, will vanish like a cloud of smoke.

◠

Will the resurrection of the body and the Last Judgment follow close upon that great event? Holy Scripture is silent on this point, and the Church has not wished to define anything. Among the interpreters of Holy Writ, some affirm it and others deny it. Suarez expresses the view that after the death of the Antichrist, the world will not subsist more than forty-five days. He bases his opinion on the prophecy of Daniel, who, after announcing that the persecution by the man of sin will last for 1,290 days, adds these words: "Happy he who has hope and holds firm until the 1,335th day."[35]

This opinion, however, does not seem to be the most certain. The most authoritative view, and the one that appears to be most in harmony with Holy Scripture, is that, after the fall of the Antichrist, the Catholic Church will once again enter upon a period of prosperity and triumph. In fact, does not St. Paul, the inspired Apostle — of all the sons of Israel, the one who saw most clearly into the future and destiny of his people — seem explicitly to affirm this doctrine? Does he not affirm it when — recalling the effects of the grace and blessing obtained by the conversion of the Jews, who, in accordance with the prophecy of Malachi,[36] will not be brought back to the truth until they are enlightened by the preaching of Enoch and Elijah — he exclaims, moved by a holy transport: "If the fall of the Jews, which brought about the conversion of the Gentiles, was the strength of the Church and the richness of the world, how much more will their resurrection enrich the world; and if their loss has become the salvation of men, what will their return be if not a resurrection for the world from death to life?"[37]

These words are formal, and appear to leave no room for doubt. They are in harmony with those of St. John: "I then saw . . . those who had won the victory over the beast and its image and also the number that signified its name . . . They sang the song of Moses, the servant of God, and the song of the Lamb."[38]

In other words, the Christians and the remnant of the Jews henceforth have only one spirit and one faith, they address the same praises and blessings to the Son of God and, together, proclaim His glory, saying, "Mighty and wonderful are Your works, Lord God Almighty! Righteous and true are Your ways, O King of the nations!"[39]

Is it really credible that the day when all people will be united in this long-sought harmony will be the one when the heavens shall pass away with great violence — that the period when the Church Militant enters her fullness will coincide with that of the final catastrophe? Would Christ cause the Church to be born again, in all her glory and all the splendor of her beauty, only to dry up forthwith the springs of her youth and her inexhaustible fecundity?

However, if it may be granted that, after the Antichrist, the end of the world will not come for some centuries still, the same cannot be said of the supreme crisis that shall bring about the great unity; for, if we study but a moment the signs of the present time, the menacing symptoms of our political situation and revolutions, as well as the progress of civilization and the increasing advance of evil, corresponding to the progress of civilization and the discoveries in the material order, we cannot fail to foresee the proximity of the coming of the man of sin, and of the days of desolation foretold by Christ.[40]

⌒

Holy Scripture gives us three main features that will mark the dominance of the Antichrist. First, he will be emperor and absolute master of the universe. Secondly, he will have Jerusalem as his capital. Thirdly, he will be as clever as he is violent, and the war he will wage against the saints will be, primarily, one of deceit and seduction.

First, the Antichrist will be lord of the world. It is abundantly clear that the effect of all the events of the present time is to prepare the social setting in which the dominance of the man of sin will be exercised.

On the one hand, the railway has reduced barriers and triumphed over distance. The telegraph allows an oppressive ruler to transmit his orders from one point of the universe to the other with the instantaneousness of thought. Moreover, the peoples of the diverse races are mingling: Russian and American, Japanese and Chinese meet on the same ships, rub shoulders, and cross one another's paths, in our great cities, and in the commercial centers of Europe, California, and Equatorial Africa.

Already, the distant peoples are adopting our inventions, casting rifled guns, and beginning to build armored ships and arsenals. China — that vast empire swarming with people, where, each day, the seas and rivers engulf a huge excess of human beings whom the rich, fertile soil can no longer feed — she has her mechanics, her engineers, and is learning our strategy and industrial progress. Now, have our latest wars not shown that, at the present time, the issue of battles lies above all in numbers, and that, in armies, as in the realm of politics, what determines success and wins the victory is the brutal, inexorable law of superior numbers?

Thus, the hour bids to be not far off when these millions . . . who populate the east and north of Asia will have at their disposal more soldiers, more ammunition, and more military leaders than all other peoples; and the day can be foreseen when, having become fully conscious of their number and strength, they will hurl themselves in countless hordes upon our Europe, enfeebled and forsaken by God. There will then be invasions more terrible than those of the Vandals and Huns ... Provinces will be pillaged, rights violated, and small nations destroyed and ground down like dust. Then, a vast agglomeration of all the inhabitants of the earth will be observed, under the scepter of a single leader, who will be either the Antichrist, or one of his immediate predecessors. That day will see the death of human freedom.

The unity of all peoples will be rebuilt, for the last time, upon the ruins of all the suppressed nationalities. The empire of evil will be accomplished. Divine Providence will scourge the world, by subjecting it, body and soul, to one master ... who will be moved solely by hatred of men and contempt of God.

Accordingly, any careful observer of the events of the present time cannot escape the conviction that everything is being done to bring about a social environment where the man of sin, by combining in his person all the depravity and every false doctrine of his age, will be produced spontaneously and effortlessly, like the parasitical tapeworm that breeds naturally in gangrenous flesh and organs.

Yet the apparently incomprehensible thing that, at first sight, no sign seems to presage, is that the seat of his empire will be Jerusalem.

Well, it is easy to see that, if the materialistic, atheistic civilization, whose impending coming the free-thinkers and the irreligious press are always predicting, ever dawns on the world, its center of action and seat of public power will be Jerusalem.

In fact, when the Christian Faith has finally died out in the hearts of men — when pleasure and well-being have become the gods of the day — human activity will then have a single goal: the power of the state; one single lever and stimulus: public opinion;

one inspiration and driving force: and this stimulus, this sinew, this driving force, will be gold. Gold will take precedence over religion and morality, becoming the basis of politics and the keystone of all institutions. The pontiffs and kings will be the financiers; and the people who possesses the most gold will be the ones who will soon exercise the greatest control over us.

Now, after fifty centuries of existence, nineteen of them in misfortune, a certain people is found everywhere, scattered in every quarter of the globe, meeting on the most distant shores, mingling with the whole human family, still enduring, still in search of their Messiah, dreaming of rebuilding their temple and, despite all changes and upheavals, unshakable in their homogeneity and in the pursuit of their goal.

It must be said, in justice to them, that they are an active, temperate, and hard-working race. If we speak of them, we do so in the abstract and solely from the point of view of their destiny and of their providential and historical mission . . . this people of illustrious ancestry, which has given to the world Christ, the Apostles, and the Immaculate Virgin.

We, Christians and children of Israel, are closer to one another than we think. As one well-known speaker has said: Christianity is Judaism with its apex; Judaism is Christianity without its apex.

Nevertheless, the facts are there, and it is impossible for the Christian philosopher to ignore or disguise them . . . Judaism is really a confessional faith and doctrine grafted onto one nationality and race. All other peoples — Frenchmen, Italians, Germans, Spaniards — if they live for a certain time subject to the same government and form of administration, if they are ruled by the same laws and institutions — do not take long to merge, unite their interests, mix their blood, and acquire the same aspirations and patriotic spirit. The Jew is *not able to be integrated*: he is planted among the other peoples in the position of a *tenant*, as a famous writer has said; or, rather, he considers himself an exile and captive amidst the other nations. Instead of a *real* motherland, he has only an *ideal* motherland, Palestine. Jerusalem is the only permanent city for which he yearns. In his speeches and writings, on every page of his newspapers and reviews, he manifests the hope he has never ceased to cherish of rebuilding a new, Jewish Kingdom, either at Jerusalem or in the surrounding area . . .

. . . Now, if we take Israel as a whole, leaving aside the men of that nation who have fallen into rationalism and unbelief, the nucleus of the Jewish race have not ceased to nourish the same illusions we have just indicated: still expecting a Messiah, whom they continue to see as a powerful conqueror who will subdue the earth. Not long ago, one of the most authoritative exponents of the Talmud dared to say, "A new messianism must be born; a Jerusalem of a new order, set reverently between East and West, must replace the twofold city of Caesars and Popes."[41] Furthermore, it is an established fact that the majority of orthodox believers have retained, as their slogan and watchword, the remark once uttered by a famous rabbi: "Jerusalem is still the pivot of our hopes and of our faith."

Now, is it improbable that, in social conditions like ours, in which the most dreadful and unforeseen events loom up with the rapidity of steam and lightning, there may live a man who will take advantage of the chaos into which our revolutions will have cast us, and succeed in beguiling the masses and gaining mastery over minds and hearts; then, pledging himself to regenerate mankind, will send out a rallying cry to which all his co-religionists will respond, thus achieving the conquest of universal power, a stupendous dominion over minds and bodies, a dominion accepted enthusiastically by the universality of misled, seduced peoples?

Lastly, may we not believe that this powerful and wicked man, who will imprison the world in the jaws of an indescribable, unrestrained despotism and unify the human race through the enslavement of consciences and the humbling of spirits, will be the personage portrayed and predicted by St. John as the Antichrist, and that he will be the man whom Divine Providence has desired to use in order to undeceive Israel, who will at first have acclaimed him as her Messiah and King?

⌒

Finally, what will be the characteristic marks of the persecution under the Antichrist? Its main features have been described by Cornelius à Lapide and Suarez, in accordance with Scripture and the Fathers.

At the outset, what is certain and should be taken in faith is that, of all the persecutions the Church has had to suffer, that of the Antichrist will be the most terrible and the most violent.

First, because this persecution will be general, and will extend over the whole earth. It is written: "They spread over the whole country and surrounded the camp of the saints and the beloved city."[42]

St. Augustine, in book 20 of the *City of God*, explains this text from St. John by saying that all the infidels, heretics, sectarians, and depraved men, scattered over the surface of the earth, will unite with the Antichrist to make war on the saints and to persecute those who are faithful to God.

Secondly, this persecution will be the most severe and violent of all because it will be inspired not by superstition or fanaticism, nor by a blind attachment to the worship of idols, as were the persecutions unleashed by the pagan emperors. Its purpose will not be to assuage pride, or to satisfy an unbridled lust for power, like the persecution of Mohammed. Nor will it be aroused by the unrestrained lusts of the flesh and by the lure of plunder, like the one to which the German princes subjected the Church under Protestantism and in the lifetime of Luther. It will be a persecution inspired solely by hatred of God, in which God and His Christ will be directly challenged, and its sole objective will be the extermination of the divine kingdom, the complete annihilation of Christianity and of all positive religion. Thus, the Tiberiuses, Neros, and the most frightful tyrants of paganism at least acknowledged an apprehension and, as it were, a distant reflection of the divinity in the idols, which they sought to compel the Christians to adore; but, in the times of which we are speaking, it will no longer be permissible to accord even a modified and corrupted adoration to any divinity. All men without exception will be forced to honor and render a cult of worship to Satan himself, personified in the Antichrist — that is, in the most evil and abominable man that humanity has ever produced.

Thirdly, this persecution, which will mark the last ages, will be waged with an irresistible seductiveness, "insomuch as to deceive (if possible) even the elect."[43] Cornelius à Lapide says, "He will excel at all the crafts, forms of guile, and practices of politicians." At first, the Antichrist will convince the Jews that he is the Messiah. In order to deceive them the more successfully, he will hide behind a mask of moderation and feigned holiness. When St. Paul tells us that he will have himself worshiped *in the temple of God*, he seems to imply that he will rebuild the temple of Jerusalem, utterly destroyed by Titus; consequently, he will prescribe circumcision and, for a time, restore the bloody sacrifices and the other rites of the Judaic religion.

As for those who are foreign to the Jewish religion, he will draw them to himself, first, by persuasion and eloquence. He will be

skilled in artifice and will be taught by the Devil himself all knowledge useful for the ends for which the evil spirit destines him. St.
Anselm tells us that he will be acquainted with all the natural
sciences and will know all the sacred texts by heart.[44] In the second place, he will win men over by lavishing gold and riches. He
will be the wealthiest person on earth. Satan will deliver to him all
the treasures concealed in the bowels of the sea and in the hidden
depths of the earth.[45]

Fourthly, he will fill all men with admiration by his genius, and
by the amazing rapidity of his elevation to the height of fortune
and omnipotence. As for the ignorant and the multitude, he will
fascinate them by marvels, *cujus est adventus secundum operationem
Satanae, in omni virtute et prodigiis mendacibu* — "whose coming is
according to the working of Satan, in all power, and signs, and lying wonders."[46] St. Thomas says that, just as Christ worked miracles in confirmation of His doctrine, so also the man of sin will
work false miracles in confirmation of his errors; and just as the
true Christ worked wonders by the power of God, the author of all
truth, so, too, His adversary will work, as we have indicated above,
by the power of Satan, the father of fraud and lies.

Thus, the man of sin will not perform true miracles, like Jesus
Christ, but will perform false and apparent ones. All his wonderful
works will be, in reality, mere illusions and works of fantasy; so
that, as St. Athanasius[47] says, when he appears to resurrect a dead
man, either the man whom he resurrects will not really have been
dead, or else, if he had been dead, he will not really be restored to
life.

Lastly, the same saint continues, the works performed by the
Antichrist that appear to transcend the laws of nature will not be
miracles in the true sense, but effects and phenomena of the physical order, performed through the intermediary of certain secret,

hidden, and natural causes. In order to better captivate men, the Antichrist will permit lasciviousness and the licentiousness of the flesh, and will stimulate the most intoxicating pleasures, *totus erit in libidinibus et concupiscentiis feminarum* — "he shall follow the passions and lust of women."[48]

Fifthly, the persecution under the Antichrist will be the bloodiest and most barbarous of all those which Christianity has ever suffered. Jesus Christ so assures us, when He says, "For those days will be more filled with anguish than any from the beginning of the world until now or in all ages to come."[49] This can be surmised if we refer back to two causes. The first is the vast power and the stupendous instruments of force and destruction that the Antichrist will have at his disposal and, with these, the evil and fury of the men appointed to execute his commands. The second will be the terrifying wickedness of the Devil, because in those days, says St. John, God will allow him to leave the fiery prison where he is chained, and will give him full permission to seduce and satisfy his hatred of the human race.[50] Whence it follows, says St. Cyril, that there will then be multitudes of martyrs, more glorious and admirable than those who formerly fought with lions, in the amphitheaters of Rome and Gaul.

These had to struggle against mere agents of the Devil, but the confessors of the last ages will have to struggle against him who is a *murderer from the beginning*. To torment them, the old enemy will practice monstrous tortures with unheard-of refinements, unparalleled in past centuries, which the human mind could never have contrived to invent by itself.

Finally — the last feature of the persecution under the Antichrist — it will be so violent that it will succeed in making almost the entirety of Christians apostatize. "And it was given unto him to make war with the saints, and to overcome them."[51] "For, as I watched, that horn made war against the holy ones and was victorious . . ."[52] St. Paul informs us that Christ will not return until the great apostasy has come.[53] Interpreting these words of the apostle, St. Augustine tells us that if, in every age, we have seen believers renounce Christ on account of the wiles of heretics and the fear of persecutors and tyrants, nevertheless the defection that will take place under the Antichrist is called the apostasy, properly speaking, because, in number and extension, this apostasy will exceed all that has been seen in previous times.

However, it would not be correct to conclude from this testimony that there will be none of the elect left on earth, and that the Son of God will fail to keep the promise made to His Church, when He said, *Propter electos, dies breviabuntur* ("because of the elect, the days will be shortened"). Moreover, St. John, in his Revelation adds, "And he [the beast] will be worshiped by those who dwell upon the earth whose names are not written in the book of life."[54]

St. Augustine tells us that, in the reign of the Antichrist, there will be multitudes of martyrs who will display a heroic constancy, and also a number, more or less large, of confessors who will manage to escape into caves and high or sheer mountains, and God will see to it that these sanctuaries shall elude the vigilance and investigations of the persecutors, and will not permit the Devil to point them out to them.

Daniel tells us that, at the time when this terrible persecution breaks out, the abomination of desolation will openly sit enthroned in the holy place. "The king shall do as he pleases," says Daniel. "He shall exalt himself and make himself greater than any god; he shall utter dreadful blasphemies against the God of gods . . . He shall have no regard for the gods of his ancestors . . . for no god shall he have regard."[55]

In other words, once the man of sin has cowed the human race by his threats and entangled it in the meshes of his lies and wiles, he will observe no restraint, show his hand, and act openly. He will not permit anyone to worship or invoke any other god than himself, and will proclaim himself sole lord of heaven and earth. Wherever he is not present in person, men will be obliged to pay homage to his image or statue: *Et elevabitur, magnificabitur adversus omnem Deum.*[56] He will tolerate neither the Mosaic religion, nor natural religion itself. He will persecute with equal thoroughness Jews, schismatics, heretics, deists, and every sect that recognizes the existence of a supreme being and the immortality of the life to come. Yet God, in His wisdom, will draw good from evil. The horrible tempest that His justice has allowed to be unleashed upon the earth will result in the disappearance of false religions. Along with Judaism, it will abolish the remains of Mohammedanism, idolatrous superstitions, and every religion hostile to the Church.

It will deal the finishing blow to the sects of darkness. Freemasonry, Carbonarism, Illuminism, and all subversive societies will vanish in the vortex of wickedness which will be their work, and which they had prepared for centuries in the belief that it would be their definitive, supreme triumph. They will have assisted unintentionally in the establishment of the reign of unity foretold by our Lord: "There shall be one flock then, and one shepherd."[57]

The triumph of the wicked one will be of short duration, but the consolations that follow will be universal, abundant, proportionate to the extent of the tribulations the Church will have suffered.

However, the final consummation will not come yet, as it is written:

And then the seventh angel blew his trumpet, and loud voices in heaven cried out; the voices of angels and of virgins, together with the voices of confessors and holy martyrs, will hail Christ with praise and acclamations, giving thanks for His victory over the Antichrist, and for the extermination of the wicked. All men, now become worshipers of one and the same God, all professing the same faith, united in the same adoration, sharing the same table, will exclaim in chorus, "The kingdom of this world now belongs to our Lord and to his Anointed One . . . We praise you, O Lord God Almighty, who is and who was and who are to come; because You have assumed your great power, and You have begun Your reign."[58]

⌒

Notes

1 Tertullian (c. 160-225), ecclesiastical writer.

2 St. John Chrysostom (c. 347-407), Archbishop of Constantinople and Doctor; named Chrysostom, or "Golden Mouth" for his eloquent preaching.

3 2 Thess. 2:1-4.

4 St. Augustine (354-430), Bishop of Hippo and Doctor; St. Thomas Aquinas (c. 1225-1274), Dominican philosopher, theologian, and Doctor.

5 St. Robert Bellarmine (1542-1621; Jesuit cardinal, teacher, writer, and Doctor), *De Pontifice*.

6 Cf. Dan. 11:37: "He shall have no regard for the gods of his ancestors."

7 Cf. Gen. 49:17.

8 Cf. Jer. 8:16.

9 John 5:43.

10 2 Thess. 2:10-11.

11 St. John Damascene, *De fide orthodoxa*.

12 "It is plausible, however, that the Antichrist will have such tremendous malice, will be so habituated to thinking and doing evil, and will have so great a

bond of familiarity with the Demon that he will scarcely ever have regard for a good inspiration, the spiritual action of the guardian angels, or God's grace" (Suarez, *Disputationes*).

[13] Cf. 2 Thess. 2:4.

[14] St. Thomas Aquinas, *Summa Theologica*, III, Q. 8.

[15] Cf. Acts 8:9-24.

[16] 2 Thess. 2:10, 11, 12.

[17] Rev. 13:5, 8.

[18] It is well known that the devils, deprived of their original beauty and goodness, have not lost any of their powers. They can act on the elements, condense clouds and vapors, project lightning and unleash storms. As for miracles properly so called, God alone can perform them. A miracle is a derogation of the laws of nature which surpasses every created force, whether human or angelic. Thus, the Antichrist will not work true miracles, but only false and apparent ones.

[19] 1 Tim. 4:1.

[20] Cf. Daniel 7:25.

[21] Luke 2:34-35.

[22] Cf. Rev. 13:16.

[23] Matt. 24:21.

[24] Cf. Matt. 24:24: "False messiahs and false prophets will appear, performing signs and wonders *so great as to mislead even the chosen if that were possible*."

[25] Mark 13:12.

[26] Cf. Rev. 13:5.

[27] Cf. Dan. 12:11.

[28] St. Irenaeus (c. 125-c. 203), student of St. Polycarp, missionary, bishop of Lyons, and Church Father.

[29] Cf. Rev. 13:18.

[30] It is clear from the context that, by the two candlesticks and the two olive trees, St. John does not mean any two saints or preachers, but two definite personages, endowed with an extraordinary power and holiness. Now — pondering all the facts and circumstances foretold to us about the life and death of these personages, and recalling all that we are told about them by Scripture, especially in Sirach, chapter 48 and by the prophet Malachi, concerning the mission they will one day be called upon to fulfill — Bede,

St. Anselm, St. Augustine, and a large number of the Fathers assure us that the two witnesses of whom Revelation speaks are none other than Enoch and Elijah, and that they were miraculously preserved from death for no other purpose than to fight against the Antichrist, and bear testimony to Jesus Christ, at the end of the world.

[31] Rev. 11:5-6.

[32] Sir. 48:9-10.

[33] Cf. Rev. 11:7-13.

[34] Cf. 2 Thess. 2:8.

[35] Cf. Dan. 12:12.

[36] Cf. Mal. 3:23-24: "Lo, I will send you Elijah, the prophet, before the day of the Lord comes, the great and terrible day, to turn the hearts of the fathers to their children, and the hearts of the children to their fathers . . ."

[37] Rom. 11:11-12: "I further ask, does their stumbling mean that they are forever fallen? Not at all! Rather, by their transgression salvation has come to the Gentiles to stir Israel to envy. But if their transgression and their diminishing have meant riches for the Gentile world, how much more their full number!"

[38] Rev. 15:2-3.

[39] Rev. 15:3.

[40] It is undeniable that all governments at the present time are at work accomplishing this abominable operation of apostasy, and that they are striving to banish Jesus Christ from the school, the army, and from the very abode of justice! Are not His Cross and His adorable name blasphemed and held up as a symbol of ignorance and fanaticism? Has not the Church been outlawed and excluded from the councils of governments and deliberative assemblies? Are not all the laws that are formulated marked with the seal of odious intolerance toward her, and have they any other purpose than to diminish her authority and influence? Blasphemy is raised to the level of a privilege and a right. Parallel with the destruction of Christianity, we see the reappearance of paganism, in the form of base materialism, marked by the exaltation of all that flatters the senses, and the glorification of the basest and most brutish instincts; a paganism that pervades industry, the arts, and literature, and predominates in all public institutions. Christianity is declared to be the enemy, and at the same time, materialism is presented to the aspirations of peoples as the moving force of progress, and the god of the future. Now, if the extremes of evil do not meet with a prompt and vigorous

response, if the defection continues on its course, it may be predicted that this war on God must inevitably end in total, consummated apostasy. It is but a small step from the cult of the state — that is, the utilitarian spirit and the worship of the god-state which is the religion of our time, to the worship of the individual man. We have almost reached that point . . . and, proceeding from these facts and observations, we must conclude that the hypothesis of the proximity of the Antichrist's coming is more probable than the hypothesis that considers his coming as remote.

[41] *Archives Israelites.*

[42] Cf. Rev. 20:8-9.

[43] Cf. Matt. 24:24.

[44] St. Anselm (c. 1033-1109), Archbishop of Canterbury and Doctor.

[45] Dan. 11:43.

[46] Cf. 2 Thess. 2:9.

[47] St. Athanasius (c. 297-373), Bishop of Alexandria and Doctor.

[48] Cf. Dan. 11:37.

[49] Matt. 24:21.

[50] Rev. 20:7-8.

[51] Rev. 13:7.

[52] Dan. 7:21.

[53] 2 Thess. 2:3.

[54] Rev. 13:8.

[55] Dan. 11:36-37. It is true that the prophet also intends, by these words, to depict the persecution by Antiochus and the fury against the Lord's people which will fill this prince. Nevertheless, as Suarez observes, Antiochus was only the image of the Antichrist, and the evils to which he subjected the faithful Jews are meant to be a brief outline of those which the Christians of the last days will endure.

[56] Cf. Dan. 11:36.

[57] John 10:16.

[58] Rev. 11:15-17.

The Resurrection of the Dead and the General Judgment

*Ecce mysterium vobis dico: . . . in momento,
in ictu oculi, in novissima tuba (canet enim tuba),
mortui resurgent incorrupti.*

≈

*Now I am going to tell you a mystery . . .
in an instant, in the twinkling of an eye,
at the sound of the last trumpet;
the trumpet will sound
and the dead will be raised incorruptible.*

1 Corinthians 15:51-52

The world must have an end, and that end will not take place until the Antichrist has appeared.

Protestantism and unbelief reject the individuality of the Antichrist. They consider him to be a mere myth, an allegorical, imaginary person; or else they see this man of sin, foretold by St. Paul, as nothing more than the leader of the anti-Christian fight, the chief and messiah of Freemasonry and the sects, raised up in order to bring civilization to its zenith, by liberating it forever from the darkness of superstition — in other words, eliminating all positive religion and every revealed truth from the whole surface of the earth.

Among the truths relating to the end of our destiny in time, there is one that is particularly repugnant to human passions, one that rationalism and free-thinking assail ceaselessly and remorselessly, making it the target of their most astute sophistry and of their most audacious denials. That doctrine — the most glorious and most consoling of all doctrines for our human nature — is the future resurrection of our bodies. Sometimes, as St. Paul found at Athens, unbelieving science seeks to crush the doctrine beneath the weight of its derision and sarcasm; at other times, as happened at the tribunal of the praetor Felix, it turns pale on hearing it mentioned, and feels terror-stricken: *Disputante autem illo . . . de judicio futuro, tremefactus Felix respondit . . . Vade: tempore autem opportuno accersam te.*[1]

The End of the Present World

It is clear from this passage, and from many others recurring at various points in the letters of St. Paul, that the dogma of the resurrection of the dead was the favorite and popular subject of the apostle's preaching.

He expounded it boldly in the praetoria, in the synagogues, and in the areopagus of the wise men and philosophers of Greece. In the eyes of St. Paul, this doctrine of the future resurrection is the foundation of our hopes, the solution to the mystery of life, the principle, crux, and conclusion of the whole Christian system. Without it, divine and human laws would be devoid of all sanction, and spiritual doctrines would be an absurdity. Wisdom would consist solely in living and enjoying like the animals; for, if man is not to live again after death, the just man who fights against his own feelings and checks his passions would be senseless. The martyrs, who suffered for the honor of Christ and let themselves be torn apart by lions in the amphitheaters would have been only trouble-makers and freaks.[2]

Once it is taken for granted that the destinies of man are limited within the bounds of the present life, there is no happiness in this world except in the crassest and most brazen materialism. The only true Gospel, the only sound, rational philosophy is that of Epicurus, summed up in the words "Let us eat and drink, for tomorrow we shall die."[3]

In order to turn souls away from gross cravings, and raise them up to aspirations worthy of their heavenly origins, the apostle does not cease to instill this great truth; and, at the same time, he draws from it the consequences that bear upon the ordering of life, and the external and internal regulation of human acts.

Now I am going to tell you a mystery. Not all of us shall fall asleep, but all of us are to be changed — in an instant, in the twinkling of an eye, at the sound of the last trumpet. The trumpet will sound and the dead will be raised incorruptible, and we shall be changed. This corruptible body must be clothed with incorruptibility, this mortal body with immortality. When the corruptible frame takes on incorruptibility and the mortal immortality, then will the saying of Scripture be fulfilled: "Death is swallowed up in victory."

"O death, where is your victory? O death, where is your sting?"[4]

In the preceding verses, the great apostle explains, no less wonderfully, the theological reason and the sovereign excellence of this mystery, of which God has made him the interpreter and herald.

[The body of man] . . . is sown in corruption; it shall rise in incorruption. It is sown in dishonor; it shall rise in glory. It is sown in weakness; it shall rise in power. It is sown a natural body; it shall rise a spiritual body . . . The first man Adam was made into a living soul; the last Adam into a life-giving spirit . . . The first man was of the earth, earthly; the second man, from heaven, heavenly . . . Therefore, as we have borne the image of the earthly, let us bear also the image of the heavenly. I am telling you this, my brothers, because corruption shall not possess immortality.[5]

Here we have a statement, drawn up by a master-hand, clear and concise; and any interpretation that the human word might seek to add would serve only to weaken its vigor and clarity.

Such is also the true, Catholic faith, which the Church has inscribed in the Creed we recite, and which she ordains to be sung in her places of worship on solemn feasts.

The End of the Present World

"I believe in the resurrection of the body, I await the resurrection of the dead."

Both St. Athanasius,[6] in his creed, and the Fourth Lateran Council express this truth in terms no less precise and even more explicit: "All men," they say, "must rise again with the same bodies with which they were united in the present life."

In fact, if, after being dissolved and returned to the dust from which they came, our bodies were not to be reborn with their entire limbs and the totality of their corporeal, constituent parts; if they were not to reappear with the same faces and the same features, so that, when we saw one another again on the day of judgment, we would recognize ourselves immediately, there would then be no point in calling our rebirth a resurrection, but a new creation.

Thus, it is quite certain that, at the judgment, we shall be in every respect the same: the feet that will support us then will be the feet that have borne and sustained us during our exile and the days of our pilgrimage in time; the tongue through which we shall speak will be the one that once gave voice in divine praise or in blasphemy; the eyes that will enable us to see will be the selfsame ones that opened to the rays of the sun that shines upon us; the heart that will beat in our breasts will be the very heart that the ardors of divine love will have consumed, or which will have let itself be devoured by the impure flames of lust.

Such was the unshakable hope of Job. As he sat on his dunghill, wasted away by putrefaction but with an unruffled countenance and shining eyes, the whole span of the ages flashed through his mind. In an ecstasy of joy he contemplated, in the brightness of the prophetic light, the days when he would shake off the dust of his coffin, and exclaimed, "I know that my Redeemer lives . . . whom I myself shall see; my own eyes, not another's, shall behold Him."[7]

Evidence of the resurrection from the Old Testament

This doctrine of the resurrection is the keystone, the pillar, of the whole Christian edifice, the focal point and center of our Faith. Without it there is no redemption, our beliefs and our preaching are futile, and all religion crumbles at the base: *"Inanis est ergo praedicatio nostra, inanis est fides nostra.*[8]

☞

Rationalist writers have declared that this belief in the resurrection was not contained in the Old Testament, and that it dates only from the Gospel. Nothing could be more erroneous. We need only read through the long line of Mosaic tradition, listening to the great voices of the patriarchs and the prophets, to see that they all tremble with joy and hope at the prospect of the promised immortality, and celebrate this new life, which will become theirs beyond the grave, and will have no end. It is said in the book of Exodus, "I am the God of Abraham, the God of Isaac, and the God of Jacob."[9] In St. Matthew, Christ uses this passage to prove to the Jews the truth of the resurrection:

> As to the fact that the dead are raised, have you not read what God said to you: "I am the God of Abraham, the God of Isaac, the God of Jacob"? He is the God of the living, not of the dead.[10]

Did not the mother of the Maccabees, standing amidst the blood and the scattered, mutilated limbs of her sons, strike the evil Antiochus dumb with fear, when she said to him:[11]

> Know, O wicked and very perverse man, that you are making us die only for the present life, but the Master of the world is going to receive us, we who are dying for His laws, and He will raise us again on the day of the *resurrection.*[12]

For the saints of the Old Testament, this belief in the resurrection was not only a symbol and a speculative doctrine; it was their fundamental faith, expressed in the marvels and works of their lives, of which the institutions they left us were representative types. St. Jerome says:

> Chief among them was Abel, whose blood, crying out to the Lord, bore witness to his hope in the resurrection of the dead. Next came Enoch, carried off so that he might not see death: he is the type and image of the resurrection. Thirdly, Sara, whose barren womb, exhausted with old age, conceived and brought a son into the world, gives us hope of resurrection. Fourthly, Jacob and Joseph left instructions for their bones to be gathered up and honorably buried, thereby confessing their faith in the resurrection. Fifthly, the withered rod of Aaron which blossomed and gave fruit, and the rod of Moses which, at God's command, became alive and turned into a snake, offer us a shadow and an outline of the resurrection. Finally, did not Moses, who blessed Ruben and said, "Let Ruben live and not die," when Ruben had long since departed from this life, acknowledge that he desired for him resurrection and eternal life?[13]

And if these various testimonies were to be deemed mere allegories or mystical testimonies, we would conclude this list with the very explicit words of Daniel, which leave no doubt about the constant and universal faith of the Old Testament in the future resurrection: "Many of those who sleep in the dust of the earth shall awake; some shall live forever, others shall be an everlasting horror and disgrace.[14]

This truth, affirmed by Scripture, is proclaimed no less boldly by reason and by Christian philosophy.

Evidence of the resurrection from philosophy

Philosophy covers in its vast field all that pertains to the nature of God, the nature of man and that of the world. Now, the dogma of the resurrection belongs to the ideas that philosophy gives us on these three subjects, which fall within its realm and are the matter of its investigations.

In the first place, the dogma of the resurrection follows from the ideas that philosophy gives us on the nature of God. Christian philosophy teaches us that God is the efficient, the first, and the final cause of all the creatures in the world. Having freely created them, with absolute sovereignty and independence, He has marked them all, to a greater or lesser degree, with the character of His own likeness and His infinite perfections. However, the human body, made by His own hands and enlivened by His breath, is the epitome of His marvels, the masterpiece of His wisdom and divine goodness. By the beauty and elegance of its construction, the nobility of its bearing and the splendors that shine through it, the body of man is infinitely superior to all the material beings that have come from the hands of God.

It is *through the body* that the mind reveals its power and exercises its kingship. It is the body, Tertullian says, that is the organ of the divine life and the sacraments. It is the body that is washed by the water of Baptism, so that the soul may obtain its purity and clarity. It is the body that is anointed by the oil and the unction of the Holy Spirit, so that the soul may be consecrated. It is upon the body that hands are imposed, so that the soul may be enlightened and can communicate blessings. It is the body that receives the Eucharist and quenches its thirst with divine Blood, so that man, becoming one with Christ and sharing with Him the same life, may live eternally.[15]

Again, it is the body that crosses the hands in prayer and bows in adoration. It is the body that is emaciated by fasts and mortification, that offers itself as a holocaust on scaffolds and stakes, and is consumed in martyrdom, which state is not absolute and irrevocable until it is sealed by death and expressed in blood. And could the body of man — instrument of the most heroic deeds, channel of all graces and blessings, champion of Christian witness, priest and altar of sacrifice, and *virginal spouse of Christ* — be like the grass in the fields, bursting forth into life for a moment, only to become the prey of worms and the guest of death forever? That would be a blasphemy against Providence and an affront to His infinite goodness.

The dogma of the resurrection of the dead follows from the ideas that Christian philosophy gives us about God; it follows, in the second place, from the ideas this philosophy gives us about the nature of man.

Man is really composed of two substances: spirit and body. These two principles are united by links so intimate and profound — there is between them such a close reciprocity and interrelationship — that, were it not for the instrumentality of the body, the spirit, by its very nature, would be unable to exercise any of its functions.

It would be like a puff of wind that, in the absence of an organ, could not resound, or a lyre with loose and broken chords, that would no longer disturb the air and would remain without tune or echo.

Thus, without the body, the soul cannot enter into a relationship with the exterior, visible world; it has neither the use of sight, nor the use of hearing; it cannot exercise its action and its sovereignty over matter, nor gain control over the elements, nor savor fruit, nor breathe in fragrance.

Evidence of the resurrection from philosophy

The mouth itself — the mouth, which was perhaps heard speaking in golden accents, which has so often opened to teach or to praise — is no more than a withered, arid member that the soul can no longer use to move hearts and enlighten minds. No doubt, as St. Thomas teaches, God will confer upon the separated souls after their death, a form of existence that will enable them to know one another, to hold communication among themselves, without the aid of corporal organs of which they will have been deprived. That, however, will be a marvelous and exceptional means, beyond the normal conditions and laws of human beings.

What is certain is that, in itself, and leaving aside that capacity which God, by His power, will add to our inner constitution after death, the soul deprived of its body is but an isolated, mutilated substance, cut off from all communication with the world of the living.

If you ask why God saw fit to unite, in one and the same creature, two principles so disparate, so different in their essence and properties, as mind and body; why He did not wish man to be, like the angels, a pure spirit, I will reply that God so acted in order that man might be truly the king and the epitome of all His works; so that he might, after the manner of Christ, *recapitulate* in his personality *the totality of created elements and beings*, so that he might be the center of all things and, by bringing together mind and body, the visible and invisible order, serve as interpreter of both, and offer them simultaneously to the Most High, in his homage and adoration.

Hence it is that, if man were to be deprived forever of his body, the material and visible creation would no longer have any mediator or pontiff, no longer have any voice to address its hymn of gratitude and love to God, and the link that unites inanimate being to the Creator would be irreversibly broken.

The End of the Present World

So, if God has not resolved to cast His work back into nothingness forever, if this earth, sanctified by the footsteps of Christ, is destined, once radiant and renewed, to remain forever, then man must rise again in a future life to reconquer its scepter and kingship. Hence, once more, it follows that death means not ruin but restoration. If God has decreed that our earthly abode shall one day be dissolved, it is not for the purpose of despoiling us of it, but to render it subtle, immortal, serene. His aim may be compared to that of an architect, says St. John Chrysostom, who has the inhabitant leave his house for a short period, in order to have him return with greater glory to that same house, now rebuilt in greater splendor.

⌒

The propriety and the necessity of the resurrection follow from the nature of man; they follow, lastly, from the laws and nature of the world.

The law of the world, says Tertullian, is that everything is renewed and nothing perishes. Thus the seasons follow one another in their course, the trees shed their fruit in autumn, and their leaves turn yellow and dry, like an adornment that has faded; but, when autumn gives way to spring, the trees become green again, their buds spring forth, and their leaves adorn themselves with a new crown of flowers and fruit. Thus the grain and the seed, laid in the furrows of the land, wither and appear to dissolve, from the effect of humidity and the action of the air; but, by the time of the harvest, they will have broken through the surface of the soil, and been born again in greater splendor, rejuvenated and renewed, as an ear of corn. In the same way, the sun, at the close of the day, disappears in the shades of its twilight, and seems to sink beneath the depth of the ocean; but in the morning it appears anew at the appointed time, to illuminate the earth and enkindle the air with its light and fire.

Death is only slumber, and a latent state. It is a state of rest and silence, where creatures, apparently motionless and buried, take on a new shape and assume a new vitality and a new energy: in the tomb where they sleep, they undergo a process of incubation and recasting, from which they will emerge more free and transformed, like a torch that has gone out and is rekindled with greater brilliance by the vivifying breath of men; or again, like the insect that pulls itself over the mud of the ground and, having been enclosed in its shell, emerges with a new strength, spreads out its shining wings, and thereafter rests only upon flowers.

At this point, certain questions need to be clarified. It is said that the dead will awaken at the sound of the trumpet. It is said that all will rise again, but that all will not be changed. Finally, it may be asked whether men will rise again in the state and at the same age as when they died in this world.

In the chapter on the fear of the judgment, quoting the words of St. Paul, ". . . at the last trumpet, for the trumpet shall sound," St. Jerome says, "At the sound of the trumpets, the whole earth will be stricken with fear," and, further on, "Whether you are reading or sleeping, writing or keeping watch, let that trumpet always resound in your ears."[16]

Will this trumpet, the echoes of which will penetrate the murky caverns of the abyss and awaken the fathers of the human race from their long slumber, give out an audible sound? It seems probable. The angels who, on that day, will assume aerial bodies in order to be seen by all men, may also construct, out of the elements and diverse substances of the air, material instruments capable of emitting real sounds. However, if we feel reluctant to accept this explanation, we can keep to the interpretation of St.

The End of the Present World

Thomas, who tells us that St. Paul uses the term *trumpet* only alle-gorically, as an image. Just as, among the Jews, the trumpet was used for summoning the people to the great feasts, urging on the soldiers in battle and giving the signal to strike camp, so the voice of the angel is called a *trumpet* by analogy, by reason of its power and glitter, and the ability it will have to summon all men, in an instant, to the same place.

Secondly, it is said that all men will rise again, but that not all will be changed. It is certain that the damned will rise again, possessed of all their physical and intellectual faculties and all their limbs, and that their bodies will not be subject to any illness or change; but, lacking the nuptial robe of charity, they will not be clothed in the qualities of the glorified bodies. They will be reborn neither trans-figured, nor luminous, nor subtle, but such as they were on earth — passable, opaque, shackled to matter and to the law of gravity. They will not feel the intensity and violence of the fire any the less thereby; and this fire will cause them the greater suffering because, being in a perfect state of health and in full possession of their physical and intellectual vigor, they will be all the more conscious of its energy and action. The fire of the damned is a fire lit by the breath of God's justice, created solely to punish; consequently, its severity is not at all proportionate to the weakness or diversity of temperaments. It is measured according to the number and gravity of the crimes to be punished, as it is said: *ignis eorum non extinguetur.* This fire will consume without destroying. It will cling to its victims as to a prey, without their organs being affected by it, and without their flesh ever feeling any tear or injury.

Lastly, will men rise again the same age as they were when they died? The most probable opinion, and the one most in harmony with Scripture, is that they will rise again "in the state of perfect man, according to the age of the fullness of Jesus Christ: *in virum perfectum, in mensuram aetatis plenitudinis Christi.*"[17] In other words, when all men have been restored to the type and image of Christ, at least as far as befits the number and degree of their merits, they will be reborn in the maturity of manhood, in the full development of their being and physical constitution, just as Christ on the day of His Resurrection and Ascension, when, entering upon His beatitude, took possession of His eternal sovereignty.

Finally, will Jesus Christ be the sole author of the resurrection, or will it be brought about through the ministry of the angels? We say that it will be accomplished directly by the power of Christ, but that the angels, too, who are His ministers, will be called upon to cooperate and lend their assistance. For it is said in St. John, ". . . an hour is coming, and has indeed come, when the dead shall hear the voice of the Son of God."[18] Furthermore, it is said in Matthew: "He will dispatch his angels with a mighty trumpet blast (and a great voice); and they will *assemble his chosen* from the four winds . . ."[19]

Thus, Jesus Christ, as king and leader, will give the signal; He will utter His command and leave His angels the task of gathering together the scattered elements that have belonged to our bodies, and which are destined to reconstitute them.

⌒

To these truths founded on Holy Scripture, mocking, skeptical science raises objections, drawn from the laws that bind the present order, and which it considers decisive and irrefutable.

How, they say, will the angels or, indeed, any other superior beings, however great be their degree of perception, ever manage to gather up and separate the remains and particles of human bodies, scattered over every continent, dispersed beneath every firmament, engulfed in the seas, some dissolved, others turned into vapor or vegetable sap, some of them having served in turn to form a multitude of organized, living beings? Since the same particles of substances will have belonged at different times to an infinite diversity of bodies, will it be within the power of an angel to assign them to one particular person, rather than another?

It is easy for us to reply that, when the angels receive the command to gather together the ashes of the dead, whether with the aid of their natural knowledge or assisted by a revelation from above, they will immediately know which are the elements and material parts that must form each human body; they will know in which place on sea or land these material parts lie, and in what form they subsist. There is a pious belief that each angel will concern himself particularly with the human creature whom God had once entrusted to his care. Can it be supposed that these good angels forsake the remains of those creatures over whom they had watched with such loving kindness and solicitude? That they do not follow them through all their transformations and that, at the required moment, they do not have the means and the power to find the ashes?

Furthermore, are not the angels God's delegates? How, then, can it be admitted that God, who sees all things, who is present in the atom, in the blade of grass, in each grain of sand on the seashore, will be unable to make them distinguish the particles of our bodies, which His gaze embraces, and in which He lives substantially by His immensity?

Let us note, however, that the ministry of the angels will be limited to gathering together, at the appointed place, the remains and particles of our bodies; as for the arrangement of these different pieces — the spirit of life that will again be infused into our reconstituted bodies — that, says St. Thomas, is a creative work which exceeds the power of the angelic nature itself, and which will be wrought by the direct, immediate power of God.

Hence, the reason the resurrection will be instantaneous: it will be accomplished in the twinkling of an eye, says St. Paul, in an imperceptible instant, in a flash. The dead, asleep in the slumber of many centuries, will hear the voice of the Creator, and will obey Him as promptly as the elements obeyed Him during the six days: *Dixit et facta sunt.*[20]

They will shake off the binding-clothes of their age-long night and free themselves from the grip of death, with greater nimbleness than a sleeping man awakening with a start. Just as, of old, Christ came forth from His tomb with the speed of lightning, cast off His shroud in an instant, had the sealed stone of His sepulcher lifted aside by an angel, and hurled the guards, half-dead with fright, to the ground, so, says Isaiah, in an equally imperceptible space of time, death will be cast forth: *Praecipitabit mortem in sempiternum.*[21]

Ocean and land will open up their depths to eject their victims, just as the whale that had swallowed up Jonah opened its jaws to throw him out on the shore of Tharsis. Then human beings, free, like Lazarus, of the bonds of death, will rush transfigured into a new life, and will insult the cruel enemy that had felt sure it would keep them fettered in endless captivity. They will say, "O death, where is your victory? O death, where is your sting? *Absorpta es, mors, in victoria tua.*"[22]

But there is one senseless and crass objection, which we think it right to point out; it is the one raised by the materialists of our time.

The human body, they say, is composed and recomposed unceasingly, through age, sickness, changes of elements, and especially by nutrition. It is subject to constant and perpetual loss and renewal. The limbs can wither or grow fat; the hair falls out and grows again. It is noticed that the flesh of an elderly man does not contain a single particle, a single atom, of the blood and fluids that formed his material structure when he was just a child.

Will all this dust, all these different and incalculable remains that have gone to form his organic life, be restored to man once he arises from his ashes? If they are not given back to him, if he is still deprived of them, how can it be said that he will be born again, with the same body to which he was united in this life? If, on the other hand, he rises with the totality of the elements that have gone to make his constitution, then the bodies of the resurrected elect, which, it is said, must be filled with harmony and perfection, will in fact be just a mass of shapeless, defective elements.

True science has long since made short work of the inconsistency and absurdity of such a theory. In our times, a publicist of great profundity, an eminent theologian, knowledgeable in the natural sciences as well as in the sacred sciences, has disproved by an irrefutable argument these doctrines, which are as base as they are presumptuous and foolish:

> In the body of a man [he says], there is both something essential and something secondary and accessory. The essential part is what he shares with no one, what he alone possesses and will possess forever; it is the part of him that existed at the moment he was formed, animated and vivified by his soul. These essential elements he will always keep; they will always be his. The rest, that which is produced by nutrition, digestion, and assimilation, is not he. He can lose it, and does lose it, without ceasing to be himself. It will be with these essential, personal elements that God will resurrect the glorious, spiritual bodies, as also He will resurrect the immortal corruption of the damned. The soul being the same, the real kernel, the constitutive element

remaining the same, the rest is of little importance and its identity will remain eternally.

Moreover, it has been painstakingly demonstrated, first, that in a body as large as the earth, there are enough gaps and pores for it to be conceived as being reduced to the volume of a grain of sand; secondly, that, conversely, in a grain of sand, there are enough separable parts, atoms, and molecules for a globe as large as the earth to be formed from them. In view of these two utterly overwhelming mysteries of nature, dare we dispute the possibility or impossibility of the reconstitution of the human body, with its essential original elements?[23]

Let us conclude this account of the resurrection by recalling its magnificence and sublimity. The resurrection will be a grand, imposing spectacle that will surpass all those ever seen on earth, and eclipsing even the solemnity of the first creation. The most beautiful picture depicted for us comes from the prophet Ezekiel:

The hand of the Lord came upon me, and He led me out in the spirit of the Lord and set me in the center of the plain, which was now filled with bones. He made me walk among them in every direction so that I saw how many they were on the surface of the plain. *How dry they were!* He asked me, "Son of man, can these bones come to life?" "Lord God," I answered, "You alone know that." Then He said to me, "Prophesy over these bones, and say to them: *Dry bones, hear the word of the Lord!* Thus says the Lord God to these bones: See! I will bring spirit into you, that you may come to life. I will put sinews upon you, make flesh grow over you, cover you with skin, and put spirit in you so that you may come to life and know that I am the Lord."

I prophesied as I had been told, and even as I was prophesying, I heard a noise; it was a rattling as the bones came together, bone joining bone. I saw the sinews and the flesh come upon them, and the skin cover them, but *there was no spirit in them.* Then He said to me, "*Prophesy to the spirit, prophesy, son of man, and say to the spirit:* Thus says the Lord God: From the four winds come, O spirit, and *breathe into these slain that they may come to life.*" I prophesied as He told me, and the spirit came into them; they came alive and *stood upright, a vast army.*

Then He said to me, "Son of man, these bones are the whole house of Israel. They have been saying, 'Our bones are dried up, our hope is lost, and we are cut off.' Therefore, prophesy and say to them: Thus says the Lord God: O my people, I will open your graves and have you rise from them, and bring you back to the land of Israel. Then you shall know that I am the Lord, when I open your graves and have you rise from them, O my people!"[24]

⁐

With the resurrection accomplished, the immediate consequence is the judgment, which will take place without delay. It is impossible to imagine the innumerable members of the human family, made up of the long line of generations, massed together over the confined space of the surface of the earth, trying to recognize the traces of the places where they once dwelt, and again reduced to watering them with the sweat of their brow and wrangling over their vestiges.

It is evident that mankind, once resurrected, will enter upon another mode of existence, and that divine goodness is bound to open up new abodes, new habitations.

These habitations will be of different kinds, according to the merits or demerits of each person. The just will enter Paradise, the damned will fill up the dark abysses of hatred and malediction.

It is pointless to refute those godless men who deny this supreme manifestation of justice and solemn climax of human destiny. The general judgment is a certain fact, announced by the prophets; it is a truth that Jesus Christ constantly stresses, a truth ratified by reason and consonant with the law of conscience and every idea of equity.

In Holy Scripture, each time the judgment is spoken of without any qualification and each time this day of judgment is designated by the words *dies Domini, dies irae*[25] or other similar terms, these expressions must be understood as referring to the general judgment, which will take place at the end of the times. Thus, it is written, "I assure you, it will go easier for Tyre and Sidon than for you on the day of judgment"; "I assure you, it will go easier for Sodom than for you on the day of judgment"; "The day of the Lord is coming like a thief in the night"; "We beg you, brothers," says St. Paul, "not to be so easily agitated or terrified . . . into believing that the day of the Lord is here."[26] The prophets are full of similar words: "The great day of the Lord is near," says the prophet Zephaniah. "That day is a day of wrath, a day of tribulation and distress, a day of calamity and misery, a day of darkness and obscurity, a day of clouds and whirlwinds, a day of the trumpet and alarm."[27]

Christ speaks more explicitly in St. Matthew: "Let them grow together until harvest; then at harvest time I will order the harvesters, 'First collect the weeds and bundle them up to burn, then gather the wheat into my barn.' "[28]

Elsewhere, in the same Gospel, He says, "The reign of God is also like a dragnet thrown into the lake, which collected all sorts of things. When it was full, they hauled it ashore and sat down to put what was worthwhile into containers. What was useless, they threw away. That is how it will be at the end of the world. Angels will go out and separate the wicked from the just and hurl the wicked into the fiery furnace, where they will wail and grind their teeth. 'Have you understood all this?' 'Yes,' they answered."[29]

⌒

Let us add to these texts from Scripture the testimony of St. Thomas Aquinas, who gives us three theological reasons for the opportuneness and propriety of a universal judgment.

The first of these reasons consists in the fact that the works of man, whether they are good or bad, are not always isolated, transitory acts; more often, especially in the case of the leaders of nations and those who are invested with public authority, they continue to subsist after they are concluded, either in the memory of other men or in public acclaim, as a result of the consequences they have had and the scandal they have caused. Thus, at first sight, a particular, secret crime seems to be only a private, personal deed; but it becomes *social* on account of its effects.

Certainly it is of faith that there is a particular judgment, and that every man, at the instant of his soul's departure from the body, appears before the tribunal of God to hear his eternal sentence pronounced. Yet this judgment cannot suffice, and it is essential that it should be followed by another public judgment, in which God will not examine the actions in isolation and taken in themselves, but will examine them in their effects upon other men, in the good or evil deriving from them for families and peoples — in a word, in the consequences they produced and which those who perpetrated them ought to have foreseen.

The second reason given by the Angelic Doctor for this public manifestation relates to the false judgments and mistaken appraisals of human opinion. Most men, even the wisest and most enlightened, are easily outwitted and deceived by others. They do not discern the innermost depths of souls, and cannot reach what is secret and interior in them; hence, it happens that they generally form their judgments on appearances, on what is visible and exterior. Again, it follows that good men are often treated with undeserved severity, that they are unappreciated and injured in their reputation. On the other hand, the wickedness of a large number of men remains unknown, they everywhere enjoy public esteem and trust, and the world accords them that consideration and praise which is due to the just alone. So a judgment is necessary that exposes every pretense, unmasks all hypocrisy, and lays bare hidden ruses and all false and base virtues.

This judgment, St. John tells us, will not take place "according to the flesh, nor according to that which the eyes see and the ears hear"; it will be accomplished in the dazzling splendor of the light of God, in the discernment of all intentions and all desires, the full intuition of the most secret and mysterious recesses of the heart: *corda omnium intuendo.*

Lastly, a third reason given by St. Thomas is that God governs men by means adapted to the circumstances of their nature, and will judge them according to the promises He made them and the hopes He aroused in them; whether rewarding or punishing them. He owes it to His wisdom to keep to the laws and limits of distributive justice such as He has fixed them in this life. Now, St. Paul himself calls the present life a race, an arena;[30] he portrays man as a traveler on this earth, under the figure of a soldier or an athlete rushing after his crown; he holds forth before us the prospect of eternal life, which he calls by the names of "palm, trophy, crown of justice, crown of life and glory." In order, then, that the reward may really match the promise, it has to be bestowed at a public assembly, with a pomp and ceremony worthy of Him who confers it, in the presence of all those who have taken part in the battle, of all the enemies over whom the saints have triumphed, following the manner in which ancient Rome and Greece used to act toward their victorious warriors and heroes.

In what place will the last judgment be held? No one knows with the certainty of faith, but the general opinion of the Fathers, and that of St. Thomas Aquinas, is that it will be in the valley of Josaphat.

Holy Scripture gives this name to the region through which flows the Cedron torrent, which includes within its boundaries the town of Jerusalem and also Calvary, and extends as far as the Mount of Olives.

Is it not, indeed, fitting that Christ should manifest Himself in His glory in the very places that were the scene of His agony, where He appeared in His sufferings and humiliations? Such was what the angels implied, when they said to the disciples, "This Jesus who is taken up from you shall so come."[31] Is it not also most appropriate that the part of the earth where the first man was created,[32] where the Son of God wrought the redemption and salvation of men, should likewise be the one where the saints will receive the fullness of the fruits in His Passion and death, where they will take part in His glorious Ascension, and where Jesus Christ will exact a just vengeance on His persecutors, and on all those who have refused to wash their souls by the infinite power of His Blood?

It is for this reason that the prophet Joel exclaims, "The Lord roars from Zion, and from Jerusalem raises His voice." Again, in the same chapter, he says: "I will assemble all the nations and bring them down to the valley of *Josaphat*, and I will enter into judgment with them there on behalf of my people and my inheritance . . ."[33]

It is useless to object that our view cannot be sustained and that it is sufficiently refuted by the fact that the valley of Josaphat occupies a space less extensive and more confined than most of the Alpine valleys; and that, consequently, it could not possibly hold the thousands of millions of human beings who have followed one another, or will yet follow one another, on earth.

St. Paul, in his letter to the Thessalonians, resolves and throws light on this difficulty; he reminds us that on the day of judgment the resurrected elect will not be massed together on earth, but "will be caught up . . . to meet the Lord in the air."[34] Our Lord Jesus Christ will descend into the region of the air, situated above the valley of Josaphat, and there, surrounded by His angels, He will sit on the throne of His majesty. Is it not indeed fitting that, by reason of His dignity, the judge should be raised above all, on an elevated spot, from where He can be seen and heard by all men? Is it not equitable that, in consideration of merit and perfection, an honorable place nearer the Sovereign Judge should be assigned to the elect, who have been released from the laws of gravity and, possessing glorious and subtle bodies, will no longer need the earth for support?

The reprobate alone will be detained on earth;[35] but, as Suarez points out, we would be wrong to imagine them restricted and confined within the narrow limits of the valley of Josaphat; their enormous number will extend, so far as necessary, into the surrounding area, to the Mount of Olives, the mountain of Zion, the site where Jerusalem stood, and perhaps to remote areas.

If it is said that the judgment will take place in the valley of Josaphat, this is because Christ will set up His throne above it, and because this valley will be the place in which mankind will begin to assemble.

☞

By whom will the judgment be executed? By Christ Jesus; not precisely by Christ Jesus as God, who shares the same substance and the same life with His Father, but by Christ Jesus inasmuch as He became incarnate in time and is called the *Son of Man.* It is said in St. John, "The Father Himself judges no one, but has assigned all judgment to the Son, so that all men may honor the Son just as they honor the Father."[36] He gave Him power to judge, "*because He is the Son of Man.*" Indeed, as God, Jesus Christ is equal to the Father, the expression and image of His sovereign power, and possesses, *co-naturally* with the other two Divine Persons, the right to judge which They have. From this point of view, Christ does not have to receive a second investiture, and it is only in considering Him as a man that St. John could say that He will be honored by all, because of the judicial power conferred upon Him by His Father.

In the following verse, St. John teaches us that Christ has received the power to restore the dead to life: "I solemnly assure you, an hour is coming, has indeed come, when the dead shall hear the voice of the Son of God."[37]

This passage makes clear that the power to resurrect, conferred upon the Son of Man, is a consequence of His capacity as judge. It is essential for the exercise of judicial authority, that he who is invested with it should have the means of summoning the guilty and bringing them up before his tribunal. As the judgment has to be executed over men, observes St. Thomas, it must be adapted to their capacities; it must take account of the demands and inclinations of their nature. Man, however, is composed of a soul and a body; he apprehends spiritual and invisible things only through the agency of tangible things. That being so, is it not essential that man should be judged by a man, by a being who appears in the flesh, whose face he can see and whose voice he can hear? Rightly, St. John tells us, "The Father has given over to Him power to pass judgment, because he is the Son of man."[38]

Furthermore, if we study things after our way of thinking, must not the judge be seen by all men summoned to his bench? Now, inasmuch as He has a human form, Christ will be seen by the just and the wicked simultaneously; inasmuch as He has a divine form, He can show Himself to the elect alone. Lastly, God the Father has entrusted the judgment to Jesus Christ, as man, in a spirit of kindness, in order to temper the brilliance of this awesome manifestation, and to soften its severity and rigor; for the Church tells us in her liturgy:

> *What horror will invade the mind*
> *When the strict Judge, who would be kind,*
> *Shall have few venial faults to find!*[39]

If Christ were to appear in the aspect of a superior and altogether celestial nature, what human being would manage to bear the weight of His majesty and the fire of His gaze? He will appear, then, with the face and form He had during His mortal life; He will have His Cross and the other marks of His humiliations precede Him; He will let the scars of the wounds in His feet and hands be seen: *Videbunt in quem transfixerunt;*[40] the reprobate will no longer dare to oppose His justice, and the good in their turn will feel drawn to Him in deeper trust. The heart of St. Paul was filled with joy and hope: as he reflected that Christ was to be his judge, he felt all his fears and distrust vanish. "Who shall bring a charge against God's chosen ones?" he said. "God, who justifies? Who shall condemn them? Christ Jesus, who died, or rather was raised up, who is at the right hand of God and who intercedes for us?"[41]

As for the manner of this second coming, it will be like the first: *sic veniet quemadmodum vidistis eum euntem in coelis;*[42] it will be the same Christ and the same man, and His features and appearance will be the same as during His mortal life; it will be enough for those who lived and spoke with Him to set eyes on His person in order to recognize Him. However, this second manifestation will not come in weakness and humiliation, but in majesty and glory. St. Matthew's Gospel says, "But I tell you this: Soon you will see the Son of Man seated at the right hand of the Power and coming on the clouds of heaven."[43] In other words, Jesus Christ will appear surrounded by the pomp and apparel of divine kingship. The glorified elect and the multitude of angels will form a resplendent court around His throne, such as no mind could portray. Those who have fought with the greatest constancy, who have followed Him the most closely in the arena of His sufferings, will be the nearest to His person. "Then the righteous man will stand with great confidence in the presence of those who have afflicted him," says the book of Wisdom.

We can imagine the regrets and despair of the damned by virtue of the picture that the same inspired author draws of them:

> Seeing this, they shall be shaken with dreadful fear, and amazed at the unlooked-for salvation. They shall say among themselves, rueful and groaning through anguish of spirit: "This is He whom once we held as a laughing-stock and as a type for mockery, fools that we were! His life we accounted madness, and His death dishonored. See how He is accounted among the sons of God; how His lot is with the saints! We, then, have strayed from the way of truth, and

the light of justice did not shine for us, and the sun did not rise for us."[44]

The apostles, martyrs, Doctors, and thousands of the just, who have fought for the honor of God and for the interests of the Faith, will unite with their leader in proclaiming the truth of His sentences and the equity of His judgments.

⌒

This judgment is rightly called *universal* because it will be exercised over all members of the human race, because it will cover every crime, every misdemeanor, and because it will be definitive and irrevocable.

In the first place, the last judgment will be exercised over all members of the human race.[45]

The men of every nation, every tribe, and every tongue will appear at it. There will be no more distinction of wealth, birth, or rank among them. Those whose names were Alexander, Caesar, and Diocletian will be jumbled together with herdsmen who, at this moment, are grazing their flocks on unknown, deserted shores, where the ashes of these masters of the world lie scattered. Men will then be ruled by concerns other than those of curiosity and empty admiration. Far more serious spectacles will hold their gaze and attention; the figure of the world will have passed away, and the victories of great captains, the works conceived by genius, the enterprises and great discoveries will be deemed mere shams and child's play.

Just as in the theater, says St. John Chrysostom, when an actor goes off the stage, it is not because of the part he has played that people admire him; they praise neither the fact that he has imitated the personality of a king, nor the fact that he has acted a lackey or a beggar: rather, they praise his skill, and they applaud only the perfection with which he has played his part. So at the last judgment, a man will not be honored because he was a king, an eloquent orator, a minister, and a great statesman. All these honors and distinctions, which the world holds in such high esteem, will be deemed of no merit and of no value. Men will be praised solely for their virtues and good works: *Opera enim illorum seguuntur illos.*[46]

Secondly, this judgment is called universal, because it will cover every crime and offense. Only then will human history begin. In the clarity of the light of God, all the crimes, public and secret, that have been committed in every latitude and in every age, will be seen clearly and in detail. The whole life of each human being will be laid bare. No circumstance will be omitted: no action, word, or desire will remain unknown. We shall be reminded of the different periods we have gone through; the lustful man will have his disorderly living and libertine speeches set out before him; the ambitious man, his devious, Machiavellian ways.

The judgment will unravel and bring out all the strands and the duplicity of those intrigues, so cleverly hatched; it will set out in their true light all those base repudiations of principles, those craven acts of complicity, that men invested with public authority have sought to justify, whether by invoking the specious pretext of reasons of state, or by covering them up with the mask of piety or disinterestedness. The Lord, says St. Bernard, will reveal all those abuses people concealed from themselves, all those unknown dissipations, those planned crimes where the only thing lacking was the actual commission; those pretended virtues and those forgotten, secret sins, blotted out from the memory, will appear suddenly, like enemies darting out from an ambush: *Prodient ex improviso et quasi ex insidiis.*[47]

Without doubt there are men so hardened in evil that the thought of this terrible manifestation has little effect upon them. Being familiar with crime, they treat it as a subject of amusement and boasting. They probably boast in assessing the judgment with the same insolence, to defy by their cynical and arrogant attitude the majesty of God and the conscience of humankind. Vain hope! Sin will no longer be viewed from the opinion of carnal men, ready to excuse the most violent outbursts because they do not harm any neighbor, either in his goods or in his life. The foulness and disorder of sin will be revealed in the ineffable clarity of the light of God. Sin, says St. Thomas, will be judged as God Himself judges it: *Tunc confusio respiciet aestimationem Dei quae secundum veritatem est de peccato.*[48]

Three main classes of men will draw attention to themselves. The first of these will be the sons of justice and light, whose merits and good works will be extolled, and given public praise and approval by the perspicacious and infallible Judge, whose testimony can admit of no error or contradiction.

In the second class will be the sons of Voltaire, the leaders of free-thought and revolution who, at the present time, are hatching dark and sacrilegious plots against Christ and His Church. They will be terror-stricken, and they will tremble with unspeakable horror, when they see appear in His glory and omnipotence Him whom they had wished to crush, whom they had stigmatized by calling Him the *enemy, fool,* and the *infamous one.* They will utter a final scream of rage and malediction, crying out like Julian the Apostate: *Thou hast conquered, Galilean!*

Finally, the third category of men who will be given special attention at the judgment will be composed of the sons of Pilate, the worshipers of the golden calf and the *chameleons* of wealth and power. Clouds without water, as St. Jude calls them,[49] drifting along with every opinion and doctrine, with no other religious or political compass than that of their ambition, always ready to ride rough-shod over their conscience and their principles; speculating on the blood of souls, for lack of gold, and delivering up Christ like the Roman money-lender, in order to purchase the honors and goodwill of the master of the moment.

This hideous, repellent type recurs continuously, with the same characteristics, at every period of crisis and social unrest. St. John, in his Gospel, has popularized this archetype of lying and cowardice in a figure of speech forever popular and living, in which all our Pilates in legislation and government, who sell the just man for the sake of procuring favors and lucrative honors, will be eternally recognized. Such men as these will learn at the judgment that it is not expedient to serve two masters. They will curse the straw Caesars to which they rendered that which they refused to render to God, and will exclaim: "*Ergo erravimus.* We have erred then."[50]

Finally, the last judgment is called universal, because it is definitive and irrevocable.

This judgment is irrevocable, because there is no level of jurisdiction higher than God's, and there can be no appeal from absolute justice to relative and limited justice. So there will be no reinstatement, no partial or complete amnesty. Divine sentences are irrefutable, unchangeable, and He who sees all things, who has foreseen the crux and conclusion of human destiny in the eternal decrees of predestination, is not a being likely to go back on His judgments. What He has said, He will fulfill; what He has done, He will confirm. What He once desired will remain eternally fixed, for heaven and earth will pass away, but the Word of God will not be subject to any error or change: *Coelum et terra transibunt, verba autem mea non praeteribunt.*[51]

These great truths make little impression on us, because the day of their fulfillment is only a faint prospect, set in the distant future, and because we fondly imagine that, between now and the time when they are fulfilled, we shall mitigate their severity. It is true that the deliberations of these great assizes[52] still lie ahead of us, but the preliminary examination has begun and it continues. It is written, "The eyes of the Lord are upon those who fear Him . . . The Face of the Lord scrutinizes the evildoer. The Lord carefully watches the just and the wicked, and he who loves iniquity is the murderer of his soul."[53]

Just as, in our times, the telegraph has become a marvelous means of communication among men, instantaneously transmitting our orders and our every word from one point of space to another with the rapidity of lightning, so there is likewise a divine telegraph: each of our thoughts, the very moment it is conceived, each of our words, as soon as it is uttered, is immediately transcribed in indelible letters, and with frightening accuracy, into that great book mentioned in the sacred liturgy, where it is said, *Tunc liber scriptus proferetur, in quo totum continetur, unde mundus judicetur.*[54]

Let us not, then, be intimidated by the arrogance and dark threats of the wicked, we who, at this moment, are subjected to violence and oppression, whose rights are unrecognized and trampled underfoot, and who, exposed to the ruses and machinations of faithless men, suffer the odious excesses of despotism and force. If God is silent and seems at this moment to be asleep, He will unfailingly awaken in His own time. We repeat, the examination has begun, the files of evil men are complete, the witnesses have been summoned, and the evidence has been requisitioned. If the most solemn hearing of all has been adjourned, it is for a short period only.

The story is told of a proud, valiant, and high-minded prince of Brittany who was defeated and taken prisoner by a fierce rival and sent to languish in a dark dungeon, where he was kept short of air, bread, and sunshine; his end was not long in coming, amidst horror and under the pressure of a coldly calculated, slow torture. On the point of death, the victim addressed a summons to his murderer in these terms: "I appeal against your violence and your barbarism to the Supreme Protector of the oppressed, and in a year and a day I shall summon you to appear with me at His divine tribunal." When the day came, the murderer did indeed pass from life to death.

We are not a prophet, and we should not venture to summon at such short notice all wicked men, the pamphleteers of free-thought, the instigators of unjust laws, those who violate the honor and liberty of the family, and the rights and virtue of children; but that those men who defy God and deride His threats will one day have a minute and rigorous account to render to His justice . . . is an absolutely certain truth . . . and, sooner or later, they will settle that account. On the day of solemn reparation, the wicked who called the just fools, who glutted themselves on their tortures and tears, like starving men devouring bread, will learn to their cost that God does not suffer Himself to be mocked, and that there will be no impunity or license for the benefit of crime and evil.

All wrongs will be strikingly redressed. The blood of Abel, which washed the earth, will gush out over Cain, and raise an accusing voice against him. St. Peter will demand an account of Nero for the torture to which he sentenced him. Mary Stuart will call down the divine vengeance upon the head of Elizabeth of England, her murderer. All the saints will cry out with one voice to God: *Usquequo, Domine, non judicas et non vindicas sanguinem nostrum de iis qui habitant in terra.*[55]

It will be a great court of appeal, to which an immense number of cases, famous on earth, will be referred, where an infinite number of judgments that fear, ambition, or self-interest have dictated to men, will be irrevocably annulled; where, in a word, Providence, against which fools blasphemed on earth, with accusations that it was harsh, unjust, and blindly partial, will provide complete justification for its ways, as it is written: *Ut vincas cum judicaris.*[56]

It is said that there was a man in Germany who lived by himself, and was held in renown on account of his holiness and his works; he cured the sick, restored the sight of the blind, and drew the people of the surrounding area to his dwelling. The Emperor Otto determined to go to visit him; captivated by the words of wisdom that flowed from the saint's lips, his admiration knew no bounds: "Father," he said, "ask of me what you please and, were it half my kingdom, you will receive it."

The saint's expression became solemn, and, majestically, he raised his head, crowned, as it were, with a diadem of nobility and virtue; placing his hand upon the emperor's breast, he solemnly replied, "Prince, I have no use for your crown and your treasures; but I ask of you one favor, that, amidst the pomp and fascination of your omnipotence and majesty, you should withdraw each day, for a few moments, into the hidden recesses of your heart, in order to reflect upon the account you will one day render to God; for, as St. Clement, the pope, says, 'Who shall be able to sin if he always places before his eyes the judgment of God which will certainly be exacted at the end of the world?' "[57]

Let us do likewise and say with the prophet, "I consider the days of old; the years long past I remember. "[58] Let us judge ourselves severely, and we shall not be judged. Let us live with the Lord Jesus all the days of our life, and then we shall be freed from all fear, for there is no condemnation upon those who dwell with the Lord Jesus: *Nihil ergo nunc damnationis iis qui sunt in Christo.*[59]

Notes

[1] Cf. Acts 24:25.

[2] 1 Cor. 15:32.

[3] *Manducemus et bibamus, cras enim moriemur.*

[4] 1 Cor. 15:51-55.

[5] Cf. 1 Cor. 15:42-50.

[6] St. Athanasius (c. 297-373), Bishop of Alexandria and Doctor.

[7] Job 19:25, 27.

[8] 1 Cor. 15:14.

[9] Exod. 3:6.

[10] Matt. 22:31.

[11] Translator's note: It was actually her seventh son who said these words.

[12] Cf. 2 Macc. 7:34-36.

[13] St. Jerome, *Epistle contra Samaritanos*.

[14] Dan. 12:2.

[15] "The flesh, indeed, is washed, in order that the soul may be cleansed; the flesh is anointed, that the soul may be consecrated; the flesh is signed (with the cross), that the soul, too, may be fortified; the flesh is shadowed with the imposition of hands, that the soul also may be illuminated by the Spirit; the flesh feeds on the Body and Blood of Christ, that the soul likewise may fatten on its God" (Tertullian, *De Resurrectione Carnis*).

[16] St. Jerome/Hieron, *De timore judicii*.

[17] Cf. Eph. 4:13.

[18] John 5:25.

[19] Matt. 24:31.

[20] Ps. 148:5.

[21] Isa. 25:8.

[22] Cf. 1 Cor. 15:54.

[23] Moigno, *Splendeurs de la foi*.

[24] Ezek. 37:1-13. Translator's note: This English translation, taken from The New American Bible, Saint Joseph Edition, is a bit different from the old French version of this scriptural passage.

[25] "The day of the Lord, the day of wrath," from the Hymn of St. Columba.

[26] Matt. 11:22, 24; 1 Thess. 5:2; 2 Thess. 2:1-2.

[27] Zeph. 1:15.

[28] Matt. 13:30.

[29] Matt. 13:47.

[30] 1 Cor. 9:24.

[31] Acts 1:11.

[32] It is not of faith that Adam was created on Calvary, but simply a tradition.

[33] Cf. Joel 4:2, 16.

[34] 1 Thess. 4:17.

[35] "One doubt remains to be explained: if all the just will be in the air, the damned indeed on the earth, how is it to be understood literally that the former will be on the right, the latter indeed on the left of Christ. One can respond in two ways. First, by understanding it literally, it can be said that all reprobates, even if they are on the earth, are to be placed on the left side of Christ, the good indeed in the air on the right. In the second and better way 'right and left' is said to signify, according to the usage in Scripture, happiness and unhappiness, the place of honor or of abjection. Anselm explains Matthew 25:34 in this way: 'on the right', that is, in eternal beatitude; 'on the left', that is, in eternal misery" (Suarez, *Disputationes*).

[36] John 5:22-23, 27.

[37] John 5:25.

[38] John 5:27.

[39] From *Dies Irae*.

[40] John 19:37.

[41] Rom. 8:33-34.

[42] Cf. Acts 1:11.

[43] Matt. 26:64.

[44] Wisd. 5:1-6.

[45] "From thence he shall come to judge the living and the dead" (Apostles' Creed).

[46] Rev. 14:13.

[47] The preceding line is a rough translation of this Latin phrase.

[48] "Then the confusion, which, according to the truth, is from sin, will look to the judgment of God."

[49] Jude 1:12.

[50] Wisd. 5:6.

[51] Matt. 24:35.

[52] Court sessions.

[53] Ps. 33:18; 11:5. Cf. Douay-Rheims translation (Ps. 10:6): "The Lord trieth the just and the wicked: but he that loveth iniquity hateth his own soul."

[54] Text from the Office of the Dead: *Dies Irae*. Then the written book shall be brought, in which all is contained, whereby the world shall be judged.

[55] Rev. 6:10.

[56] Ps. 50:6.

[57] St. Clement (d. 101; fourth Pope), *Epistle to James*.

[58] Ps. 77:6.

[59] Rom. 8:1.

The Place of Immortal Life and the State of Glorified Bodies After the Resurrection

Et dixit qui sedebat in throno:
Ecce novo facio omnia.

༄

The One who sat on the throne said to me:
"See, I make all things new!"

Cf. Revelation 21:5

The visible sky and the earth where we live are no more than a place of passage, a mobile tent pitched for a day, the preparation for and rough sketch of a better world. The present world is like a worksite where everything is in progress and action. The elements break against each other and are decomposed to take on new forms; they run about, seek each other; all beings groan and must endure the pains of childbirth: "Yes, we know that all creation groans and is in agony even until now."[1] They sigh for the day when, delivered from bondage and corruption, they will enter into the glory and freedom of the children of God, when the Creator will renew them in a more perfect and harmonious order. That is why the world will have an end, in the true sense of the word, and, by transforming heaven and earth, this end will make the universe the *place of immortality*. One of the leading lights of contemporary science has spoken these sublime words: "The earth, in its perpetual revolutions, probably seeks its resting place."

Leibnitz already stated, "The world will be destroyed and reconstructed within the space of time which the spiritual government deems fitting." Again, a writer of the Protestant school has said, "It is probable that this rich variety is seeking its unity. All creatures will gather in a school of goodness and beauty. The flowers of all worlds will be assembled in the same garden."[2]

There is, moreover, one of our Master's sayings, which makes this expectation a certainty. The Lord tells us, "heaven and earth shall pass away . . . the stars will fall from the sky, and the hosts of heaven will be shaken loose." The prophet David had once said, "Of old you established the earth, and the heavens are the work of your hands. They shall perish, but you remain though all of them grow old like a garment. Like clothing you change them, and they are changed."[3]

What will be the state of creation and all beings, when they have irrevocably broken their ancient fetters and bloomed into repose — into full and consummated life? Will the earth still turn upon its axis? Will the heavenly bodies, moving along at a dizzying speed, revolve around their center as they do now? Will the stars continue to emit only a faint, cold gleam amidst the immensity of space?

These are grave and mysterious questions, which it would be futile for human reason to seek to resolve, if it were not aided by the light of revelation. Yet, no one will dispute that this study on the place of immortal life and of man's dwelling place in the age to come is a study incomparably more serious and worthy of our attention than those narrow studies that captivate men, the sole object of which is to snatch from the changing, ephemeral nature of this world a few of its vain, worthless secrets.

Men such as rationalists and pantheists, who do not share our hopes but who, nevertheless, accept immortality and a future life, do not know how to define the circumstances in which the spirits will live after death. They imagine them as useless, erratic figures, wandering around in ethereal, undefined space, not restricted to any fixed abode, like shadows bereft of their consciousness and personality, immersed in that supreme being called the *all in all*; or like rivers, drowned in the depths of the ocean. A fantastic and imaginary immortality, which is simply a cold picture of eternal gloom, a dark dream of fatality and nothingness.

Sacred Scripture contradicts all these fables and idle hypotheses. It teaches us that at the time of the Second Coming of Jesus
Christ, the earth in which we live and the sky, which gives us
light, will be the scene of two opposing changes.

The first of these changes will be the complete destruction of
the present physical order. St. Peter says, "The day of the Lord will
come like a thief, and on that day the heavens will vanish with
great violence; the elements will be destroyed by fire, and the earth
and everything on it will be consumed by fire."[4] Thus, this visible
world, once engulfed by the waters of the Flood, is destined to perish once more, and will be set aflame. The same cause that brought
about the Flood will produce the final cataclysm; the earth will be
destroyed, because the sins of men have soiled it. The elements
will be entirely dissolved because, albeit without their own voli-
tion, they were made subject to vanity. The heavens will be hurled
back with extraordinary swiftness because they, too, in the words
of Job, are not pure in the sight of the Lord.[5]

⤸

The second change, however — the total restoration of creation — will take place as soon as the ruin of the universe has been
consummated. This radiant, predestined temple, which the Lord
will build as the most striking manifestation of His glory, cannot
for a single moment be darkened and profaned by the presence of
the reprobate. It will be only when these have been engulfed in the
depths of the earth, and when the words *infernus et mors missi sunt
in stagnum ignis* — "Then death and the netherworld were hurled
into the pool of fire"[6] — have been fulfilled, that material creation
will be set free and God will proceed with the great renovation.

St. Augustine says, "When the judgment has been accomplished, heaven and earth will cease to subsist." St. Peter declares,

"What we await are new heavens and a new earth, where, according to his promise, the justice of God will reside."[7]

The universe will then be subjected to other laws; the sun and the heavenly bodies will no longer execute their revolutions, and the heavens and the earth will remain stable and at rest. False science vainly protests against the affirmations of the Sacred Books, and alleges that they are at variance with the laws of matter and the principles governing the elements; but how do we know that movement is an essential property of the elements and matter? Matter and the elements created for man are only his servants and auxiliaries: the Creator desired to adapt them to our circumstances and mode of existence. Now, when we are travelers and live in impermanence, matter is subject to alteration and change; but when man comes into the realm of the perpetual and absolute, the elements will be brought into harmony with the new life with which he will be endowed. Time will be no more — *quia tempus non erit amplius* — nor will there be henceforth any vicissitudes of years and days. "No longer shall your sun go down," said Isaiah, "or your moon withdraw. For the Lord will be your light forever, and the days of your mourning shall be at an end."[8]

Thus, creation will not perish: the temple of immortality will not be an ethereal, incorporeal place, as some imagine and teach, but a material abode and a city. St. Anselm describes this new earth when he says, "This earth, which sustained and nourished the holy body of the Lord, will be a paradise. Because it has been washed with the blood of martyrs, it will be eternally ornamented with sweet-smelling flowers, violets, and roses that will not wither."[9]

William of Paris, after declaring that the animals, plants, and mineral substances themselves will be burned and destroyed by fire, adds, "A large number of learned men among Christians consider that, after the resurrection, the earth will be bedecked with new evergreen species and incorruptible flowers, and that a perpetual springtime and beauty will therein prevail, as in the paradise in which our fathers were placed." The following words of the prophet David seem to concur with the view expressed by these two Doctors: "When You send forth your Spirit, they are created; and You renew the face of the earth."[10]

As for the order, dimensions, and structure of the temple of immortal life, St. John depicts it for us in chapter 21 of Revelation. In fact, in order to give us a picture of such transcendental realities, which go beyond the conceptions of our mind, he has to resort to enigmatic images and to obscure, mysterious expressions. To bring out the perfection and harmony of this glorious city, he tells us that it is built entirely of polished, hewn stones. To describe its richness and splendor, he tells us that

> its wall, massive and high, had twelve gates at which twelve angels were stationed . . . The city is perfectly square, its length and its width being the same . . . Its wall measured a hundred and forty-four cubits in height by the unit of measurement the angel used. The wall was constructed of jasper; the city was of pure gold, crystal-clear. The foundation of the city wall was ornate with precious stones of every sort: the first course of stones was jasper, the second sapphire, the third chalcedony, the fourth emerald, the fifth sardonyx, the sixth carnelian, the seventh chrysolite, the eighth beryl, the ninth topaz, the tenth chrysoprase, the eleventh hyacinth, and the twelfth amethyst. The twelve gates were twelve pearls, each made of a single pearl; and the streets of the city were of pure gold, transparent as glass . . .[11]

All these expressions and images are to be understood in the figurative sense and interpreted allegorically. There are, however, certain characteristics to be kept in mind, which signify that the abode of the glorified elect will present no analogy with the places where we live in this world. St. John tells us in the same chapter that there will be no temple, for the all-powerful Lord God and Lamb are themselves the temple.[12] Nor will there be sun or moon any more, because the brightness of God is the light, and the immolated Lamb is Himself the lamp.[13] We may, by analogy and induction, conclude that there will be no courts of law, because there will be no wars or strife. Nor will there be any more despots or tyrants, since the Lord will be the strength and the ornament of the inhabitants of this city, and will ordain that they shall reign eternally: *Quoniam Dominus illuminabit illos, et regnabunt in saecula saeculorum.*[14] St. John himself gives grounds for all these various interpretations when he tells us that "nothing profane shall enter it, nor anyone who is a liar or has done a detestable act," and when he informs us in the preceding verses that "during the day its gates shall never be shut, and there shall be no night. The treasures and wealth of the nations shall be brought there."[15]

What is certain is that everything in this city will be peaceful and divinely ordained. Sorrow and envy will be forever banished from it; for, as St. Augustine explains, "sorrow and envy proceed from our evil passions and desires, which make us covet another's goods; but, in the city of God, there will no longer be any desires, since all those [desires] that the elect have ever felt will be entirely satisfied: the Lamb will quench their thirst in the stream of living water, and their thirst will be fully quenched."[16] Secondly, there will be no such goods to covet. In the Holy City, the goods and the wealth will be none other than the God-Charity, who will give Himself wholly to each of the elect in accordance with the degree and extent of his merits. Thus, the totality of angels and men will be associated in perfect unity, by virtue of Him who is called the first-born of creation, the head of the body of the Church, who has received the primacy of all things,[17] so that God may be all in all: *Ut sit Deus omnia in omnibus.*[18]

Such are the sentiments and teaching of the Faith and the Sacred Books; but, from the same texts we have quoted, sacred theology infers and prominently sets out applications that are equally certain, and points of view that are just as illuminating.

⌒

Theology starts from the principle that, after the resurrection, the elements and material nature will be adapted to the circumstances of the glorious bodies; consequently, we need only recall what we are taught about the state of the glorious bodies for our minds to be able to open upon new horizons, and form a clearer and more precise idea of this palace of the renewed creation, destined one day to be our domain and dwelling-place.

The first prerogative that the resurrected bodies of the elect will enjoy will be that of *subtility.* Just as the risen Lord passed through a tomb that was sealed, and, the following day, appeared suddenly before His disciples in a room where the doors were closed, so our bodies, when they are no longer composed of an inert and gross substance, but are vivified and penetrated at every point by the spirit — *corpus spirituale* — will pass through space like a ray of sunshine, and no corporeal object will have the capacity to hold them back.

The second property of the glorious bodies will be *agility.* They will dart about like sparks through stubble.[19] They will have the ability to move with the swiftness of thought itself, and, wherever the mind wishes, the body will convey itself immediately.

Thus, our bodies will no longer be bound to the earth by the force of attraction but, freed from all corruption and all gravity, they will spring up according to their desire; and, just as the Lord was taken up to heaven, so shall we be raised up to meet Him in the air, and we, too, will fly, seated upon clouds.

Even now, the present physical order offers us an image and a faint reflection of this new state to which our nature will one day be raised. Do not imponderable elements, such as electricity and magnetism freely pass through the densest and most opaque substances, and do they not move rapidly and effortlessly through granite and metals? It will be likewise with our bodies after the resurrection. Matter will no longer be able to stop or circumscribe them. Baseness will be absorbed in glory, the tangible in the spiritual, the human in the divine.

There will be no more disease, no more death, and therefore no nourishment, no procreation, and no differentiation of sex. Our flesh, at present weak and subject to a thousand ailments, will become impassible, endowed with a strength, solidity, and consistency that will free it forever from all change, weariness, and alteration.

Lastly, the resurrected elect will possess *brightness*. They will be encompassed with such splendor that they will appear like so many suns: *Tune justi fulgebunt sicut sol in regno Patris eorum.*[20] In fact, this brightness will be distributed in different degrees among the elect, according to the inequality of their merits; for the brightness of the sun is one thing, that of the moon is another, and that of the stars yet another. The stars themselves differ from one another in brightness. So shall it be at the resurrection of the dead.[22]

The elect who appear surrounded with most glory will be the Doctors: "But the wise shall shine brightly like the splendor of the firmament, and those who lead the many to justice shall be like the stars forever."[23] The brightness with which the elect will be adorned will unceasingly cast out new reflections, increasing every moment: the glorified saints will eternally communicate to each other the goods they possess, and they will reflect upon one another the streams of splendor that illuminate them. The source and center of this divine brightness will be none other than God Himself, who, in the words of St. John, is all "light" and in whom there is no admixture of imperfection and darkness.[24]

The vision of God, which the elect will contemplate face-to-face, in its essence, will inundate their souls with its most ineffable irradiations, and their souls, in turn, will illuminate their bodies, which will appear surrounded with as much brightness as created nature can contain.

From this entire doctrine, we may draw the certain conclusion that our bodies will enter a mode of existence utterly different from their way of life on earth, that they will be ennobled, embellished and transfigured to such an extent that, between this new state and the present one, there will be an infinitely greater difference than between an inert rock and the most brilliant sunbeams, or between the purest gold and the foulest, murkiest slime.

Furthermore, it is written that the bodies of the saints will be modeled and formed after the risen body of Christ.[25] Jesus Christ in the Eucharist gives us an image and likeness of what the glorious bodies will be like one day. Without leaving heaven, where He is seated at the right hand of His Father, He is substantially present every day on earth, in a thousand places. He is entire, without reduction or diminution, in each particle of the Host and in each drop of the Chalice. By this supernatural and incomprehensible mode of existence, does He not show that those who have launched into the new life are no longer bound or governed by the laws of the present physical nature, and that inert matter can place no obstacle against the goodness and infinite power of God?

The End of the Present World

As we look over the lives of the saints, we again find innumerable analogies of that state to which we shall be raised in the life to come.

As soon as a soul has soared toward God and the spirit from above has come down into it, raising it beyond the tyranny of the senses and the bondage of the lower appetites, it happens that the flesh experiences the aftereffects of the new life with which the soul is endowed, and often feels the anticipated effects of that glorious freedom which the children of God will enter. Saints like Teresa and a multitude of ecstatic souls, interiorly consumed by the fire of the Seraphim, have risen up of themselves, unsupported, into the air. St. Maur, the disciple of St. Benedict, used to walk dry-shod over the water.[26] Others, such as St. Francis Xavier and St. Alphonsus Liguori, were released from the laws of space and were seen simultaneously preaching, praying in a town, attending a sick person, or going to the aid of shipwrecked men in the most distant places.[27]

On other occasions, the light that the spirit of God has poured into the souls of the saints becomes visible on their features, their clothing and their whole person, illuminating them with a halo, by which they appear gloriously surrounded. So it should be; for those who sow in the flesh reap corruption, and those who sow in the spirit reap life everlasting.[28]

There is yet another certain truth that is of faith, and it is that once the judgment has been completed, Jesus Christ will immediately ascend back to heaven, with all His elect as escort. He will point out to each of them the place He prepared for him on the day of His Ascension: *Vado parare vobis locum.*[29]

☞

For a dwelling-place, the elect will have the empyrean heaven, the one that is above all the heavenly bodies and all corporeal, visible nature. As it is written: "Then we, the living . . . will be caught up with them in the clouds to meet the Lord in the air. Thenceforth we shall be with the Lord unceasingly."[30]

Does it follow that the rest of creation, the heavenly bodies and our sublunary world will remain empty and depopulated? If this were so, why would divine wisdom rebuild them on a new plane, and adorn them with all the marvels of His splendor and beauty?

St. Thomas teaches us that heaven is destined to serve as the abode and principal habitation of the glorified saints, but they will not on that account be motionless and restricted within a fixed place. Each of the elect will have his throne, and they will occupy higher abodes and places, according to their merit, but, observes St. Thomas, the word *place* (*locum*), is to be understood rather as excellence of rank, order of primacy, than as the eminence of the place that will be assigned.

If Christ were momentarily to leave heaven, the place where He went to reside would always be the worthiest and highest, and the other places the more honorable as they were closer to the one occupied by Christ; and do not the angels, who enjoy glory, descend from heaven and return there at their pleasure? It must be concluded that the temple of immensity will blossom forth in its totality and in all its brilliance before the ecstatic gaze of the elect, and that, without leaving Christ for a single moment, they will have the power to transport themselves, in the twinkling of an eye, to the ends of the firmament. They will be free to explore the heavenly bodies, reappear on this earth, and pass again over the places where they lived and prayed, places that were the scene of their labors and immolation. This view concurs with the texts of the Sacred Books, where they tell us that there are many mansions in our heavenly Father's house,[31] that the saints will shine like stars in perpetual eternities, and that, wherever the body — that is, the sacred humanity of Christ — shall be, there also will the eagles be gathered.[32]

Here, science is in accord with faith, and helps us to form an idea of the order, extent, and magnificence of this temple, which will serve as an abode for renewed man.

In our times, the fertile and enterprising genius of man, having explored the earth over its surface and in its innermost recesses, has launched out up to the heavenly bodies, and boldly sent his voice into the heavens: *In coelo posuit os suum.*[33] Armed with the most powerful instruments human art has ever been able to construct, contemporary astronomy has, over a wide area, rent the veil of the immense expanse that had seemed impenetrable to man's understanding and, by patient study and analysis, has marked out the shores of the starry sky, and investigated their depths and secrets.

How many other mysteries there are in the immensity of space, which our feeble minds will never succeed in penetrating! Thus it is that science, as it advances, reveals to us ever more the divine greatness, and bids us exclaim, with the unbounded joy of the prophet David, "The heavens declare the glory of God; and the firmament proclaims His handiwork. Day pours out the word to day, and night to night imparts knowledge."[34] There lies man's domain, the magnificent temple destined, one day, to be his palace and habitation; once resurrected, glorious, and incorruptible, he will embrace with a single glance the riches that fill these spaces, and he will cover these vast distances at one stretch, with greater swiftness than light itself travels over them.

~

That science which is hostile to our beliefs has sought to turn these considerations to account in order to degrade man and combat his hopes and his glorious destiny.

The response to the skeptics

How can we admit, it says, that those vast spheres, inundated with light, where the elements possess all their energy and vitality, are black wildernesses, devoid of inhabitants? While our planet which, compared with other globes, is but an imperceptible speck, is supposed to serve as an abode for living creatures, capable of knowing and loving, those thousands of millions of worlds suspended above our heads are said to be composed of nothing but inert bodies, mechanically performing the law of their nature, or else of animals, slaves of their instincts and incapable of knowing the hand that feeds them? With the aid of a microscope, we can discern millions of minute animals, in a drop of water hanging from a needle; every grain of dust we trample underfoot contains perhaps as many living, organized creatures as there are over the whole surface of the earth, and we are to believe that the Creator, so prodigal with animal life, was parsimonious with intelligent life? Could these countless worlds, intended to proclaim His glory, be merely lyres suspended in the void, without a spirit capable of hearing them, and without a heart to echo them and quiver in harmony with their songs?

If, then, reason and every analogy with existing things bid us conclude that life and thought actuate all these spheres, what is man amidst all these countless beings, these races endowed like him with a soul and a body, to enumerate which defies all our calculations and suppositions? And how can it be granted that he is the center of all things, that it was for him that everything was made and that the final destiny of this multitude of creatures, probably superior in nature to himself, should be subordinated to the trials and vicissitudes of the ephemeral pilgrimage that he undergoes on this earth?

To this difficulty I answer that, on this question, the Church has defined nothing. The Sacred Books were not written to provide vain food to our curiosity. In the account they give us of creation, they speak of only two kinds of intelligent natures: the angels and men. They were not in the least concerned to inform us what might be the mineralogical structure, and the qualities of the plants and animals, in the spheres other than those we inhabit. In this matter, the Church has not condemned any system, and the field remains open to all hypotheses and all opinions.

There was a fairly general belief among the doctors of old that superior intellects were assigned to govern the celestial bodies. It is reasonable to think that beings capable of praising and blessing God fill all space, as they fill all time; thus, there is no infidelity to Catholic Tradition in linking the material existence of the stars to the existence of free, intelligent beings like ourselves.

The Church even gives us to understand that they were the scene of the first act in the providential drama of that great struggle among the higher spirits which St. John describes in his Revelation, a struggle of which our earthly strife is the continuation.[35] It was in the most luminous part of heaven, above the most brilliant stars, says Isaiah, that Lucifer tried to set up a throne for himself, from which he was cast down; it was to the summit of this heaven of heavens, says the psalmist, that Jesus Christ ascended.

However, if these views are only theological opinions, what must be held as certain and as an article of faith is that all the stars and suns were reborn in the divine blood and have shared in the grace of the Redemption. The Church affirms it in one of her solemn hymns: "Land, sea, and stars are washed by this stream."[36]

The scepter of heaven and earth was placed from the beginning in the hands of the Son of God. This multitude of worlds, the number as well as the dimensions of which surpass all calculation, are only the tiniest part of the dowry bestowed upon His humanity by virtue of its indissoluble union with the divinity: "because God,

His Father, has put all things under His feet, He has placed Him at His right hand, in the heavens, above all principality, all power, all virtue, all domination, and all that has a name, not only in this present age, but also in the age to come. He is the bond of all things visible and invisible, and all that is created only exists by Him and in Him . . ."[37]

If you ask me why, among the spheres incomparably more vast and brilliant, the Creator sought out the smallest of the inhabited stars, to make it the place of His annihilation, the scene of His labors and of the mysteries of His Incarnation and of our Redemption, I shall reply that the uncreated Word, desiring to show the depths and the excess of His love by abasing Himself to the very extreme, surged out from the bosom of His Father and from the eternal hills, as Scripture says, and, without stopping, passed through all the orders of intellectual hierarchy.

Crossing the empyrean heaven, where the angelic natures live, He did not unite Himself to them, and it was not in their abode that He established His dwelling-place: *Nusquam enim angelos apprehendit.*[38] Descending next into the highest regions of the firmament, those lit by the great suns, He deemed them, also, too sumptuous and brilliant. As it is written in the Song of Songs, "Here he comes springing across the mountains, leaping across the hills,"[39] until He came to the meanest thing there was: there to plant His mortal footsteps, to hide Himself, and to suffer. Confirming, in regard to the worlds, as to individuals, these words of the prophet David: "He raises up the lowly from the dust; from the dunghill He lifts up the poor."[40]

No doubt, from the preference Christ gave to our inferior and limited planet, and from the perpetual transubstantiation of its material substance into the body of God, which is consummated in the Eucharist, our earth has not acquired that pre-eminence in the physical order which the ancients mistakenly ascribed to it. It is the center of the supernatural world. It is the source, says the apostle, from which spreads over all the other worlds the virtue that conserves and deifies them; it gathers within its unity all the perfections that compose the universe; it restores within its totality the diversity of created existences; through it the heavens bowed down. God approached this base world, and, to use the beautiful expression of St. Ambrose, He clothed Himself in the universe as in a mantle, and became resplendent among all the creatures.

That is all we can say about the future state of the worlds and the place of immortality.

꩜

Of course, we do not intend today to describe the supreme, essential happiness of the elect, which we call the *Beatific Vision* — that possession of God, so intimate and inherent in our being, that we shall be united to Him just as iron unites with fire and, seeing Him face-to-face, at the source of the rays of His eternal essence, we shall be transformed in the resemblance of His divine splendors.

That vision, called *eternal life* because it confers upon man a direct and immediate sharing in the bliss of God, is not dependent on any space or place. God is infinite and everywhere present. The just soul is the sanctuary wherein it most pleases Him to dwell. The angels who assist and protect us on this earth see the face of the heavenly Father unceasingly, and the souls of the blessed separated from their bodies have their paradise wherever they are placed. Were they amidst the deepest darkness of the abyss, God, who possesses and completely satisfies them, would not fail to inundate them with His brightness, and the joys in which He immerses them would not suffer any diminution. If man were a pure spirit, he would not need any definite, material place beyond the present life. Earth and creation would then no longer have any purpose, and would be irrevocably destroyed; but mankind is destined to be reborn, whence it follows that the matter which served as its garment is also meant to be restored, in the same way as its rejuvenated, glorified host.

Thus, mankind as a complete body, and the whole of visible creation, will be tried by fire, and they will come out of it, dazzling and purified. Just as a metal is not cast into the furnace to be consumed and destroyed but to come out refined and in the state of pure gold, so the conflagration the world will undergo will not annihilate it, but only purify and transform it into a clearer and purer image of the idea of God realized in it.

> And I saw a new Jerusalem, the holy city, coming down out of heaven from God, beautiful as a bride prepared to meet her husband. And I heard a loud voice from the throne cry out, "This is God's dwelling among men. He shall dwell with them, and they shall be His people and He shall be their God who is always with them . . ."[41]

Oh, you must not think that, because the world will cease to turn around upon itself and ever to revolve around the same circle like a slave tied to the millstone that, in this new earth, there will be no freshness in the air, no verdure in the meadows, no flowers on the trees, and no water gushing out of the springs. You imagine, perhaps, that this nature, which now runs, moves, and seethes, full of zest and life, beneath the indirect and partial light of our dark sun, is to remain inert, fruitless, and frozen beneath the direct gaze of God!

Far from it: the new world is a living thing! The heavenly Jerusalem is the eternal Church, the daughter of God, the spotless spouse of the Lamb. The Lamb, the incarnate Word, occupies the center of its heart. It is He who is its life, its focus, its streaming water, and its ever-burning, inextinguishable torch.

As for the fortunate creatures who dwell in it, they will forever pass rapidly from brightness to brightness, from progress to progress, from one ecstasy to another. "God cannot grow, but the creature will always grow. Only, it will bind itself unalterably to its center through an immense love, and this is what will be known as its repose and immobility."[42]

What practical and moral lessons are to be drawn from these teachings, for the guidance of our lives and the rule of our actions?

The first is this: that it is the height of human folly to become attached to the perishable and corruptible goods of this life.

What would you think of a great king, lord of a vast empire, who, spurning his sumptuous treasures and the glitter of his crown, kept his eyes and all his thoughts fixed on a handful of sand or a piece of slime, and set his heart and all his affections unwaveringly on this base matter? The story is told of a Roman emperor who, instead of commanding his armies and dispensing justice, spent his time killing flies. So it is with the majority of men called to possess a kingdom that encompasses the whole range of the firmaments: they excite themselves and engage in senseless fights to the death over objects more trifling than the flimsy web spun by the spider, than shriveled grass, or than the paltry, worthless life of the worm, crawling along at our feet.

The second of these consequences is that suffering in this life is only a relative evil. There are cases of profound sorrow, of intolerable, raw bruises, and heart-rending, indescribable separations on this earth. History affords us the spectacle of mothers who with their own eyes saw their children branded, degraded, and delivered to wretches worse than demons, who tortured their bodies, and strove, by countless contrivances, to kill their souls. It has portrayed the spiritual anguish, worse than torture and death, which they endured. A great poet has said, "He who lives in a hovel, and he who lives in a palace — all in this life suffer and mourn; queens have been seen weeping like ordinary women, and the quantity of tears in the eyes of kings has brought astonishment."[43]

Yet all this heartbreak and suffering are but a laboratory and a crucible, into which divine goodness has cast our nature, in order that, like coal, black and base, it may emerge in the form of a precious, sparkling diamond.

Jesus Christ has said, "When a woman is in labor, she is sad that her time has come. When she has borne her child, she no longer remembers her pain for joy that a man has been born into the world. In the same way, you are sad for a time, but I shall see you again; then your hearts will rejoice with a joy no one can take from you."[44]

Thus it is with every part of creation. It is in pain that it sows the harvest to come amidst tribulation and tears, but, sooner or later, there will rise over it the sun of that other world, the dawn of which we can glimpse by faith, and all that now lies buried and overwhelmed beneath the weight of sin and death, all that sighs in pain amidst malediction and corruption, will be filled with light and joy, and will rise up again in the glory of a boundless, endless bliss.

The third consequence of our doctrine is that we must not allow ourselves to be perturbed by the noise of our social strife and the convulsions of our revolutions. All this is but a prelude. It is the chaos that precedes harmony; it is motion seeking rest, twilight on the move toward day. The city of God is being built, invisibly but surely, amidst these shocks and heartbreaking convulsions. Public disasters and great scourges are none other than the sword of the Lord and the harbinger of His justice, separating the chaff from the good seed. Our wars, mortal combats, and civil commotions hasten the day of deliverance, when the city of God will be perfect and complete; and, when the turmoil of the ages has passed, there will come a great calm and a great pacification. Then there will follow progress and growth, the eternal dwelling-place of free, intelligent creatures, the unity that will make all people a single soul in the life and eternal light of God.

St. Augustine, after his baptism, having considered in what place he might serve God most usefully, determined to return to Africa with his mother, his brother, and a youth named Evodius. When they reached Ostia, they stopped there to rest after the long journey they had undertaken from Milan, and were preparing to embark.

One evening, Augustine and his mother, leaning upon a window that looked onto the garden of the house, were conversing most graciously, forgetting the whole past and directing their gaze upon the heavenly future. That evening the night was calm, the sky clear, the air still, and in the light of the moon and the gentle twinkling of the stars the sea could be seen, extending the silvery azure of its waves to the distant horizon.

Augustine and Monica were seeking to discover what eternal life would be like. In a single movement of the mind they scaled the stars, the sky, and every region where bodies lived. Next, they swept past above the angels and spiritual creatures, felt themselves transported to the very throne of eternal Wisdom, and had, as it were, a vision of Him through whom all things exist and who is Himself always, without any distinction of time.

How long did their ecstasy last? To them it seemed as fleeting as a flash, and they felt unable to estimate its duration. Having recovered consciousness, and being obliged once more to hear the noise of human voices, Monica exclaimed, "For my part, I find no more pleasure in this life, and I do not know what I am doing or why I still remain here."

That scene has remained famous and popular. Great masters have immortalized it in their masterpieces of art. The paintings and images they have drawn of it have been reproduced a thousand times, and have left, vivid and imperishable, this sublime episode in the life of Monica and Augustine.

On the following day, Monica caught an illness that led to her death, and nine days after the ecstasy that had entranced and raised her above the senses, she went to contemplate face-to-face that sovereign beauty, whose radiance and image she had glimpsed on earth.[45]

In that abode of blissful life St. Monica glimpsed, Christ will be truly king; not only as God, but, inasmuch as He is visible and clothed with our human nature. He will rule over the house of Jacob forever.[46]

His taking possession of His kingdom will not be definitive, and the glory with which He is invested at the right hand of His Father will not be perfect and consummated, until He has finished laying His enemies at His feet.[47]

Then, all things will be subjected to Him, and He Himself will be subjected to the One who has bound every creature to Himself. Hitherto, Christ fought in union with His Church, and was busy conquering His kingdom, whether by eliminating the wicked from it, or by calling to Himself the just through the ineffable attraction of His mercy. His kingdom in heaven will be built on a completely new foundation, and on a model very different from the one on which it is established here below.[48] In that new life Jesus Christ will no longer be represented by a teaching Church, and the elect will not need to be enlightened and aided by the good angels, nor to have recourse to the sacraments for their sanctification. Their state will be a pure, perpetual contemplation of the divinity, in which Christ, the head of humanity, will bear within Himself, to the bosom of His Father, the totality of its members, in order to subject them to Him, to whom He is Himself subject: *Et tunc Filius erit subjectus Patri, ut sit Deus omnia in omnibus*.[49]

There will be no domination but that of one God, extending to all men, and there will be but one glory, the glory of God, who has become the possession of all. Just as the present life is subjected to various constraints and requires for its support certain kinds and conditions of air, clothing, and food, so, as St. Gregory of Nyssa says, in the kingdom of Christ the divine vision will compensate for these different needs. The elect will find therein all they are capable of loving and desiring; it will be their clothing, their food and drink, and will satisfy all the demands of their renewed life.[50]

Happy is he who can forget the cares of the present for a moment, and turn his hopes toward this blessed abode, raising himself up in thought to these high spheres of contemplation and love.

But, O my God, how far these ideas are from the thoughts of most men, and where is he who will even lend a cursory attention to the few things we have endeavored to stammer out? The greater number, blinded by their passions, consumed by greed and pride, are far removed from any concern for their souls and their future. Children of men, how long will your hearts be burdened, how long will you seek your sustenance in lies and shadows? When will you cease imagining death as a curse, and cease regarding it as the abyss of darkness and destruction? Let us try today to understand that it is not the obstacle, but the means; it is the paschal transition that leads from the kingdom of shadows to that of reality, from the life of movement to the life of immutability and indefect-ibility. It is the good sister, whose hand will one day cast off the clouds and idle phantoms, to lead us into the holy of holies of certitude and incomparable beauty.

Ah, perhaps in this discourse we have been permitted to have an inkling and a glimpse of what will take place in the land of glory. So far as forming an exact idea of it is concerned, we can no more do so than the person who, having lived since his mother's womb in an underground cave, could picture to himself the light of a beautiful day.

In drawing an image of the kingdom of Christ, we have been able to speak only in riddles and metaphors; but these riddles and metaphors represent great and true things, an eloquent, irrefutable commentary on these words of the apostle Paul: "Eye has not seen, ear has not heard, nor has it so much as dawned on man what God has prepared for those who love him."[51]

Here, speech fails. Beyond what we have said, reason is powerless to conceive anything. Man can only believe, hope, love, and hold his peace. "The angel said to me, 'These words are trustworthy and true.' "[52]

We have obeyed you, O Lord my God, we have spoken these things, we have written them, and we have preached them. May those who have heard them, and we with them, by a holy, sinless life obtain one day their perfect fulfillment!

⌒

Notes

[1] Rom. 8:22.

[2] Herder, *Idée sur la Philosophie*.

[3] Ps. 102:26-27.

[4] 2 Pet. 3:10.

[5] Job 15:15.

[6] Rev. 20:14.

[7] 2 Pet. 3:13.

[8] Isa. 60:20.

[9] *Terra quae in gremio suo Domini corpus confovit, tota erit ut paradisus, et quia sanctorum sanguine est irrigata odoriferis floribus, rosis, violis immarcessibiliter erit decorata* (St. Anselm, *Elucid*).

[10] Ps. 104:30.

[11] Rev. 21:11-21.

[12] Rev. 21:22.

[13] Rev. 21:23.

[14] Rev. 22:5.

[15] Rev. 21:26, 27.

[16] St. Augustine, *City of God*.

[17] Col. 1:18.

[18] 1 Cor. 15:28.

[19] Wisd. 3:7.

[20] Matt. 13:43: "Then the saints will shine like the sun in their Father's kingdom."

[22] Cf. 1 Cor. 15:41-42.

[23] Dan. 12:3.

[24] 1 John 1:5.

[25] Phil. 3:21.

[26] St. Maur (d. 584), founder and abbot of abbey at Glanfeuil; St. Benedict of Nursia (c. 480-c. 547), abbot who founded the monastery of Monte Cassino.

[27] St. Francis Xavier (1506-1552), Jesuit missionary to the East Indies; St. Alphonsus Liguori (1696-1787), bishop, Doctor, writer, and founder of the Redemptorists.

[28] Cf. Gal. 6:8.

[29] John 14:2: "I go to prepare a place for you."

30 1 Thess. 4:16.

31 John 14:2.

32 Cf. Luke 17:37: "Wheresoever the body shall be, thither will the eagles also be gathered together" (Douay-Rheims translation).

33 Cf. Ps. 73:9: "They have set their mouth against heaven" (Douay-Rheims translation: Ps. 72:9).

34 Ps. 19:1-2.

35 Isa. 14:12-13: How have you fallen from the heavens, O morning star, son of the dawn! How are you cut down to the ground, you who mowed down the nations! You said in your heart, I will scale the heavens; above the stars of God I will set up my throne . . ." Rev. 13:7: "The beast was allowed to wage war against God's people and conquer them. It was likewise granted authority over every race and people, language and nation."

36 *Terra, pontus, astra hoc lavantur flumine.*

37 Cf. Eph. 1:19-23.

38 Heb. 2:16: "Surely He did not come to help angels (but rather the children of Abraham)."

39 Song of Sol. 2:8.

40 Ps. 113:7.

41 Rev. 21:2.

42 Gratry, *De la Connaissance de l'Âme.*

43 Chateaubrand, *Genie du Christianisme.*

44 John 16:21-22.

45 St. Augustine, *Confessions.*

46 Luke 1:32-33.

47 Ps. 110:1.

48 For then all ministries, new illuminations in the blessed, accidental joys from the conversion of sinners, and similar things will cease. But there will be as it were a certain pure divine contemplation in the same way stable and perpetual, by which the whole Christ, that is, the head with all its members, will be taken up in God and be made subject to Him. And to this exposition a fourth reason is added by Paul: And then the Son will be subject to the Father, that

The End of the Present World

God may be all in all; that is, that one God may rule and be glorified in all, and all may have in God something holy and just that they can love and desire" (Suarez, *Disputationes*).

[49] Cf. 1 Cor. 15:28.

[50] St. Gregory of Nyssa (d. c. 395; bishop and writer), *Liber de Anima et Resurrectione*.

[51] 1 Cor. 2:9.

[52] Rev. 22:6.

Fifth Conference

~

Purgatory

Miseremini mei, miseremini mei, saltem
vos amici mei, quia manus Domini tetigit me.

~

Pity me, pity me, O you my friends,
for the hand of the Lord has struck me.

Job 19:21

How beautiful religion is, how admirable and consoling in its teachings and in the glorious obscurity of its mysteries! While letting us die on earth through the deprivation of our bodies, it does not make us die in our hearts by the rupture of friendships, which are their joy and support.

Does not the merciful Savior, who, out of a feeling of exquisite delicacy, deigned to call Himself the God of Abraham, who promised His Apostles to bring them to rest one day in the bosom of Abraham, Isaac, and Jacob, seem to give us to understand, by this religious remembrance given to ancestors, that death does not have the privilege of breaking the lawful ties of life, and that holy affections are not extinguished by the cold hand of death?

Our task today is a difficult one: we must make you love and fear purgatory. Purgatory deserves to be feared. It is, in all truth, the workshop of infinite justice. Divine severity and rigor are exercised there with an intensity that, to us on earth, is unknown. Stern Doctors of the Church assure us that all the cruelties practiced on the martyrs by their executioners, and all the sufferings and afflictions heaped upon men since the beginning of time, cannot be compared to the lightest penalty in that place of atonement. On the other hand, purgatory is the masterpiece of the heart of God, the most marvelous artifice of His love, so much so that we could not tell you whether the consolations enjoyed there are not more abundant than the torments themselves.

The End of the Present World

The state of the holy souls whose laments we wish to let you hear is incomprehensible and ineffable. Their bliss is not that of heaven, where joys are unmixed; their torments are not those of hell, where suffering is unremitting. Their pains bear no comparison with those of the present life, where happy days alternate with days of desolation and sorrow.

These souls are happy and unhappy at the same time. The most extreme tribulations, the greatest anguish the soul can feel, are indissolubly united to the most authentic and most exhilarating joys imaginable, excepting those of heaven.

Oh, do not accuse the Lord of cruelty toward these souls, whom He will one day immerse in the ocean of His radiance, and make them drink the torrent of His pleasure: *De torrente voluptatis potabis eos.*[1] Rather, wonder how love and justice are united by a mutual disposition in this great work of amendment and purification.

In the glow of those terrible flames, we shall realize the profound degree of evil contained in the faults we consider slight and unimportant. On the other hand, the consolations, which God's infinite clemency condescends to extend to these dark places of fire will help us to calm the fears that will grip us at our last hour; at the moment of our death, they will set our souls at peace and inspire us with courage, confidence, and true resignation.

So, in a few words, purgatory is pleasing and consoling, a blessed abode, worthy of our greatest solicitude and predilection, inasmuch as the torments there endured are visited upon holy souls, beloved of God. Purgatory is a scene of affliction and anguish, inasmuch as God's justice gains compensation for the portion of sacrifice and love we have refused Him here below.

Holy angels, guardians of those blazing chasms, help me to call to mind those souls, so holy and resigned, from the bowels of the flames that torment them. Make us recognize among them our fathers, our mothers, our sisters and brothers. Let their cries, so tender and heart-rending, capable of splitting the mountains and mollifying cruelty itself, reach and penetrate our ears.

Oh, if our hearts have not been turned to stone, if one drop of Christian blood still runs in our veins, we shall understand that there is no greater distress to be relieved, no devotion more meritorious or more compelling to be practiced!

☞

The existence of purgatory is explicitly attested by Holy Scripture and by the constant tradition of the Jewish and Christian Church. It is said in the books of Maccabees that it is a holy and wholesome thought to pray for the dead, so that they may be freed from the faults and imperfections by which they sullied themselves in life: *ut a peccatis solvantur.*[2] Speaking of easygoing and presumptuous preachers who, in the exercise of their ministry, are led astray by love of praise and yield to thoughts of vanity and feelings of self-satisfaction, St. Paul says that they will be saved, but after having first been tried by fire: *sic quasi per ignem.*[3] St. Gregory teaches that souls guilty of trespasses for which they have not sufficiently atoned during their life will be baptized in fire: *ab igne baptizabuntur.* It will be their second baptism. The first is necessary in order to introduce us into the Church on earth, the second to introduce us into the Church in heaven.

According to St. Cyril and St. Thomas, the fire of purgatory is of the same kind as that of hell. It has the same intensity, and differs only in that it is temporary. Lastly, the sacred liturgy teaches us that purgatory is a frightful abyss, a place in which the souls are in anguish and cruel expectation, a brazier where they burn unceasingly, subjected to the effect of subtle fire, lit by the breath of divine justice, the strength of which is the measure of His most just and most dreadful vengeance: *Dies irae, dies illa . . . Lacrymosa dies illa, qua resurget ex favilla judicandus homo reus.*[4]

In the Canon of the Mass, the Church offers her petitions to God in order to obtain for these souls *locum lucis*, a place of light: whence it follows that they are in the night, and enveloped in dense, impenetrable darkness. She seeks for them *locum refrigerii*, a place of refreshment; whence it follows that they are in intolerable, burning pain. Again, she asks for them *locum pacis*, a place of peace: whence it follows that they are consumed by fears and inexpressible anxieties.

This simple description makes our whole being shake with horror. Let us hasten to say that the consolations these captive souls experience are also inexpressible.

It is true that their eyes are not yet refreshed by the sight of the gentle light, and the angels do not descend from heaven to transform their flames into a refreshing dew; but they have the sweetest treasure, one that is enough by itself to raise up the man most despondent beneath the weight of his afflictions, and bring the dawn of calmness to the most doleful and dejected countenances: they possess the good that, on earth, is left to the most wretched and deprived of men, when he has drained the ever-filling cup of all afflictions and pains: they have hope. They possess hope in the highest order, in that degree which excludes all uncertainty and apprehension, which sets the heart at rest, in the deepest and most absolute security: "a merited crown awaits me."[5]

These souls are assured of their salvation. St. Thomas gives us two reasons for this unshakable certainty which is so consoling that it makes them, in a certain sense, forget their pains. In the first place, these souls know that it is of faith that the reprobate can neither love God, nor hate their sins, nor fulfill any good work: now they have an inner awareness that they love God, that they hate their faults and can no longer do evil. Moreover, they know with the certainty of faith that souls who die in a state of mortal sin are cast into hell without delay, the very moment they utter their final sigh. They spend their days in wealth, and in a moment they go down to hell.[6]

Now, the souls of whom I speak are not given up to despair, do not see the faces of the demons, do not hear their curses and blasphemies: from this fact, they infallibly conclude that they did not die in a state of mortal sin, but are in a state of grace and pleasing to God.

Also, what a source of happiness it is for them to be able to exclaim with St. Paul's confidence: "No more relapses into sin! No more separation between God and myself: *Certus sum enim!* For I am certain! No more terrifying doubts about my predestination. Ah! it is over, I am saved . . . I have heard from the very mouth of my God the irrevocable declaration of my salvation; I know so as never again to doubt it that one day the gates of the heavenly city will open for my triumphal entry and that heaven, earth, the principalities and powers together are powerless to separate me from the charity of God and dispossess me of my eternal crown; 'for I am certain that neither death nor life, neither angels nor principalities, neither the present nor the future, nor powers, neither height nor depth nor any other creature, will be able to separate us from the love of God that comes to us in Christ Jesus our Lord.' "[7]

Oh, no doubt this soul will exclaim: How sharp my pains are! Nothing can be compared with the violence of my punishment; but this punishment and these sufferings are powerless to take me away from God, to destroy the fire of His love within me: "Who will separate us from the love of Christ? Trial, or distress, or hunger?"[8] Oh! My weakness is now no longer liable to reveal itself in outbursts of temper, in impatience and murmuring. Resigned to

God's will and pleasure, I bless the hand that chastises me; I accept joyfully all my torments.

These torments cannot crush my soul or make it uneasy, bitter, or anxious: *Non contristabit justum quidquid ei acciderit.*[9] I know that they are ordained and moderated by that Divine Providence which, for the good of creatures, arranges all things with love and equity.[10]

I will say more: I should prefer my torments to the delights of heaven, if it could be granted to me to enjoy them against the desire of that sovereign will to which I am henceforth absolutely and irrevocably subject. My wishes and aspirations are summed up in a single motto: "All that God wishes, as He wishes it, and at the time He wishes it." O God of my heart, my treasure and my all, what am I that Thou deign to come down to me and, with Thy paternal hand, purify an ungrateful and unfaithful soul!

Oh, cut deep into the flesh, drain the unimaginable cup of Thy torments! Listen only to Thy honor and the interest of Thy justice, and, until this is fully satisfied, pay no heed to either my groans or my complaints.

Poor souls! They have but one passion, one burning desire, one wish: to break the obstacle that prevents them from springing forward toward God, who calls them and draws them to Himself with all the energy and all the violence of His beauty, mercy, and boundless love.

Oh, if they could, they would willingly stir up the flames that consume them, and vie with one another in accumulating torment upon torment, purgatory upon purgatory, in order to hasten the happy day of their deliverance. In these souls there are residual traces of sin, an alloy of afflictions, blemishes, and defects that do not permit them to unite with the divine substance. Their imperfections, the venial faults with which they allowed themselves to be tarnished, have darkened and maimed their inner eye. If, before their complete purification, the bright, dazzling light of heaven met their sick, enfeebled eyes, they would feel an impression a thousand times more painful and burning than those they feel amidst the deepest darkness of the abyss. God Himself would like to transform them immediately into the likeness of His glory by illuminating them with the pure rays of His divinity; but these rays, being too bright and dazzling, could not penetrate them. They would be intercepted by the dross and the remains of that earthly dust and mire with which they are still sullied. It is essential that, having been cast into a consuming crucible, they should lay aside the rest of human imperfections, so that, from being like base, black carbon, they may emerge in the form of a precious, transparent crystal. They must be made subtle, purged of every admixture of shadow and darkness, and become capable of receiving, without opposition, the irradiations and splendors of divine glory that, flowing in superabundance within them, one day, will fill them, like a river without banks or bottom.

Imagine a person afflicted with a hideous ailment that gnaws his flesh and makes him an object of ostracism and disgust for those around him. The doctor, seeking to cure him, applies forceps and fire unsparingly. With his terrible instrument, he probes to the very marrow of the bones. He will attack the source and root of the disease in its innermost depths. So violent are the convulsions of the patient that he nearly expires; but, when the operation is over, he feels reborn, the disease has disappeared, and he has recovered his beauty, youth, and vigor. Ah! Far from flying into a rage with complaints and reproaches, he has no words or blessing great enough to express his gratitude to the skilled man who, by making him suffer a thousand woes, gave him the most precious of things: health and life.

So it is with the souls in purgatory. They quiver with joy as they see their stains and filth vanish through the marvelous effect of that reparatory punishment. Under the action of those purifying flames, their more or less disfigured being is refreshed and restored. The fire itself, St. Thomas says, loses its intensity in proportion as it consumes and destroys the faults and imperfections that feed its strength. A barrier of imperceptible size still separates these souls from the place of recompense. Oh! They feel indescribable transports of joy, as they see the wings growing that will enable them soon to rush forward toward the abodes of heaven. Already they glimpse the dawn of deliverance. Oh! They are not yet within reach of the promised land; but, like Moses, they draw up a mental picture of it. They have a presentiment of its lights and pleasant shores, and breathe in its fragrance and its sweet-smelling breezes in advance. Each day, each moment, they see the dawn of their deliverance rising in a less distant horizon; they feel the place of their eternal repose come nearer and nearer: *Requies de labore.* What else shall I say? These souls have charity which, this time, has taken complete and absolute possession of their hearts; they love God, they love Him so intensely that they are willing to be dissolved and annihilated for His glory.

St. John Chrysostom says, "The man who is inflamed with the fire of divine love is as indifferent to glory and ignominy as if he were alone and unseen on this earth. He spurns all temptations. He is no more troubled by pincers, gridirons, or racks than if these sufferings were endured in a body other than his own. What is full of sweetness for the world has no attraction for him, no taste; he is no more liable to be captivated by some evil attachment than is gold, seven times tested, liable to be tarnished by rust. Such are, even on this earth, the effects of divine love when it firmly takes hold of a soul."

The sufferings and consolations of purgatory

Now, divine love acts upon the souls of whom I am speaking with all the greater force, in that, being separated from their bodies, deprived of all human consolations, and abandoned to a thousand martyrdoms, they are compelled to have recourse to God and to seek in Him alone all that they lack.

One of the greatest of their sufferings is the knowledge that the pains they endure bring no benefit to them. Night has come for them, when they can no longer labor or acquire anything: "The night comes on when no one can work."[11] The time when man is able to make satisfaction himself for his sins, accumulate merit, and increase his heavenly crown ceases with death. The moment he enters the other life, every human being receives the pronouncement of his eternal sentence.

His fate is immutably fixed, and he no longer has the option of accomplishing good or bad works, for which he can once more be answerable at God's tribunal. Yet, if the souls in purgatory cannot grow in holiness and amass new merits by their patience and resignation, they nevertheless know that they can no longer lose merit, and, for them, it is a sweet joy to suffer out of a free, altogether disinterested, love.

Without doubt this peculiar mixture of happiness amidst the most cruel torments is a state our dull minds cannot comprehend; but ask the martyrs: the Teresas, the Lucians, the celestial lovers of the Cross. They will tell you that, most often, it is in sorrow and amidst afflictions and the most cruel spiritual desolations that he who seeks to live in God alone experiences a kind of foretaste of paradise, and feels the sweetest and most exhilarating joys and delights pour into his heart.

The souls in purgatory love God; furthermore, they are loved by the churches of heaven and earth, who maintain continuous contact and relations with them. The Catholic Church appeals to the charity of her children, and, through their mediation, lavishes her petitions and aid upon them day and night. Every moment the charity of the good angels bestows upon them the heavenly dew that the good Jesus sends down from His Heart. They love one another, and console each other by ineffable conversations.

No unfathomable gulf separates these souls and their friends on earth, and we are free at every moment to bring them that drop of water which the rich fool sought in vain from the pity of Lazarus.[12]

St. John once had a wonderful vision: he saw a temple, and, in the sanctuary of this temple, perceived an altar, and beneath this altar, the multitude of suffering souls: *vidi subtus altare animas interfectorum.*[13] These souls are not *in front of the altar*, as one commentator remarks; they are not permitted to be there. They participate in the fruit of the Eucharistic Sacrifice only indirectly, by means of intercession. They are *below the altar*, and await, resigned, although in torment, the portion we are willing to convey to their lips.[14]

☞

The Catholic Church has made no declaration on the location of purgatory. Different opinions have been expressed on this point by the Doctors and Fathers, and we are free to choose any of them without lacking in orthodoxy or departing from the true Faith.

St. Thomas, St. Bonaventure, and St. Augustine teach that purgatory is situated in the center of the earth. They quote, in support of their opinion, the words sung by the Church's command: "Lord, deliver the souls of the faithful departed from the pains of hell and the deep pit."

Likewise, these words from Revelation: "But no one in heaven or on earth *or under the earth* could be found to open the scroll or examine its contents."[15] From these words of St. John, it is certain that only just men were invited to open the mysterious book. Now, by this reference to those who are *below the earth*, does not the apostle John seem to give us to understand that there are some just people who are detained for a time in these dark depths? Elsewhere, in Sirach, it is said: "I shall enter into the lower parts of the earth, and shall visit those who sleep, and the hope of salvation shall appear in their sight."[16] Scholars have shown that the inspired author intended in this passage to indicate limbo, where the Patriarchs and saints of the Old Testament rested in the bosom of Abraham. This explanation confirms, rather than invalidates, the view of St. Thomas and St. Bonaventure.

In fact, if the Patriarchs and the just of the Old Testament, once purified of all their actual sins, had the lower regions of the earth as their abode until the day when the sin transmitted to our race by Adam had been completely erased on the Cross,[17] it seems all the more fitting that souls guilty of actual sins for which they have not sufficiently atoned should be punished and detained in the depths of the earth: *Inferiores partes terrae.*

The testimony of St. Augustine adds a further degree of probability to this opinion: in his Epistle XCIX, *ad Evodium*, he states that, when Christ descended into hell, He went not only to limbo but also to purgatory, where He delivered some of the captive souls, as seems to be indicated in the Acts of the Apostles: *Solutis doloribus inferni.*[18]

The second opinion concerning the location of purgatory is shared by St. Victor and by St. Gregory the Great in his *Dialogues*. Both maintain that purgatory is not a fixed place, and that a large number of deceased souls atone for their faults on earth, and in the same places where they sinned the most frequently.

Sacred theology reconciles these different testimonies by establishing, first, that purgatory is a fixed place, with given bounds, situated at the center of the earth, where the majority of souls go in order to atone for the faults by which they were sullied.

Nevertheless, purgatory is not restricted to this one single place. Whether by reason of the gravity of their sins or through a special dispensation of divine wisdom, there are a considerable number of other souls who do not languish in that prison, but undergo their punishment on earth, and in that place where they had sinned. This interpretation, which comes from great theologians, explains and confirms a multitude of apparitions and revelations made to the saints, several of them having marks of truth that make it impossible to dismiss them.[19]

In order fully to elucidate our doctrine, we shall select, among all the revelations quoted by St. Gregory in his *Dialogues*, those of which the authenticity is beyond all question.

In the annals of Citeaux, it is related that a pilgrim from the district of Rodez, returning from Jerusalem, was forced by a storm to pull into port at an island close to Sicily. There he visited a holy hermit, who inquired about matters pertaining to religion in his country of France, and also asked whether he knew the monastery of Cluny and Abbot Odilon. The pilgrim replied that he did, and added that he would be grateful if he would tell him what purpose he had in asking him that question. The hermit answered, "Very near this place, there is a crater, whose summit we can see; at certain times, it belches up clouds of smoke and flame. I have seen demons carrying off the souls of sinners and hurling them into that frightful abyss, in order to torment them for a while. Now, on certain days, I hear the evil spirits conversing among themselves, and complaining that some of these souls have escaped from them; they blame pious persons who, by their prayers and sacrifices, hasten the deliverance of these souls. Odilon and his monks are the ones who seem to terrify them most. That is why, when you return to your country, I ask you in the name of God to exhort the abbot and monks of Cluny to redouble their prayers and alms for the relief of these poor souls." The pilgrim, on his return, did as he was bidden. The holy Abbot Odilon pondered and weighed everything carefully. He sought enlightenment from God, and ordained that, in all the monasteries of his order, the second day of November each year should be established in commemoration of all the faithful departed. Such was the origin of the Feast of All Souls.[20]

⌒

St. Bernard, in his life of St. Malachi, quotes another case. This saint relates that one day he saw his sister, who had been dead for some time. She was doing her purgatory in the cemetery. On account of her vanity and the attention she had devoted to her hair and body, she had been sentenced to live in the very grave where she had been buried, and to witness the dissolution of her body. The saint offered the Sacrifice of the Mass for her for thirty days; at the end of this period he saw his sister again. This time she had been sentenced to complete her purgatory at the gate of the church, doubtless because of her irreverent demeanor in the holy place; perhaps she had distracted the faithful from the Sacred Mysteries in order to draw eyes and appreciation to herself. She was exceedingly sad, wearing a mourning veil, and was in extreme anguish. The saint offered the Sacrifice once more for thirty days, and she appeared to him for the last time in the sanctuary, with unruffled countenance, radiant in a white robe. The bishop knew by this sign that his sister had gained her deliverance.

This story records the universal custom, which prevailed from the very first ages of the Church, of praying for the dead over a period of thirty days. On this point, Christianity had merely followed the Mosaic tradition.

The End of the Present World

The patriarch Jacob, on his deathbed, said to his sons, "Bury me in the double cave . . . over against Mambre, in the land of Chanaan";[21] and the grandsons of Isaac mourned their father for thirty days. On the death of the high priest Aaron and his brother Moses, the people again observed this thirty days' mourning; and the pious custom of praying for the dead for a whole month soon became a law of the chosen people. St. Clement stated that St. Peter, Prince of the Apostles, liked to have prayers said for the relief of the dead, and St. Dionysius describes, in magnificent terms, the stateliness with which the faithful celebrated the funeral rites.[22] From the very first centuries, the Church encouraged prayers for a month after the deaths of the faithful, in memory of the thirty days' mourning, observed under the Mosaic law.

Oh! You who sorrow after creatures whom you wrongly think absent, you who shed tears because you can set eyes upon those cherished faces no more — understand that the doors of their prison are wide open to your prayers and charity.

The prophet used to gain solace from the deaths of his friends who had died in the peace of God by diligently visiting them and, with incomparable confidence, repeating the words: "I will penetrate to all the lower parts of the earth, and will behold all that sleep, and will enlighten all that hope in the Lord."

Ah, we almost fear that our words may chill your devotion toward these souls; that, as you hear of their many positive consolations, your compassion may diminish, and you may not have for them all the pity they deserve. Let us, then, recall that their happiness and consolations are mingled with afflictions and torments.

⁀

We said, my dear brethren, that those souls, confirmed in grace, are marvelously consoled by the certainty of their salvation. On the other hand, as they are freed from the body that, like a thick veil, darkened their view and understanding of invisible, supernatural things, they suffer cruelly from the delay in possessing God.

In this world, the absence and remoteness of God brings to the majority of men only a faint displeasure! Captivated by the lure of the goods of this world, absorbed in the display of tangible objects, we comprehend God too imperfectly to realize how much the loss of Him means; but, when we die, the veil of the senses will be rent; all our human attachments will perish, and the inanities that bemused us will have gone forever. There will be no more amusements, pastimes, and conversation. Then, our inclinations, aspirations, and all our propensities will center upon this divine Spouse, our sole and incomprehensible treasure.

These poor souls, eager to be embraced eternally, rush toward God, who is their end, with more energy than a magnet attracts iron and with a greater impetuosity than natural things rush toward their center. Under this great ruin of death, in the complete separation from all those objects on which our life turns, the soul has nothing left save this love that bares itself, leaving only the unimaginable regret that, through his own fault, he has delayed — by a day, a year, or a century — this consummated union which, for the soul, must be the real and perfect, the sole and everlasting, happiness.

Imagine how bitter and heart-rending it is for a mother to bear the separation of a son who has left for distant lands, or has died a premature death, and whom she cannot hope to see again. From the moment when this mother's eyes cease to rest on that beloved child, a part of her life has gone: there is no joy or pleasure in the world capable of filling the deep, unfathomable void the departure or loss of that son has created in her heart.

How much more bitter and heart-rending are the cries of the unfortunate soul! Can you hear it calling out from the desolate place of its atonement: where is He who is the soul of my soul? It is useless for me to seek Him on this bed of flames where I feel only gloom and emptiness! O beloved of my heart, why keep me in this long suspense? Increase my torments — if necessary, put centuries of punishments into the minutes! How severely You punish me for my ignominy and indifference when You withdraw Yourself from my ardent soul, which longs to see You, to lose itself in You, and to dissolve in You!

☞

To this punishment of separation from God is added the punishment of fire.

Let us state, however, in order to be precise, and to express no debatable and disputed opinion, that the Church has not defined that the souls in purgatory undergo the effects of a material fire. It is merely a truth of divine faith and theologically certain.[23]

At the first session of the Council of Florence, the Fathers of the Greek Church were unwavering in their formal refusal to accept the materiality of the fire of purgatory; on the other hand, they unanimously acknowledged that purgatory is a dark place where souls, free from the punishment of fire, endure very severe sufferings and penalties, consisting chiefly in the darkness and anguish of a cruel imprisonment. The Fathers of the Latin Church, who were unanimous in maintaining the opposite opinion, did not, however, consider that the Greek Church, on this point, strayed from the Faith. That is why, in the decree uniting the two churches, there was no mention of a punishment of fire. It was stated simply that those souls which have not entirely satisfied God's justice in this life endure, in the life to come, penalties proportionate to the number and gravity of their sins, and that the sufferings they endure are attenuated or shortened by the prayers and good works of the living, and particularly by the Sacrifice of the Mass.

If, in defining the punishments of purgatory, the Council of Florence did not consider it opportune to mention the existence of fire, whether out of deference to the Fathers of the Greek Church, and in order not to hold back a long-sought reconciliation, or, in addition, because their error did not endanger the essence and substance of the dogma, the existence of a material fire in purgatory must not be held as anything less than a proven truth, which cannot be subject to any doubt or attenuation. In the first place, at this very Council of Florence the materiality of the fire of purgatory was maintained by the unanimous vote of all the Fathers of the Latin Church. So this opinion has in its favor a longer line of tradition, as well as the belief of almost all the Doctors. St. Paul appears formally to teach it in these words: "He himself will be saved, but only as one fleeing through fire";[24] and it should be noted that he does not use the qualifier *quasi* as a diminutive, but in order to better explain the manner of purification. Finally, all the visions and revelations dealing with purgatory liken the pains and the fire that are endured there to the pains and the fire of hell, with the sole reservation that this fire is not *eternal* but *temporary*.

A question arises here that is not easy to answer: how can a material fire act upon souls separated from their bodies and upon pure spirits? We reply that this is a mystery of God's justice, a secret that human reason will never succeed in comprehending. All that theology teaches us about purgatory is that this material fire is not identical with the human soul, nor united to it in substance, as, in this world, the spirit is to the body. When the saints and eminent Doctors tell us that the reprobate and the souls in purgatory are arrayed in a body of fire, they are speaking metaphorically, adopting our way of thinking. What is quite certain is that, as a number of Doctors have maintained, the fire will not confine itself to forming a sort of prison or enclosure around the souls it torments and purifies; it will not merely make them suffer from the vexations that it inflicts upon their will, and from the obstacles it will place in the way of the use and full development of their intellectual powers and their sensory faculties.

The true opinion is that the fire of purgatory, although corporeal, will act as an instrument of God's justice and, in some indescribable way, pierce the soul to the quick. This is the view expressed in the following words of St. Augustine: "Why should we not say that incorporeal substances can be really, though by means which our reason cannot comprehend or our words explain, chastened by the corporeal pain of fire?"[25] So it will act directly upon the soul. The same thought is expressed more clearly by St. Gregory when he says, "It is a visible, corporeal fire, which will cause an invisible fire and pain in the soul."

Who can ever understand how penetrating this fire is, which, unlike that of the earth, does not attack man through the medium of his material covering, but acts on the quick of the substance; this active and marvelously efficacious fire, which penetrates the most secret recesses of the soul, as far as the channels uniting it with the spirit: *Usque ad divisionem animae et spiritus?*[26] It is a fire that does not let any stain subsist; an immortal fire, which discerns even those defects the eye of the creature cannot perceive; a fixed fire, as the prophet calls it, which crushes the guilty soul, consumes and encompasses it, without granting it a single moment's rest; a fire whose intensity is not moderated by any relief, or subject to any alteration, and which puts the children of Levi to the test, like gold and silver in the furnace: *Sedebit conflans et purgabit filios Levi et colabit eos quasi aurum et argentum.*[27]

In our world, pain is intermittent. A fever is not of the same violence all the time. Sleep suspends the sick person's groans. He can turn from one side to the other on his bed of suffering, and find solace in the conversation of his friends; but the fire of purgatory consumes unceasingly and unremittingly. Every moment these souls feel and bear the whole weight and vigor of a pain they are unable to put out of their minds for a single minute, a single second.

A certain person who underwent a terrible operation had refused to be anaesthetized. She suffered without uttering a sigh, gazing upon the picture of Jesus Christ. The operation took five minutes. When it was over, she said, "It seemed to me to have lasted a century." Just as it is recognized that a feeling of intense joy makes the mind oblivious to the passage of time, so one can imagine a pain so severe as to make one minute seem like eternity. If this is so — if, in purgatory, minutes are the equivalent of years, and years the equivalent of centuries — what will it be like to remain in the depths of that dark prison for nights, for years on end, perhaps until the end of the world?[28]

⸎

O you, whose lives are so lax, who do not fear to stain yourselves with a thousand faults in order to please the world or spare your body a moment's trouble, tell us: have you understood the mysteries of God's justice, and have you meditated upon the length of the torments that await you? *Indica mihi si habes intelligentiam.*[29]

O primitive Church, cradle of Christianity, model of all ages, who numbered as many saints as faithful and, taught by the Apostles, received the oracles of the Incarnate Word at first hand: how frightful was your idea of the greatness of the penalties due to sin! You made amends in this life that astound us.

The End of the Present World

In the Church of the early ages, canon law was applied in its full rigor. There was no remission or concession. Penance and works of satisfaction were imposed strictly according to what was required in order to satisfy completely the justice of God. That penance did not consist in reciting a few short prayers; it consisted of long fasts on bread and water, daily recitation of the psalms, long and painful pilgrimages, and a considerable number of pious works. A thief, depending on the amount stolen, was sentenced to two or five years' penance, a blasphemer to seven years, an adulterer to ten and often twelve years of fasting, tears, and public prostrations on the threshold of the sacred place. On this frightful calculation, an entire life spent in the macerations of the Anchorites [hermits], even if it were as long as that of the ancient Patriarchs, would scarcely be enough to atone for the most ordinary, habitual sins of the men of our time. How long and terrible the purgatory of most sinners will be!

Without doubt, one thought capable of lightening the sorrow of those suffering souls would be that their memory is not lost, that the friends whom they have left on this earth are working to aid and deliver them. Alas, that is a consolation their hearts cherish in vain.

True, it is our custom to show the sorrow we render to their memory; and undoubtedly religion is far from condemning this honor rendered to grief. Rather, indeed, it condemns the hardness of heart of those who have no sooner lost their parents and friends than they cease to remember them. The saints used to mourn their friends, but their greatest concern was to help them. It was not tears that St. Monica asked of St. Augustine, when, on her deathbed she said to him, "Son, I bid you remember me, each time that you offer the Sacrifice at the Altar." It was not by tears that St. Ambrose sought to mark the deep attachment he felt for the Emperor

Theodosius, when he said, "I have loved this prince, and, because I have loved him, I shall not leave him until I have led him into that abode to which his virtues call him. O people, hasten hither and, together with me, bestow upon the remains of this prince the incense of your prayers, the outpourings of your charity, and the grief of your penance."

What am I saying — tears? Those tears that promised ever to flow soon dry up. Our fickle, selfish hearts grow tired of calling out names that utter no sound in answer; we grow tired of seeking to recall images that have forever vanished from our sight. Caught up in the whirlwind of the world and its frivolities, we shrink from such a grim and painful memory. Severance is followed by oblivion, and the pains of the dead are the most forgotten of all pains.

Poor deceased! After a few days spent in grief and mourning, a few courtesies paid to etiquette and convention, you will be buried once more in a tomb, crueler and colder than the one in which you were first laid; and that second tomb will be oblivion — harsh, inhuman, unrelenting oblivion, like that winding-sheet, the final clothing of the dust of your limbs; oblivion, which will envelop your silent dwelling-places, which no one will visit anymore; oblivion over your name, which no one will utter again; oblivion in your home, in the hearts of your friends and children, where no subject of conversation will evoke your memory. Yes, a deep, complete, and irremediable oblivion, and this despite the most heart-rending farewells that were addressed to you, despite the vows to your immortal memory and the declarations so full of tenderness.

One day our Lord Jesus Christ met a most unhappy man at the side of the pool. This man's face was as pale as death, his eyes were sunken and lusterless, and his limbs withered and stiff; he lay paralyzed and motionless on the bank of the pool of Probatica, trampled upon by passersby, exposed to all weathers and all the in-clemency of the air. Nevertheless he was by no means afflicted with an incurable disease. For him to be cured there was no need to consult skilled doctors, or to search the valleys and mountains for medicines, or strange and rare herbs. It was enough to give him a little push and put him down into the pool at the time when the angel of the Lord descended to stir its waters. Yet, in a town as pop-ulous as was the capital of Judea, amidst the mass of pilgrims who came from every part of the world for the feasts, there was not one relative, not one friend, to render him such an easy service.

Jesus, seeing this paralytic one day, was moved to pity, and, with emotion in His voice, said to him, "Do you want to be healed?" The infirm man replied, "Sir, I do not have anyone to plunge me into the pool once the water has been stirred up."[30] What a strik-ing picture this unhappy paralytic gives us of the soul whose com-plaints I have described! They sit by the side of the pool of that blood which has saved the world. They have no power to gather up its fruits or to administer the vivifying drops to themselves; and it may be for years that they have implored us in vain, and have been tortured, for lack of a helping hand.

In this world, no afflicted person is without recourse. The most unfortunate have at least their tears; and, when everything fails us at the same time, both divine and human, when we have to con-tend with injustice and oppression and suffer abuses and excesses of power, we still have a place of refuge in our own hearts, where God always awaits us. Each of our sorrows can become a sacrifice for us; each can be turned into a crown and treasure. To suffer in-terminably, however, knowing that nothing will come of it; to shed hot tears, and to feel that their burning dew will bring no growth, and that suffering will follow suffering, until divine justice is satisfied: that is a situation capable of softening hearts of steel; a misfortune that can be mourned only with tears of blood, and to which no one, in whose soul any feeling of humanity and compassion lingers, can remain indifferent.

Ah, if, beneath that thick soil that covers their bodies, if, from the shelter of their dark impenetrable dwelling-places, these souls could awaken for a moment, and bring their harrowing cries and groans to our very ears and hearts — what depth of feeling would there be in their wailing, and with what tones of indescribable anguish would they appeal for our aid! Ah, they would say, have pity on us, you who were our friends. Break our fetters, save us, deliver us. Arise, go over the places where we have lived; and the deeper the silence over our tombs, the louder let your voices be raised.

Priest of Jesus Christ, minister to all misfortunes, let this forgetful child hear the voice of his mother. I had reared him, I lived for him alone; he was the child of my heart. When I lay in my last agony, he would have wished to prolong my days at the cost of his own. Ask him how religion is powerless now to remind him of me.

Priest of Jesus Christ, raise your voice louder still! Do not fear to bring shame and remorse into the soul of that unconcerned husband who seeks solace for his widowhood in licentiousness. Ask him where his sworn faith is, what has become of that tenderness and fidelity of which he gave me such warm and striking demonstrations, right up to the moment of my death. Ask him how it is that today I have to beg his solicitude and support with such heart-rending cries. Ah, he is still unmoved, and provides me with bitter proof that I am forever dead in his heart.

Tell our friends — and strangers as well who are not related to us by blood but who are our brothers in faith, passing unconcernedly over that troubled sea of human life where they are swept along by the rapid waves, just as we were not long ago — tell them to stop and consider whether there exists any pain more bitter and intense and, at the same time, more neglected and solitary than ours. Ah, we beseech you — brother, father, husband, friend — from the depths of this pool of fire, we implore you . . . a drop of water, a prayer, an act of fasting or almsgiving, a helping hand, and we shall be saved. Brother, friend, father, husband: reflect that, if we are suffering, it is partly because of you.

Yes, that soul suffers because of us.

That mother suffers because she was too soft with her son, because she did not correct his faults or chastise the misdeeds of his youth. This wife suffers because she gave her heart too much to her husband — a heart that belonged to God alone — and showed a complaisance for him that was too excessive and too blind. This friend suffers because he was an accomplice in the infidelities of his friend, and because he took up his quarrels and made them his own, sharing in his disorders and licentiousness. And we leave them to bear the weight of God's justice alone! In return for the misguided leniency they had for us, we are unwilling to relieve them of one day's expiation, to spare them centuries of torture!

Ah, if you knew that at this moment your father, your mother, or your brothers — the people you love most of all — were about to perish in a fire or beneath a landslide, or that they were about to be engulfed by the sea or by flames; and if the only way to save them were to endanger your own life, run to their aid and hold out your hand to them, you would not hesitate, even if it meant risking your life, going through flames and allowing your hand to be burned. If fear, or selfishness, or any other craven feeling, made you hesitate, you would be ashamed of yourself and you would rightly consider yourself as the most heartless and thankless of men.

There is a story that, at the time of the Crusades and the wars waged by our forebears in the East, a Christian knight was taken prisoner by the barbarians. Cast into a hideous dungeon and unable to obtain the required ransom, he faced only slavery and death. Suddenly a noble thought struck his daughter, tender as she was, and in the prime of her youth. Alone and without a guide, she traversed vast areas, and succeeded in crossing over immense deserts. Arriving at the coast, she offered to work for the price of her fare. At length, she reached the shores of Europe. Taking no rest, she at once traveled through the towns, and appealed to the compassion of all, going from house to house in order to collect the sum demanded by the barbarians. As soon as she had secured it, she prepared once more to face those perilous journeys and that laborious voyage, from which she had escaped only by a miracle. Finally, she rejoined her father and, thanks to her superhuman efforts, and with the aid of the ransom obtained at the cost of so many perils and such severe hardship, managed to save her sire and snatch him from the fetters of captivity.

What courage in a young girl! What energy and strength of filial affection! Like that heroic girl, we, too, have received from God a tender, compassionate, and loving soul. When an unfortunate person, in extreme want, stretches his hand out to us, we do not ask ourselves whether he is united to us by friendship and blood; our duty, our fortune, and, especially, our heart, instantly go out to him. If necessary, we would not hesitate to deprive ourselves of food and the most essential things in order to rescue an unfortunate man from degradation, captivity, or death. Well, for the sake of our parents, those who have loved us, who are bound to us by the closest bonds, we claim neither the sacrifice of your health, nor your freedom, nor the whole of your goods, but merely the drop of water the rich man vainly asked of the compassion of Lazarus.

What else shall I add? How many are there among you who, after a dissipated, disorderly life, have lost even the courage to make amends, and the will to repent? Who shudder at the thought of the day when their soul, stripped of their body and stained with a mass of iniquity, will be exposed alive before the gaze of the Sovereign Judge? There is an easy way to obtain mercy at the last moment, and it is the one Jesus Christ Himself teaches us: "Make friends for yourselves . . . so that a lasting reception will be yours . . ."[31] Obtain for yourselves, with that gold which has served as the instrument of so many evil passions, the support and protection of the holy souls in purgatory.

There is another thing the dead say to us: you are mistaken about our desires, and the kind of relief our pains demand; you thought you were showing us your sorrow and love by arranging a magnificent funeral. On the spot of our last abode you have erected monuments, which are not so much tributes to our memory as a gratification of your pride. What is the purpose of all this ostentation and splendor? If need be, pull down those mausoleums, smash those monuments and stones, and purchase with their rubble the prayers and suffrages of the Church.

That is what the dead ask of us; and, if we listen to them, truly, I tell you, our charity will be blessed. The dead will not be thankless. One day, freed from their torments by our solicitude, they will help us by their powerful intercession, and, when we fly up toward the heavenly fatherland, they will accompany us in procession; they will sing around us the hymn of thanksgiving, and increase the joy of everlasting bliss that will be our reward and our glory.

☞

Notes

1   Cf. Ps. 36:8.

2   Cf. 2 Macc. 12:46: "That they may be freed from sin."

Notes

3   Cf. 1 Cor. 15:32.

4   According to St. Bonaventure, St. Thomas and St. Augustine, the torments of purgatory surpass in severity all the pains that man can endure in this life.

5   2 Tim. 4:8.

6   Cf. Job 21:13.

7   Rom. 8:38-39.

8   Rom. 8:35.

9   Cf. Prov. 12:21.

10 I believe it to be of the faith that those souls will not be perturbed in this way by sorrows, such that it may sustain irrational anxiety or impatience. This is proved by Proverb 12: "Whatsoever shall befall the just man shall not make him sad."

11 John 9:4.

12 Luke 16:24.

13 Rev. 6:9: "I saw under the altar the spirits of those who had been martyred because of the witness they bore to the Word of God."

14 St. Jerome and several Doctors are of the opinion that, when the Holy Sacrifice is offered for the intention of a deceased person, he ceases to suffer the pains of purgatory for the whole duration of the ceremony.

15 Rev. 5:3.

16 Cf. Ecclus. 24:45 (Douay-Rheims version).

17 According to tradition, limbo, where the just of the Old Testament were detained after their death, was situated at the center of the earth. The just of the Old Testament were not stained by Original Sin: they had the means of erasing it; yet, they were unable to enter heaven because, in consequence of the sin of Adam, this abode had been closed to all the descendants of the first man, and could not be opened again, except by the merits of Jesus Christ.

18 Cf. Acts 2:24.

19 Can the dead and the souls in purgatory appear — and do they, in fact, sometimes appear — to the living? St. Augustine declares that such apparitions may take place, and have taken place on a number of occasions, by a special disposition of the divine will. He quotes, as proof, the souls of Moses and Samuel (1 Sam. 28); the souls of

Jeremiah and the high priest Onias (2 Macc. 15), who reappeared on earth although still captives in limbo. As for apparitions of blessed souls who dwell in heaven, these are frequent in the lives of the saints. It is likely that, by virtue of the same divine disposition, the souls in purgatory sometimes appear or reveal themselves for the salvation and guidance of the living.

[20] There is one objection to the authenticity of this story. It does not appear theologically admissible that the holy souls in purgatory should be delivered up to demons to be tormented. First, it is in no way necessary that the evil spirits detain or convey these souls to the place of their expiation; once they know God's will, they obey and submit to it willingly. It is a pious belief that the souls who die in the friendship of God are led to purgatory by their good angels, and that these assist them and appear to them for their consolation. If, nevertheless, there are indeed souls, not among the reprobate, who are given over to the Devil for a time, these can only be certain great sinners, guilty of enormous crimes, who had been reconciled to God only at the moment of their last breath. The common opinion of theologians is that, as a general rule, the holy souls in purgatory are not tormented by demons.

[21] Gen. 49:29-30.

[22] Possibly St. Clement of Alexandria (c. 150-c.215), Church Father and theologian, and St. Dionysius the Aeropagite (d. c. 95), first bishop of Athens.

[23] A *theologically certain* truth is a truth that follows from Holy Scripture, has been accepted by tradition and the teaching of the majority of the Doctors and Fathers, and consequently, is founded on irrefutable evidence.

[24] 1 Cor. 3:15.

[25] St. Augustine, *City of God.*

[26] Heb. 4:12: "It penetrates and divides soul and spirit."

[27] Mal. 3:3.

[28] The Church has made no definition concerning the duration of purgatory. Certain saints have had reason to believe, through revelation, that a large number of souls were condemned to purgatory until the end of the world, and that, despite the assistance of the prayers and petitions of the Church, they have languished in that prison for some

centuries. This may be true in very exceptional cases, as with great sinners who returned to God only on the point of death; but there is no evidence or testimony to show that this view should be extended to the greater number of the faithful departed. The truth is that we cannot hazard any guesses as to the average length of time that souls spend in purgatory. Revelations on this matter apply only to special, individual cases, and we cannot draw therefrom any general, authoritative induction.

[29] Job 38:4: "Where were you when I founded the earth? Tell me, if you have understanding."

[30] John 5:7.

[31] Luke 16:9.

Sixth Conference

Eternal Punishment and the Unfortunate Destiny

Ibunt hi in supplicium aeternum.

These will go off to eternal punishment.

Matthew 25:46

There is one terrible truth in Christianity that in our times, even more than in previous centuries, arouses implacable horror in the heart of man. That truth is of the eternal pains of hell. At the mere allusion to this dogma, minds become troubled, hearts tighten up and tremble, passions become rigid and inflamed against this doctrine and the unwelcome voices that proclaim it.

Ought we, then, to be silent, leaving shrouded in oblivion an essential truth about man's most important concern: his supreme destiny beyond the short years of his exile on earth? Yet, if hell is a reality, whatever silence we might maintain over this fundamental question would not shake its certainty. All the softening and sweetening of human language will not shorten its duration. It would be the height of folly to convince ourselves that if we turn our minds away from this fatal possibility and try hard not to believe in it, we shall manage someday to avoid its rigor.

In this series of conferences, wherein we propose to deal with the things relating to the future of man and his immortal destiny, we could not leave out the punishments of the life to come without failing in our duty and acting like a false, negligent doctor who, for the sake of sparing his patient the suffering of an operation, calmly left him to die. On this subject, Christ Himself did not think it fit to speak with circumspection and reserve. He continually emphasizes the punishments reserved for sinners, and, on many occasions, speaks about exterior darkness, the fire that is not extinguished, and the prison without an exit, where there will be gnashing of teeth and unending tears.

When human justice wishes to strike down a big criminal, a scaffold is erected in the public square and the people are summoned to be present at the terrible spectacle. In several regions, the crushed body of the criminal is left for days on end hanging by the road or upon the gibbet where he breathed his last, in order that such an example may frighten wrongdoers who might be led astray by wicked passions.

Jesus Christ acts in the same way as human justice: He shows the malefactor the sword that hangs over his head, so that, being struck with fear, he may not contravene His law, and may do good instead of evil.

St. Ignatius of Loyola used to say that he knew of no sermons more useful and beneficial than those on hell. Reflections on the beauties of virtue and the delights and attractions of divine love have little influence upon coarse, sensual men. Amidst the noisy pleasures of their lives, the seductive bad examples set before them, the traps and pitfalls set beneath their feet, the threat of hell is the only curb powerful enough to keep them on the path of duty. For the same reason, St. Teresa would often bid her austere nuns to go down to hell in spirit and thought during their life, so as to avoid, she said, going there in reality after their death.

In the study we are about to undertake on this serious question of the fate reserved for those who die at enmity with God, we shall avoid all disputed opinions, proceeding by rigorous reasoning and with the aid of sound theology, taking as our sole basis Scripture and the true knowledge of tradition and of the Fathers.

In the first place, does hell exist, and is it certain that the punishments endured there are eternal? Secondly, of what nature is the punishment of hell, and where does it take place? Thirdly, can the mercy of God be reconciled with the idea of a justice that no reparation can ever appease?

No man can undertake the study of these supreme considerations without hearing the echo of these words of Scripture resounding in his innermost soul: "Be watchful, serve the Lord thy God and keep His commandments; for in this is the whole of man." He who reflects upon these awesome truths is certain to become better; he will at once feel his spirit transformed, and his nature enhanced in strength of virtue and love of good.

⁀

It is a truth formally taught by Sacred Scripture that the pains of hell are eternal; it is part of the Christian creed; numerous councils have defined it as an article of faith. St. Matthew in chapter 18, and St. John in chapter 14 of Revelation, speaking about the pains of the demons and reprobate, say that they will be of endless duration.[1] St. Mark in chapter 9, and Isaiah in chapter 66, say that their fire will not be extinguished, and their worm will not die. Quoting these words, St. Augustine remarks that the nature of this worm and the materiality or immateriality of the fire is open to discussion; but what is true beyond all dispute from the words of the prophet is that the rigors of this fire will never be moderated, and that the tortures of this worm will never diminish.[2]

When Jesus Christ speaks about the supreme sentence He will pronounce one day, He maintains and draws the same parallel between justification and condemnation; neither in the rewards of the just nor in the punishment of the wicked does He make any distinction of degree or time: "These will go off to eternal punishment and the just to eternal life."[3] Thus, if eternal life can have no limit of time, then eternal death, too, will be without limit or end.

From these various testimonies, we know that mercy is excluded from hell, and that redemption cannot reach it. Moreover, there are only three ways whereby the reprobate and the demons could be released from justice and obtain freedom or mitigation of their pains: by a true and sincere repentance; by the power of the prayers of the saints and the works of satisfaction offered up by the living; or else by the destruction of their existence — in other words, as it is absolutely impossible for God to take them to Himself, He would, by making them cease to exist, thereby bring their torments to an end.

Now, the reprobate cannot do penance. God has never granted pardon to Satan because Satan *has never repented*.

Sometimes, says St. Thomas, a person repents and hates sin in one or two ways: *absolutely* or *accidentally*. He who hates sin *absolutely*, hates it on account of its intrinsic ugliness, and because it is an offense against God; he who hates it *accidentally*, hates it, not out of love of God, but out of love of himself; in other words, he does not really detest sin, but only the pain, the evils it has brought him.

The will of the damned is still inclined to evil, and their horror and detestation of their punishment is neither repentance nor atonement.[4] Undoubtedly they are consumed by desires and dreams; but the object of these dreams is their own happiness, which they would arrange independently of God.

Such is the dream of the demons and the damned, a dream eternally futile that consumes them in unceasing despair and rage. So, the damned cannot repent.

Can they share in the prayers and merits of the living? If this were so, Lucifer and his angels would be able, in the more or less distant future, to return to favor; consequently they would become holy creatures, worthy of reverence and love, by the same right as the cherubim and the archangels, whom they would one day embrace in an eternal communion.

It would follow, too, that the Church would be obliged to pray for the demons. The demons are, in truth, our worst enemies, but the precept of charity requires us to pray for all our enemies without exception. The Church prays for the persecutors in this world because, during the present life, they can produce worthy fruits of repentance; but even on the day of judgment, when she will be filled with love and holiness, she will not pray for those sentenced by the just Judge to everlasting torments. If the reprobate can expect to be saved one day, not only must the Church pray for them but, in addition, we do not see why she would forbid the faithful to venerate them and why she would not gather up the remains of the Neros, Robespierres, and Marats to honor them on the altar, by the same right as the ashes of the Aloysius Gonzagas, Vincent de Pauls, and Francis de Saleses.

Finally, the sufferings of the reprobate will have no end, and their existence will never be destroyed. Holy Scripture depicts their pitiful state by calling it *secunda mors*, a "second death." St. Gregory says, "It will be a death that will never be consummated, an end always followed by a new beginning, a dissolution that will never bring decay."[5]

St. Augustine expresses with no less vigor and clarity the sad condition of that death which, while letting the soul subsist eternally, will make it endure its pangs and horrors in all their intensity: "It cannot be said that there will be the life of the soul in hell, since the soul will not share in any way in the supernatural life of God; it cannot be said that there will be the life of the body, since the body will there be a prey to all kinds of pains. Hence, this second death will be more cruel than the first because death can never bring it to an end."[6]

To these theological proofs, let us add the proofs from reason.

If there were not an eternal hell, Christianity would disappear and the moral order would be abolished. This truth about the eternity of punishment is linked essentially to the great truths of religion — to the Fall of man, the Incarnation, and the Redemption — which logically imply its certainty. If there were no hell, why would Jesus Christ have descended from heaven, why His abasement in the crib, His ignominies, sufferings, and sacrifice on the Cross? This excess of love on the part of a God who became man in order to die would have been an act devoid of any wisdom, and out of proportion with its declared aim, if it had been simply a matter of delivering us from a temporal, transient punishment, such as is purgatory. Man, then, had fallen irremediably upon evil days and was condemned to infinite disgrace, since only a divine remedy could raise him up again.

Otherwise we would have to say that Christ redeemed us only from a finite punishment, from which we might have freed ourselves by our own amends; and, in that case, would not the treasures of His Blood be superfluous? There would no longer be any *redemption* in the strict and absolute sense of the word: Jesus Christ would not be our Savior; the debt of boundless gratitude and love He demands of us would be an inordinate and unwarranted claim. With the God-made-man cast down from the throne of our hearts and our worship, Christianity would become a hoax, and all consistent minds would necessarily be led to reject revelation and to reject God Himself.

If there is no eternal hell, there is no moral order. The foundation of the moral order is the absolute and essential difference between good and evil. Good and evil are different in essence, because their conclusions are different and they result in opposite outcomes; but, if we abolish the eternal sanction of punishment, vice and virtue reach the same conclusion. Each, by different means, attains its last end, which is repose and happiness in the bliss of God. The same fate falls to the share of those who have been instruments of evil and to those who, right up to the end, have been incorruptible vessels of good.

You may say, "Agreed, but it will be a thousand or a hundred thousand years sooner for the just; a thousand or a hundred thousand years later for the wicked."

What does that matter? A period of atonement, however long you suppose it to be, does not constitute an essential difference between the destiny of the one and that of the other. During our fleeting, transient life, when moments, once passed, never recur, a period of a thousand or a hundred thousand years is of some consequence; but, as soon as man has entered into eternal life, a thousand or a hundred thousand years no longer have any significance: they are less than a grain of sand in the desert, or a drop of water in the ocean.

Imagine a future composed of punishments, as long as you wish; double the years, pile centuries upon centuries — so long as the end is the same for all, the past counts for nothing. Once a punishment is over, the extent of its duration, compared with *eternity*, will seem such a tiny quantity, so infinitesimal, that it will be as if it did not exist.

It would in fact be true to say — since there is no perceptible difference between one *eternity* and another *eternity* — that sin would have brought no harm upon the sinner.

For example, let us suppose that, as punishment for my sins, God hurls me into the flames for centuries. I have this consolation: I know that I have for myself a measure of comparison, mathematically equal to that of the just man. I have *eternity*; so there is an *eternity* of joy and glory for one who has served God and loved Him until death, and an *eternity* of joy and glory for the wicked man who thrilled with pleasure as he did evil, and constantly spurned the divine laws and commandments. Now, if these two final ends are the same, if, by way of evil even as by way of good, we unfailingly attain life — life lasting an eternity — the conclusion is inescapable that virtue and crime are two means toward an equal security; that it is optional for man to follow one or the other as he pleases; and that the most sordid lives and the most pure lives are of equal merit and dignity, since both lead to the same perfection and happiness.

Once such a scheme is granted, morality, public order, and all semblance of honesty must disappear from the earth. Justice is stripped of its sanction; conscience is a prejudice; virtue and sacrifice are a stupid exertion. Remove the fear of eternal punishment from mankind, and the world will be filled with crime; the most execrable misdeeds will become a duty whenever they can be committed without risk of prison or the sword. Hell will simply happen sooner: instead of being postponed until the future life, it will be inaugurated in the midst of humanity, in the present life.

As a contemporary writer has said, "There can be no middle way for society — it is either God or *the gun*." If there is no sanction beyond death, might prevails over right, the hangman becomes the pivot and cornerstone of the social order, and justice will be proclaimed in the name of death instead of being proclaimed in the name of God.

"Besides," remarks another moralist, "by virtue of what right will the courts repress crime, when it has the approbation of divine impunity, and when eternal justice undertakes not to bestir itself to impose its legitimate punishment?"[7]

Without hell, there is no moral order

The conscience of the nations has rebelled against this monstrous consequence. Amidst the explosion of error and the collapse of true belief, the doctrine of a future state of rewards and punishments has remained unshaken. It is found among the pagans. Virgil gave expression to their belief in these famous lines from the *Aeneid*:

Sedet aeternumque sedebit infelix Theseus.[8]

Rostroque immanis vultur obunco
Immortale jecur tondens . . .
Nec fibris requies datur ulla renatis.[9]

"The vile scoundrels whose souls are incurable," says Plato, "are tormented by punishments which convulse but do not cure them. Souls who have committed grave crimes are hurled into the abyss which is called hell. Such is the judgment of the gods who dwell in heaven: the good are reunited to the good, the wicked to the wicked."

How astonishing this assent among all men — poets, philosophers, peoples, kings, civilized and barbarian — to a truth that troubles our minds and that men would have so much interest in denying!

Here we might shelter behind the authority and weight of this fundamental axiom: "that which has been believed always, everywhere, and by everyone" is necessarily the truth. Every dogma has been changed except this one. All the important points of Catholic theology have given rise to dispute, except hell, which has escaped that common law. It has come down to us, without encountering one man who disputed its justice or, at least, cast doubt upon its awesome certainty. "The Protestants, who denied so many things, did not deny this. Destroyers of that which most graced the human conscience; of penance, virginity, and the efficacy of good works; they did not strip hell of its terrifying attributes. Their hand, which had not respected the door of the tabernacle wherein the Flesh of the Man-God reposes in bounty and sacrifice, stopped at this threshold of the place of suffering . . ."[10]

Contemporary rationalism alone has dared to go as far as to deny it and, strange to say, has done so by taking refuge in the very bosom of divine perfection. It has impugned the justice, greatness, and wisdom of God and, even while denying the Redemption, appeals to that very excess of love which Jesus Christ poured out as He expired on the Cross.

"God," it says, "is too perfect, too sublime, too disinterested to want to crush eternally, under the impressive display of His power, a frail creature, one who has been led into evil by an outburst of anger, or by weakness. That would be an act of vengeance and retaliation, unworthy of His glory and perfections." We reply that, if crime went unpunished, greatness would cease to be the endowment of God and would belong in its fullness to sinful man. It would rest with him, by a single act of his will, to make rebellion triumph against the divine government. So God must have been laboring under an illusion the day when, for His glory, leaving His state of repose, He enacted the fundamental law that the creature must tend toward Him in each of its aspirations, serve and love Him by constant acts of praise, allegiance, and worship? God would then no longer be our essential and final end.

Let us suppose, as some have dared to maintain, that hell is merely a place of vexation and sorrow where the captive soul undergoes only a mitigated, limited suffering. Let us imagine, on this supposition, Satan and his accomplices surpassing themselves in rebellion and pride, and saying to the God who rejected them, "We are in good shape, and we possess a tolerable enough existence for us to agree to do without You forever. It is true that we are far from possessing perfect bliss, but we have a quality of life and repose that is our own work, and we are content with it; if we are not radiant like Your angels, at least we are not Your subjects; we do not serve You or obey You."

Such would be the sentiments of every creature shut out from God's bosom if he succeeded in rejecting his heritage without experiencing pain that is intense and unending, like the happiness he freely and obstinately spurned. Were God, in order to alleviate the misery of the devils and the damned, to allow them but a shadow of good, a slender hope, or a drop of water to refresh them, they would cling to that shadow, that semblance, with all the strength of their exhausted, gasping will; they would strive with their whole soul after that crumb of solace, seeking to beguile themselves with it, and to delude themselves as to the extent and depth of their misfortune; and one would have to be ignorant of man's nature to imagine that he would not resign himself to this mitigated hell, rather than bend the knee and submit.

So if hell is not a deluge and overwhelming onslaught of unspeakable and eternal sufferings, making the guilty feel the whole weight of the hand that chastises them, then, in the fight between good and evil, man will forever be the victor; and the Lord of heaven will be the loser; every knee will not bend before Him as He foretold.

Thus, it is a prime necessity for divine glory that the man who has insulted Him by proving to be obstinately and systematically rebellious should be subjected to extreme, endless, and incomprehensible torments in proportion to the offense against divine glory. He must endure unbroken heartache and pains, together with absolute, total separation from any creature able to divert and amuse him; enveloping pains that do not permit him to see, whether above his head or at his feet or round about him, anything except desolation and terror, and this, so that he may acknowledge the greatness of the God whom he has repudiated, and that, the extremity of his anguish forcing from him the homage that goodness was unable to obtain, he may exclaim, like Julian the Apostate at his death: *Thou hast conquered, O Galilean.*

Without doubt this state of unalleviated punishment terrifies our minds, but it is the necessary sanction of the divine government. A temporary hell, such as purgatory, could not suffice to maintain its order and sanction. Indeed, how many people in this life care about purgatory? How many ungenerous, fainthearted Christians there are who would willingly bear a thousand purgatories, in order to satisfy their momentary desires! A German philosopher, talking one day with one of his friends, said, "To obtain the fulfillment of such a wish, of such an ambitious project, on which I have set my heart, I should gladly give two million years of my eternal bliss." His companion replied, "You are singularly modest in the sacrifice you offer."

Man values only that which is infinite: let a creature come to him with a seductive smile and charm, and he will at once endow her with all this infinity which is embodied in his affections and his dreams, and he will make the ideal and fascination of an immense, unending happiness rest on her. Well, in the face of all that tangible, living, palpable infinity which raises his heart to fever heat and enkindles a raging fire in his senses, set against this a punishment of infinite duration, the threat of which seems to him to lie in a distant, indeterminate future; a punishment of which he has a vague idea, but which he feels sure he will be able to make less severe before his death — this temporary hell, we say, will seem to that man a modest compensation for the unlimited delights that one minute of power or pleasure hold out to him. He will risk everything; he will stake the thousands of millions of centuries with which you threaten him; and will imagine he has got a good bargain; unless it is *eternity*, he will not haggle over the degree or the time.

Anyone who does not admit this has never fathomed the depths of human nature. An immortal being must have hopes and fears on a level with himself; everything that is not eternal vanishes before the frightful immensity of his desires.[11]

Having established our facts on the subject of eternity, let us deal with its punishments, their intensity, and the place where the devils and the damned endure them.

⌒

The pains that the reprobate undergo are of two kinds: privative and positive. The privative pain consists in the punishment of *damnation* — that is, in the loss of God; the positive consists in the punishment of *fire*.

St. Augustine tells us that the pain of *damnation* (*loss*) is the most terrible and incomprehensible of all the punishments of hell; in comparison with the sorrow and despair that it arouses, the other punishments do not deserve to be so called: *Plus torquetur caelo quam gehenna.*

The damned person has the certainty that he has lost God, that he can no longer be united to the One who created him. He is forever deprived of the supreme good and of the sight of infinite beauty; and this knowledge causes him such an acute pain that it alone would be enough to enkindle the flames that consume him.

The End of the Present World

During the present life, when we are weighed down by our earthly shell, amused and led astray by the spectacle of visible things, we cannot realize the immensity of such a loss; but when the soul is separated from the totality of creatures by death, it has no other object from which it can draw comfort. It becomes apparent to the soul that God is the only treasure and end; it rushes toward Him with all the force of its desires, and on that divine beauty concentrates its whole strength, its whole fervor, and the fullness of its aspirations.

Imagine a fish cast out of its liquid environment, or a magnetic needle swinging continuously from side to side, without managing to settle in the direction of its pole, or a derailed locomotive plunging into a void — all these comparisons give us only an imperfect picture of the indescribable state of a lost soul, cut off from its final end and powerless ever to return to the right path. There is no future for it. The poet-theologian of the Middle Ages saw these expressive words, written in black letters, on the gate of the dark, accursed place of hell:

> Through me you pass into the city of woe:
> Through me you pass into eternal pain;
> Through me among the people lost for aye.
> Justice the founder of my fabric moved:
> To rear me was the task of power divine,
> Supremest wisdom and primeval love.
> All hope abandon, ye who enter here.[12]

What is certain, and what all theologians teach, is that the devils and the damned are deprived of every grace and *supernatural* enlightenment. In this respect, they are sunk in darkness and struck with an incurable blindness; but they lose none of their strength, nor the use of their natural faculties; they remain in possession of the speculative knowledge they had acquired, and are even capable of acquiring new knowledge by *experience*.

In all their torments, their memory does not lose its retentiveness, their intellect preserves its acuteness, and their will its energy and all its activity; but all the faculties and natural abilities, which God leaves in them in order to increase their punishments, are perverted in their aim and direction, and cannot tend toward upright, useful, and serious purposes. The reason is that rectitude, beauty, and utility are reflections of, and a participation in, the divine attributes, and the soul irremediably separated from God is no longer capable of such sharing. As Suarez says, the damned lack all probity of judgment in everything relating to the direction of their thoughts and desires and the right ordinance of their actions.[13] Bowed down under the weight of their accursed state, the devils and the damned cannot adhere to the truth, and their minds aspire only to indulge in illusions and lies; their depraved hearts cannot open to love, and are always gnawed by hate; their imaginations are assailed by frightening phantoms and ever-recurring terrors.

In the ages of faith, when a minister of the altar had betrayed his sacred commitments and fallen into grave sin, he was led into the sanctuary and subjected to the penalty of degradation. The bishop would strip him of his insignia, removing from him the alb, the symbol of innocence; the stole, the sign of his jurisdiction over souls; and the chasuble, the mysterious emblem of his personification of Christ. And he would say to him, "Let these vestments of which you are unworthy be stripped from you."

Reprobate Christians are subjected to a similar degradation. When God relinquishes them at the moment of their unhappy end, He withdraws all that remains in them of theological virtues, such as faith and hope. He deprives them of their moral virtues, of strength, prudence, justice, temperance, disinterestedness, fidelity to the laws of honor, charm, and nobility of manners — virtues they have abused in order to serve their pride and its culpable satisfactions. He does not permit any trace of perfection to subsist in those whom He has rejected.

Thus, the damned are profoundly degraded beings; they do not have any respect, love, or compassion. As beings separated from the supreme good, they become supremely detestable and, like the devils, cannot inspire any feeling other than horror and execration.

To form a better idea of their lamentable fate, let us imagine a town where the Cains and Neros and all the other wicked men who have defiled the earth — men whom human justice gets rid of by casting them into dungeons and convict prisons — were put together. Let us further suppose that in this town there were no police or military to prevent these wretches from killing and tearing one another apart. Well, that would be hell such as it is described by the prophet Job: "a land . . . where no order, but everlasting horror dwells."[14]

Such is the punishment of *damnation*. Having lost God, the damned have thereby lost all hope, all dignity, and all consolation.

⌒

The second punishment of hell is that of *fire*. Is this fire of the same substance and nature as ours; or is it, as some believe, an immaterial fire, merely the effect of the intense pain caused in the soul by sorrow over its loss? As we have said, Holy Scripture constantly refers to the punishment of fire when speaking of the pains of the reprobate. As it uses this expression without accompanying qualification, there is no reason to interpret it in a distorted, metaphorical sense.

The doctrine of St. Thomas on this point is remarkable in its precision:

> It is certain that every kind of fire known to us, considered in itself and as to its substance, is material, and of the same nature as ours; although as to its effects, and in relation to the bodies subjected to its action, it may be that it is of a different kind. Thus, coal and flame, wood which is set alight, and iron, heated red-hot and glowing white, do not differ as to the heating element which passes through them, or as to their state of ignition, but only in their manner of receiving it. Iron is made red-hot, and begins to smelt, owing to external contact; sulphur, by contrast, begins to burn by virtue of an intimate, innate principle; hence there is no doubt that, considered in itself, the fire of hell is of the same kind as ours; but, as for saying that it subsists in itself, or in some extraneous substance, we can make no affirmation on that point.[15]

According to the Angelic Doctor, the fire of hell has the same principle as earthly fire, but is distinguished from ours by its properties and purpose. The fire of earth is a gift of Providence and was created for our use; the fire of hell is an instrument of divine justice and was created to punish. The fire of earth burns and consumes; the fire of hell burns without destroying or consuming. The fire of earth disintegrates the organs, reducing the flesh to ash and vapor; the fire of hell is compared by St. Mark to salt: "Everything will be salted with fire."[16] that is to say, it feeds and consolidates the flesh by burning it. The fire of earth is liable to become extinguished if it is not sustained by wood or other combustible material; but the fire of hell sustains itself, and subsists without sustenance, and, if we are to believe the testimony of Lactantius, "no smoke emanates from it; it is pure and liquid, like a lake or a pond. "[17]

The reprobate will be plunged into it, like fish into the sea, devoured by burning pains whose sharpness will never be tempered. *Quis poterit habitera de vobis cum igne devorante?*[18]

There remains one difficulty to be elucidated: whether a material fire can act on souls separated from the body and on pure spirits.

In *The City of God*, St. Augustine seeks to resolve the objection:

> Why could we not say, although the mode is incomprehensible and ineffable, that bodily pain can affect bodiless spirits? If, indeed, the spirits of men, devoid of any material elements, can be contained in bodily parts, then if, after death, they be reunited with those same bodies through unbreakable bonds, why, then, can't the spirits of the demons, although without body, be attached to bodily fires for their suffering?"

The theologian Lessius, in his treatise on the divine perfections, gives this other explanation:

> The sensory faculty with which we are endowed is not distinct from the essence of our soul, and will subsist in its entirety after death. If, by its own heat, fire can make its action felt on the spirit of man through the intermediary of the body, why could not this same fire, acting as an instrument of God, affect the spirit directly? When a man is burned, the body is only an agent for applying the heat to the spirit; for in the present order, the soul could not exercise its sensory faculty without the presence of the body; but God acts directly when he wishes, and He can, as He

desires, compensate for the absence of an agent, or Himself provide the effect of some agent."[19]

⁓

Finally, the one remaining question: *where is hell?* If we take various passages in Scripture literally, and if we hold to the general opinion of theologians, the *center* of the earth is the place where the reprobate are detained, and where, after the resurrection, they will live with the devils. St. Luke, in chapter 8, calls hell "*Abyssus,*" the abyss. St. John, in the book of Revelation, says, "An angel . . . cast the dragon into the bottomless pit."[20] He calls it the "pool of fire."[21] St. Gregory the Great says, "This abode is called hell, because, in fact, it is the lowest place: *Infernum appellari, eo quod in fra sit.*" Hugh of St. Victor adds: "This lower place, prepared for the punishment of the damned, is situated in the interior of the earth."[22]

The same opinion is expressed by St. Thomas. "No one," he says, "unless directly taught by the Holy Spirit, can know with absolute certainty the place where the reprobate are." He gives his personal opinion, in his terse, didactic style and with matchless arguments:

Those who die reprobate have condemned themselves by the disordered love of the pleasures of the flesh; it is, therefore, just that the same fate which has befallen their bodies should befall also their souls. The bodies were buried beneath the earth; it is therefore just that the soul, too, should be imprisoned within the depths of the earth. Furthermore, sadness is to the spirit as gravity is to the body: joy, on the contrary, is to the soul as lightness is to matter. Just as, in the physical order, the lowest parts are those where the bodies have the greatest gravity, so, in the spiritual order, the lowest regions are also the saddest: it follows, then, that the suitable place for joy is the empyrean heaven, and the suitable place for sadness is the center of the earth."[23]

Finally, let us quote Suarez's argument, which complements and further clarifies St. Thomas's:

> Hell is a prison that will also serve as an abode for the rebellious angels and for the demons; this abode cannot be other than the most unpleasant, obscure, and ignominious of all created places; it is fitting that it should be at opposite ends and at the greatest distance from the one destined for the elect. Now, the elect will reign eternally in the highest part of heaven, which is the empyrean heaven, and so the lowest part of the earth is the place where the damned will suffer their eternal torments.

Let us observe, however, that it is not a truth of faith that hell is situated in the center of the earth. The Church has not defined anything on this point; it is simply the most probable opinion, based upon the almost unanimous testimony of the Doctors and Fathers.

And whatever may be the case, the important thing, as St. John Chrysostom says, is not to know where hell is, but to ensure that we shall not, one day, be cast into it: *ne igitur quaeramus, ubi sit, sed quomodo eam (Gehennam) effugiamus.*[24]

Such, then, seems to be the place of hell. The fire that tortures the devils and the damned is a material fire — a material fire that makes its action felt on spirits and on separated souls. It remains for us to consider how the implacable severity of divine justice can be reconciled with its infinite mercy.

God strives to keep every sinner from perishing

⁀

A witty man once said of the wicked, "They are a great difficulty in this world and in the next." Human society feels this extreme difficulty with regard to certain criminals, and one could say, in another sense, God feels this difficulty to an even greater extent with regard to sinners.

It is of faith that God desires the salvation of all men and that, so far as it lies with Him, He excludes no one from the fruits of the Redemption. He did not willingly create hell; on the contrary, He exhausts all the means of His wisdom and all the secrets of His tenderness to forewarn us against such a misfortune, as He says by the mouth of Isaiah: "What more was there to do for my vineyard that I had not done?"[25]

If God were able to suffer, no anguish would be comparable to the sorrow His heart would feel when He is compelled to condemn a soul. The holy Cure d'Ars once said, "If it were possible for God to suffer, as He damned a soul He would be gripped with the same horror and the same tremor as a mother who was herself compelled to let the blade of the guillotine fall upon the neck of her child."

Behold Jesus Christ at the Last Supper: He gazes upon Judas with an expression that shows sadness and the bitterest grief. He is violently troubled, and in the last extremity of consternation. He understands, better than we can ever conceive, how horrible is the state of a man adrift, irremediably lost, left without any means of retracing his steps and taking his destiny back into his own hands. He tries, by every imaginable means, to avert the loss of this wretched man; He casts Himself at his feet and kisses them; He admits him, despite his unworthiness, to the feast of His sacred Flesh; and, when the darkness, which more and more engulfs the obdurate soul of Judas, has blocked every avenue by which divine grace might have forced its way in, Christ weeps. He seems to forget that this traitor has chosen Him as the victim of his dastardly greed. He sees only the horror of his fate, and says in anguish, "Better for him if he had never been born."[26]

O you that accuse the Creator of harshness, and reproach Him for not going to the extreme limits of His omnipotence in order to prevent His creature from perishing eternally, tell Him your way, teach Him your secret. What do you want God to do?

Would you ask Him to abolish hell? To abolish hell would be to abolish heaven. Do you believe that the martyrs, hermits, virgins and saints, at this moment delighting in the joys of bliss, would have kept apart from seductive pleasures, trampled upon worldly snares, sought out solitary places, come through persecutions, and braved the hangman and the sword, if they had not had in mind the Master's word: "Do not fear those who deprive the body of life but cannot destroy the soul. Rather fear him who can destroy both body and soul in Gehenna"?[27]

Divine love awoke in them only when, by courageous mortification, they were detached from sin and sensual habits. The starting-point of their justification was fear: "*Initium sapientiae timor.*"[28] The thunder that aroused them from their slumber and lethargy was the terrifying word: *eternity.* It was then that they looked upon their luxurious houses and the gilded paneling of their palaces, and said, "This is where every day we amass treasures of wrath, where all seductions come together for our perdition. Hatred of God, flames, an endless curse for a day's pleasure — this is what awaits us . . ."

The next day these men would go barefoot, dressed in sackcloth, seeking the road that leads to the wilderness and the desert. Without these merciful fears, the City of God would never have filled up; we should all have strayed from the right path; no one would have done good, *non est qui faciat bonum, non est usque ad unum.*[29]

God cannot abolish hell without abolishing heaven. Shall He then wait, pardon, and keep on pardoning? That is just what He does. In this life He never abandons even the person who spurns Him. He pursues him right into the sanctuary of his conscience, through an inner voice that does not cease for a single instant to make itself heard. In the face of the temptation that incites us to evil, this voice rings out and calls to us: *Beware!*

If we turn a deaf ear, He does not hasten to cut the thread of our life, as would be His right. He does not watch out for the moment when we go astray in order to make this the final moment of death for us. He comes back to us. He makes us feel the sting of remorse and, not disheartened by our refusals, waits for years.

He lets the years of maturity succeed the wildness of youth, and the icy hand of old age replace the illusions that beguile even manhood; and all His efforts are in vain. A man's last hour finally rings; most often it is preceded by illness, the premonitory sign of his approaching end. This man is still obdurate. One minute before his last sigh, God still offers to take him to Himself and save him from the fires of the abyss. His voice has no more strength, and his condition is desperate. It would be enough that, in the intimacy of his heart, he should utter these simple words: "I love You, and I repent." These words would be his saving grace . . . and the sinner stubbornly refuses to say them.

We ask: What can God do? Shall He, to sanctify the hardness of heart of this creature, overturn the whole plan and all the counsels of His wisdom, annihilate the darkness by a foolish act of omnipotence, because a confused man has blinded himself so as to have no part in the divine light? Ah, God has the right to wash

His hands and say, "O Israel, thy perdition is thy work, and not mine. *Perditio tua ex te, Israel.*"

Yet why should grace and redemption be excluded from hell? When a man's eyes have been opened, as he sees the last of his illusions crumble, and, terror-stricken, he realizes the full extent of his wretchedness, why would God not let a final ray of His mercy fall upon him? Why would He not hold out a hand to this unfortunate man, who would grasp it with a love and gratitude proportionate to the immensity of his deliverance?

We do not hesitate to reply that God cannot — He cannot, at least, without losing His infinite dignity. He would be obliged to bow down, of His own accord, before a rebellious, obdurate creature who, far from appealing to Him, hates and curses Him. Death has placed the sinner in a position that leaves him no choice. He knows it with a certainty that overwhelms his free will. He remains hardened in hatred and pride, magnified by his tears and despair. To arouse a salutary, meritorious sorrow in him, he would require a grace. That grace he does not seek, does not want. True, he abhors his punishment, but he has a supreme hatred of God, as well as of the gifts and lights emanating from the heart of God.

And yet, is God just, and does He not go beyond all proportion, when He punishes a passing fault, committed in a single moment, with an eternity of pains? Here, reason is powerless, for God is the greatest of mysteries. Sin is a mystery as unfathomable as the majesty of Him whom it offends; and the punishment due to its evil is another immeasurable mystery that the human mind will never succeed in solving.

◌

All we can say is that, if we consider the person of God, the insult offered to Him by sin is an *infinite* insult. Now, since man, on

account of the limitations of his nature, cannot sustain a punishment infinite in *severity* and *intensity*, it is only just that he should
suffer a punishment infinite in *duration*. Human justice is the image and configuration of divine justice. The right to punish and
sentence a guilty man to death is conferred upon earthly tribunals
for the service and good of men. They pass sentence for crimes,
not because of their intrinsic deformity and because they offend
God, but because they are harmful and prejudicial to the common
good and the right ordering of human society. Yet they have the
right to inflict a perpetual punishment upon a murderer whose
crime was committed in a single moment, to remove him forever
from human society because he has violated the moral and human
order.

All the more reason God has the right to inflict a perpetual
punishment upon one who has violated the universal and divine
order, and to banish him forever from the society of heaven.

It is in no way repugnant, observes St. Augustine, that God
should restrict His mercy to the years of the present life, so that,
when these have passed, there will be no place for pardon. Do not
the princes of the earth act in the same way, when they refuse to
reprieve men locked up in prison even though they show repentance and sincere detestation of the crimes they have committed?

Among the various schemes devised in order to reconcile
God's mercy with justice, the most rational, the most acceptable,
and the one which, at first sight, appears to provide a satisfactory
solution to the formidable problem of human destiny, is the
scheme conceived by Pythagoras and the Oriental sects, according to which, instead of casting a man into endless ignominy, God
will introduce him to a second period of trials where, as in the preceding ones, there will be a mixture of light and darkness, the path
of freedom will be open to him, and in it there will be temptations,

divisions, and conflict between God, dimly perceived, and creatures who parade their seductions.

Let us at once admit that, of all the doctrines opposed to Christianity, the doctrine of metempsychosis or transmigration of souls is unquestionably to be preferred. At a superficial glance, it appears to leave belief in an immortal life intact, and seems not to impugn the divine attributes nor to deprive human law of its sanction. But, if we look at this doctrine in detail, we see clearly that it places us back amidst all the preceding difficulties, and raises others still more insolvable. As an illustrious Christian philosopher observes:

> If this second life to which you introduce man is not purer than the first — if his soul dies there a second time through sin — to which period will God confine Himself? Shall the soul have an inexhaustible right to retrace the course of its migrations, without God ever being able to restrain and punish it other than by giving it the right to continue to offend Him? Instead of that frightening prospect in which the judgment is seen as life's awesome barrier, the sinner would go to the grave, feeling as secure as a man passing under a portico, and would say to himself, with all the derision of his impunity, "The universe is large, the centuries are long; let us first complete our passage through worlds and times. Let us go from Jupiter to Venus, from the first heaven to the second, from the second to the third. And if, after spaces and periods beyond number, it should happen that there are no more suns left for us, we shall present ourselves before God and say to Him, 'Here we are, our time has come; make us new heavens and new stars; for, if You are weary of waiting for us, we are not weary of cursing You and of managing without You.' "[30]

God has the right to condemn the unrepentant to hell

Finally, we may say, love is all-powerful, with its own secrets and excesses, of which our hearts can have no inkling and, whatever may be said, cannot consent to condemn forever a creature made by its own hands, redeemed by its own blood. Ah! We might indeed set love against justice if it were justice that punished. But justice was propitiated nineteen centuries ago, on Calvary; at the foot of the Cross, it forgave men the debts they had incurred for their crimes, casting away the sword of rigor, never to wield it again.

Let us listen to St. Paul: "Who shall bring a charge against God's chosen ones? God, who justifies? Who shall condemn them? Christ Jesus, who died, or rather, was raised up, who is at the right hand of God and who intercedes for us?"[31]

But it is because damnation issues from love that salvation is not possible. If it were justice that punished, love might intervene once more on the mount and say, "Mercy, Father, spare man and, in exchange for the death that is due to him, receive the homage of my flesh and blood!"

However, when it is the very one who is to us more than a brother, more than the most affectionate friend, who tightens this heart consumed with tenderness and turns it into an abode of inexhaustible hatred, how can the ingratitude of the man who has wrought this transformation (all the more terrible as it is unnatural) dare to expect hope and refuge?

O you who, at one time or another on this earth, have loved with a love that is sincere, ardent, and boundless; you know the demands and the laws of love. Love offers itself for a long time, insistently and abundantly; it suffers, dedicates itself unreservedly, humbles itself, and becomes small. But one thing that renders it implacable, and that it never forgives, is obduracy in contempt, contempt maintained until the end.

The End of the Present World

Go, then, ye cursed, the Savior will say on the day of His judgment: *Ite maledicti*. I did everything for you; I gave my life, my blood, my divinity, and my person for you. And in return for my infinite generosity, I asked only for these simple words: I obey and I love You. You have constantly spurned me and have responded to my approaches solely with these words: Go, I prefer my gross interests and my brutish sensual pleasures to You.

Be your own judges, the Savior will add. What sentence would you pronounce against the most dearly beloved creature who displayed the same indifference and same obstinacy toward you?

It is not I who condemn you; it is you who have damned yourselves. You have chosen, of your own free will, the city where egotism, hatred, and revolt have established their dominion. I return to heaven, where my angels are, and thither I bring back this heart, the object of your insults and scorn. Be the children of your own choice, stay with yourselves, with the worm that does not die and the fire that is never extinguished.

Let us tremble, but let us also be penetrated with a lively and unshakable confidence! Damnation is a work of love. It is the incarnate mercy that will determine our fate and convey the eternal sentence. It is easy to avert it while the present life lasts. Love in this world never requires a perfect parity between the fault and the penalty. It is content with little — a sigh, a sign of goodwill. Jesus Christ opens His Heart to us; we are the price of His blood and His conquest. He destines *eternity* for us; not an eternity of tears and suffering, but an eternity of bliss that we shall possess with Him, in the bosom of His Father, in union with the Holy Spirit, and in the very center of His glory. Amen.

Notes

[1] Cf. Revelation 14:11: "And the smoke of their torment shall rise forever and ever. There shall be no relief day or night . . ."

[2] St. Augustine, *Ad Orosium*.

[3] Matt. 25:46.

[4] St. Thomas Aquinas, *Summa Theologica*, Supp., Q. 98, a. 11.

[5] St. Gregory the Great, *Morals*.

[6] St. Augustine, *City of God*.

[7] Lacordaire, *De la Sanction du Gouvernement Divin*.

[8] "There sits, and to eternity shall sit, unhappy Theseus."

[9] "A great vulture with hooked beak / feeds on his indestructible liver . . . / No respite given to the ever-renewing tissue."

[10] Lacordaire, *De la Sanction du Gouvernement Divin*.

[11] Nicolas, *Études sur le Christianisme*.

[12] *Per me si va nella città dolente;*
Per me si va nell' eterno dolore;
Per me si va nella perduta gente.
Giustizia mosse 'l mio fattore;
Fecemi la divina potestate
La somma sapienzia, e 'l primo amore.
Lasciate ogni speranza voi che intrate (Dante, *Inferno*, Canticle III).

[13] Suarez, *De Angelis*.

[14] Cf. Job 10:22: "The black, disordered land where darkness is the only light."

[15] St. Thomas Aquinas, *Summa Theologica*, Supp., Q. 97, a. 6.

[16] Mark 9:49: "Everyone will be salted with fire."

[17] *Divinarum Institutionum*.

[18] Isa. 33:14: "Who of us can live with the consuming fire?"

[19] Lessius, *De Divinis Perfectionibus*.

[20] Cf. Rev. 20:3.

[21] Cf. Revelation 20:15: "the pool of *fire* . . ."

[22] Hugh of St. Victor, *De sacramentis*.

[23] St. Thomas Aquinas, *Summa Theologica*, Supp., Q. 98, a. 7.

[24] St. John Chrysostom, *Homily on the Epistle to the Romans*.

[25] Isa. 5:4.

[26] Matt. 26:24.

[27] Matt. 10:28.

[28] Ps. 111:10: "The fear of the Lord is the beginning of wisdom."

[29] Cf. Rom. 3:12: "All have taken the wrong course, all alike have become worthless; not one of them acts uprightly, no, not one." See also Ps. 14:3 and 53:4: "All alike have gone astray; they have become perverse; there is not one who does good, not even one."

[30] Lacordaire, *De la Sanction du Gouvernement Divin*.

[31] Rom. 8:33, 34.

Eternal Beatitude and the Supernatural Vision of God

Hae requies mea in saeculum saeculi,
hic habitabo quoniam elegi eam.

This is my resting place forever;
here I will dwell, for I have chosen it.

Cf. Psalm 132:14

Our destiny is an enigma, which reason alone cannot explain; but faith elevates our thoughts, strengthens our courage, and inflames our hope.

It tells us: have no fear; you are not wandering along some lost and uncertain path. Beyond our mortal years, there is a new life, of which the present one is only a representation and an image. On this earth, we are travelers; but, beyond the stars and all space, our heritage and native land is found up above.

Pilgrims and exiles, we now live under tents; in the world to come, the Lord will build us permanent dwelling-places.

The fool, who has no understanding of our destiny and our hopes, accuses the Creator of injustice, pointing out signs of imperfection in the designs of divine wisdom. He is like a savage or an inhabitant of a remote island who one day goes into one of our building yards. There he sees stones scattered about, materials lying on top of one another, workmen carving metals and cutting away marble; and in the spectacle presented by this activity, he sees only a picture of confusion and ruin. He does not know that the apparent disorder will, one day, engender an order of admirable perfection.

In the same way, we err in our judgments on the conduct of God toward men; we see nothing more than a pointless harshness in the mystery of suffering; we bear the burden of life without courage or dignity, because we do not know how to raise our eyes and our hopes above the limited sights and perspectives of the present life, and because we do not reflect upon their destiny and end.

Our destiny is the possession of God and eternal life: to live in that abode from which all evil is absent and where we enjoy a multitude and abundance of every good, a place that is commonly called *heaven*.

✑

Heaven: this is the torch before which the vivid appeal of earthly things fades, the light that, by transforming our judgments, makes us cherish poverty, sickness, and the insignificance of our state of life as a good, and makes us regard riches, the glamor of honors, the favor and praise of the world as an evil. The thought and expectation of heaven impelled Paul to face the most arduous labors and the most formidable perils, giving him a superabundance of joy amidst his sufferings and afflictions. The thought of heaven enkindled a holy thirst for martyrdom among the confessors and made them indifferent to worldly honors and comforts.

When they beheld the royal pomp and the magnificence of courts, Polycarp, Ignatius of Antioch, Anthony, and their like were filled with aversion and, with disdain in their hearts, they exclaimed: *Earth, how vile you appear to me when I contemplate heaven!*

Consider the traveler who returns from distant lands, bathed in perspiration and exhausted by his long journey. He walks painfully, bent over with fatigue and leaning upon his stick, but, once he reaches the summit of the hill, and discerns, far away in the distance, at the farthest horizon and merged with the clouds, the steeple of his hamlet, the roof that saw his birth and the trees that shaded his childhood games — at once all weariness fades away and, finding again the vigor of his youth, he runs as if on wings. In the same way, when our constancy weakens and we no longer feel equal to the sacrifices that the law of God requires of us, let us lift up our eyes and turn our thoughts and hearts toward our heavenly Homeland . . .

Yet, how can I describe the marvels of the City of God, that vision and those joys beyond words, which no language can express and which surpass all the conceptions of human understanding?

Heaven is something that we have not seen. We travelers, wandering in this valley of darkness and tears, are reduced, like captive Israel on the banks of the Euphrates, to hanging our harps and zithers upon the weeping willows of this wretched, human life. No human voice, no lyre can ever succeed in producing songs and tunes in unison with the melodies and sweet harmonies with which that indescribable city resounds. We can speak of it only obscurely, by way of rough and defective comparisons. Our sole resource is to call to mind the sketches to be found, here and there, in the Sacred Books and in the treasury of the Doctors, as well as in the dim and incomplete insights the Fathers had on that happy abode.

Nevertheless, let us hope that divine grace, coming to the aid of the weakness of our understanding, will compensate for the insufficiency of our words, and that, to some extent, we shall be able to turn souls away from base affections and make them yearn to possess the everlasting Homeland.

Let us observe that Holy Scripture calls heaven *requies*, a rest. Furthermore, we are told that there are two kinds of inhabitants in this abode: first of all, God, of whom heaven is the temple and throne; then the angels and men, called to be united with God and to share His supreme happiness, His beatitude. Thus, heaven is a place of rest for man, a twofold truth we propose to elucidate and develop.

The End of the Present World

In Sacred Scripture, God calls heaven His rest. Heaven is the end and termination of created things, in nature and in time; the supreme glorification of the infinite Being in His intelligent creatures, when, raising them to the ascending heights of all progress and perfection, He will, through His seal, crown the irrevocable greatness of our destiny.

In order to retrace — insofar as our weakness permits — the splendors of this repose of the Almighty, when He will have brought to completion the work of His wisdom that animated the unfolding of the centuries, let us imagine an artist who has just finished a masterpiece and, in a surge of genius, has erected on earth a monument destined to be the climax of his fame, and an inimitable challenge for future ages. In his work he has exhausted all the secrets of his art. The world applauds and admires. The artist, on the other hand, gives way to a feeling of discouragement and sadness, grieving that he is merely a man. In the bold flight of his imagination, he has caught an image, glimpsed a perfection or an ideal that he is unable to express in any form on the chill canvas or the mute stone, and upon which all the cold strokes of his brush and all the power of his art come to nothing. Our artist, seeing the delighted crowds fall at his feet, remains pensive and mournful amidst their praise and acclaim; he is not satisfied, and enjoys no rest.

If, however, the hand and the power of our artist were equal to the breadth and thrust of his spirit; if he were the master of nature and able to bend it to his exaggerations and dreams, to transform it into a perfect, living image of the ideal conceived in his mind; if he had the ability to animate the marble and to infuse it with feeling and life and if a light more brilliant than that of the sun were to radiate from the gold and precious stones arranged in such profusion and with such perfect art; if, finally, matter, released from its gravity, rose of its own accord to that level in the air whither the wings of his genius had raised it, then that monument erected by a great architect, that canvas produced by the brush of a genius, and that marble sculpted by an incomparable artist would be finished works, excelling in beauty all that our language has in its power to depict or our mind to conceive. At such a spectacle all mankind would be lost in breathless wonderment from which no other marvel could rouse them. The artist would have achieved his supreme ideal; he would be satisfied and would enjoy repose.

Heaven is not the ideal of a human intellect: it is the repose of the divine intellect, the ideal and masterpiece of God, whose power fecundates the void; who, by virtue of one word, can make a thousand beautiful things appear in an instant such as we could never remotely imagine; a thousand worlds, in comparison with which the earth and sky are less than mud and foul smoke. God is as much superior to man as His ideal is above that which the noblest and keenest mind could possibly conceive. We lack the elements necessary to form even an imperfect sketch of it. All the pictures we might seek to paint are mere vain and crude shifts, similar to the efforts of a man born blind who, in order to form an idea of light, from which he is cut off, seeks comparisons and analogies in the dense, impenetrable darkness that presses down upon his eyelids.

St. John, on the island of Patmos, was transported in spirit beyond the bounds of time; and God revealed to him, as it were, a shadow and a reflection of the *ideal* of eternal life. As a matter of fact, so as to bring his visions within the capacity of our feeble minds, he recounts them in figurative language, with images borrowed from nature and the present life. These images are not to be interpreted in a material sense; nevertheless, they contain striking analogies. It is possible for us to find therein a pale semblance of that glory and those splendors, which surpass all experience and all words.

And I, John, saw a new Jerusalem, the holy city, coming down out of heaven from God, beautiful as a bride prepared to meet her husband. And I heard a loud voice from the throne cry out, "This is God's dwelling among men . . ." This city is built of living stones, all cut . . .[1] All *ailments* are excluded from this tranquil place . . . and a river can be seen there, with quick running water, clear as crystal, and gushes forth from the throne of God and the Lamb. At the center of the city and on both sides of the river is seen the tree of life, which bears twelve fruits and yields its fruit each month, and the leaves of this tree are meant to heal the nations from all defilement. The throne of God and of the Lamb shall be there, and His servants shall serve Him faithfully. They shall see Him face-to-face and bear His name on their foreheads. The night shall be no more. They will need no light from lamps or the sun, for the Lord God shall give them light, and they shall reign forever.

A throne was standing there in heaven, and on the throne was seated One whose appearance had a gemlike sparkle as of jasper and carnelian. Around the throne was a rainbow as brilliant as emerald. Surrounding this throne were twenty-four other thrones upon which were seated twenty-four elders; they were clothed in white garments, and had crowns of gold on their heads. From the throne came flashes of lightning and peals of thunder; before it burned seven flaming torches, the seven spirits of God. The twenty-four elders fall down before the One seated on the throne, and worship Him who lives forever and ever. They throw down their crowns before the throne and sing, "O Lord our God, You are worthy to receive glory and honor and power! For You have created all things; by Your will they came to be and were made!"

After this, I saw before me a huge crowd which no one could count from every nation and race, people and tongue. They stood before the throne and the Lamb, dressed in long white robes and holding palm branches in their hands. They cried out in a loud voice, "Salvation is from our God, who is seated on the throne, and from the Lamb!" . . . Then one of the elders told me, "These are the ones who have survived the great period of trial; they have washed their robes and made them white in the blood of the Lamb . . . He who sits on the throne will give them shelter. Never again shall they know hunger or thirst, nor shall the sun or its heat beat down on them, for the Lamb on the throne will shepherd them. He will lead them to springs of quick running water, and God will wipe every tear from their eyes."[2]

What marvelous descriptions! What human brush could produce a more colorful and expressive picture of the place of light, serenity, and sweet transports! Truly, it is the most vivid and striking image of the sweet thrills of joy that God destines for His beloved ones. Beyond this happiness and these radiant feasts, speech is powerless, the mind is lost and cannot conceive of any other triumph or splendor capable of pleasing human intelligence. At the sight of this, St. John felt transported in ecstasy: in his inebriation and wonder he cast himself down on his face to adore the angel who had revealed to him such sublime mysteries.

Yet to say that these sights and harmonies are God at His best would be an affront to the sovereign goodness and omnipotence. Even the inspired word itself cannot rise to realities that extend beyond the bounds of reason and surpass all the strength and capacity of our nature.

Let us listen to the great apostle Paul, immersed in the most exalted raptures, conveyed in spirit as far as the third heaven, and into splendors more profound and ineffable than those experienced by the Eagle of Patmos, as he exclaims: *Heaven is not as you tell us; it is a thousand leagues above the analogies and descriptions you are offering us.* "Eye has not seen, ear has not heard, nor has it so much as dawned on man what God has prepared for those who love him."[3]

O inspired prophet, when you tell us that *eternal life* is the collection of all the attractions of the world, of all the beauties portrayed in the Sacred Books, and when you teach us that the flowers of spring, the tint of meadows, and fresh-flowing clear waters are to be found there, you are assuredly not straying into fable and imaginary pictures. That is indeed what heaven is: all our riches, beauties, and concords, but infinitely more than these. When you describe the elect in heaven as being subtle, immortal, impassible, and clothed in a sweet light or, rather, in a divine glory that dwells in them and penetrates them more subtly than the sun penetrates the purest crystal, you are not being deceived by some illusion. Heaven is that, too; it is our subtleties, our lights, and our glory, but infinitely more than these. Lastly, when you compare the future bliss to the sweetest and most intoxicating transports of the soul, to a joy ever new, freed from all disquiet and passion and maintaining its intensity and strength through all eternity, you do not feed us with false hopes; for heaven is our transports and all our joys, but raised beyond all measure, expression, and comparison.

The eye of man has not seen, nor the ear heard, anything comparable or close to it. The reason is that the good things God prepares for us surpass all that our senses can perceive, all that our experience is capable of acquiring, all the thoughts of our minds and the desires that will ever arise in our hearts.

St. Bernard, in his *Sermon 4 on Christmas Eve*, says, "Never has man seen the inaccessible light, never has his ear heard the inexhaustible symphonies, nor his heart tasted that incomprehensible peace." "There," adds St. Augustine, "a light shines that no place can contain; there praises and songs resound that are unlimited in duration. There are fragrances the air does not blow away, savors that never fade, goods and sweet joys unaccompanied by any distaste or surfeit. There, God is contemplated continuously, is known without any error of apprehension, and praised without weariness or diminution."[4]

Heaven is a kingdom of such beauty, a bliss so transcendent, that God has made it the sole object of His thoughts; to this creation, the only one truly worthy of His glory, He directs the universality of His works; the destiny and succession of empires, the Catholic Church, with her dogmas, sacraments, and hierarchy, are ordered toward the consummation of this heavenly life. Faith teaches us that the divine assistance of grace is indispensable to man for him to accomplish the smallest meritorious work, such as a Sign of the Cross or the mere invocation of the Name of Jesus; all the more reason why eternal life, which is the end to which all supernatural works tend, deserves to be called the crowning and the apex of all the graces bestowed upon us. In the words of St. Paul: "The gift of God is eternal life."[5]

The plan and the whole ordinance of the Incarnation requires that the state of bliss, which is its end fruit, should be of a more perfect order and beyond all natural happiness, such as, outside the divine order of grace, would have been the recompense for morally good works accomplished in the pure state of innocence. When, at the time of the six days, the Creator willed to establish the heavens and lay the foundations of the earth, adorning it with everything that could make it precious and attractive, He spoke just one word: *Dixit et facta sunt*;[6] but, when He willed to construct the City of God, He brought to bear all the treasures of His wisdom, chose His own Son as architect, and bade Him work with His own hands at this important task and not to spare His blood, sweat, or tears in His labor. He tells us that nothing defiled shall enter the sanctuary of all justice. He desires that the guests at the eternal banquet should feed on His flesh, wash in His blood, transform themselves and raise the powers and capacities of their souls by becoming, even in this life, as one divine nature and disposition.

In short, in the construction of the immortal dwelling-place, He deigns to take infinite pains, exhausts the depths of His knowledge and carries preparation to the extreme. He wishes this incomparable abode to be truly His house, the highest manifestation of His attributes and glory, so that on the last day, when He contemplates His supreme work, this great God, so jealous of His honor, may be able in all truth to say: This is well done. I have brought the greatest of my designs to its perfection; beyond it, I see no kingship, no greatness, that can be bestowed upon the creature whom I have destined to reign with me through all eternity. I am satisfied; I have achieved my ideal and obtained my repose: "Since, on the seventh day, God was finished with the work He had been doing, He rested on the seventh day from all the work He had undertaken."[7]

Heaven is God's ideal, the repose of His intellect. Let us add: it is the repose of His heart. The heart goes further than the mind. It has aspirations and impulses, unknown to genius, which go beyond all the bounds of inspiration and thought. Thus, a mother sees her son rich and honored; the most brilliant crowns glitter on his head; the mother cannot conceive of any new fortunes or new empires for her child. Her reason says, "Enough!" Yet her heart calls out, "More! The happiness of my child is greater than all the dreams in which my mind can indulge; it does not come up to the limits and presentiments of my love, nor attain my heart's ambition."

As no mother ever loved her dearest son, so the Lord loves His predestinate. He is jealous of His dignity and could not permit Himself to be outdone by His creature on the score of fidelity and generosity.

Oh! The Lord cannot forget that the saints, when they once lived on earth, paid homage to Him by the total donation of their repose, their happiness, and their whole being; that they would have liked to have had an inexhaustible flow of blood in their veins, in order to shed it as a living and imperishable pledge of their faith; that they would have desired a thousand hearts in their breasts, so as to consume them in the unquenchable fires of their love, and to possess a thousand bodies, in order that they might deliver them to martyrdom, like victims unceasingly renewed. And the grateful God cries out, "Now it is my turn! The saints have given me the gift of themselves: can I respond other than by giving myself, without restriction and without measure? If I place in their hands the scepter of creation, if I surround them with the torrents of my light, that is a great deal; it is going beyond their highest hopes and aspirations, but it is not the utmost endeavor of my heart. I owe them more than paradise, more than the treasures of my knowledge; I owe them my life, my nature, my eternal and infinite substance. If I bring my servants and friends into my house, if I console them and make them thrill with joy by enfolding them in the embrace of my charity, this satisfies their thirst and their desires superabundantly, and is more than the perfect repose of their hearts requires; but it is not enough for the gratification of my divine heart, for the repletion and perfect satisfaction of my love. I must be the soul of their souls, I must penetrate and imbue them with my divinity, as fire penetrates iron; by showing myself to their spirits, undisguised, unveiled, without the intervention of the senses, I must unite myself to them *in an eternal face-to-face*, so that my glory illuminates them, exudes and radiates through all the pores of their being, so that, 'knowing me as I know them, they may become like Gods themselves.' "[8]

"O my Father," exclaimed Jesus Christ, "I have asked of You that, where I am, those whom I have loved may be there with me. May they be engulfed and lose themselves in the ocean of Your splendors; may they desire, possess, enjoy, and then desire again; may they be plunged into the bosom of Your beatitude, and may it be as if nothing remained of their personality except the knowledge and experience of their happiness."

Here human language fails, and the intellect is amazed and overwhelmed. Is our doctrine a kind of mysticism? Are the hymn and the hopes that such sublime prospects arouse in our innermost hearts just a poetic dream; or is *the vision of God* we have just set forth a truth and a certain fact, resting on a syllogism that the Fathers have attested to us and proved irrefutably by their imagery and inspired words?

We must have recourse to theological argument, and suspend for a moment our songs and transports; for it is good to strengthen disturbed and wavering souls by dealing with this subject as it deserves, and by combating all the objections that naturalism and cold reason seek to raise in order to obscure or contest it.

Is the created being capable of uniting itself so closely with God that it sees Him face-to-face, *facie ad faciem?* What will the mode of this vision be? When we see God as He is, shall we know Him in His integrity and without restriction? These are three important questions that must be resolved.

If we consider things from the narrow compass of our reason, God cannot be seen by any creature. God is the uncircumscribed, unlimited being. In order that an object may be known, says St. Thomas authoritatively, it must be contained in the mind of the person who knows; and it can be contained therein only in accordance with the forms and capacity for knowledge which that mind possesses.[9] Thus, we cannot see and know a stone, except insofar as the image of this stone, transmitted by our senses, is made present and, as it were, contained in our understanding. Hence the axiom: "Nothing is in the intellect which is not first in the senses."[10] St. Paul expresses the same truth when he says: "invisible realities . . . have become intelligible by the sight of visible things."[11]

To take the angels: they are endowed with a nature more perfect than ours; they have no need of the aid of tangible things in order to rise to the perception of intellectual truths; they are an admirable likeness of the divinity, and need only contemplate their own being and nature in order to rise to the knowledge of the existence of God and of His divine attributes. This mode of knowledge always occurs by representation, *per speculum et in enigmate.*[12] For man, it is external and material creatures that act as a mirror. For the angels, it is their cogitative nature, and, although pure spirits, they do not have the power to rise to the knowledge of God directly, and without intermediary, *facie ad faciera.*

That is why no one has ever seen God.[13] God "dwells in inapproachable light; whom no human being has ever seen or can see."[15] God is at an infinite distance from men and angels, and is invisible in Himself.

Nevertheless it is of faith that man will one day see God, as He is, in the brightness of His essence. Jesus Christ has said, "He who loves me will be loved by my Father; I, too, will love him and reveal myself to him."[16] God said to Abraham, "I myself shall be your great reward" — *Ego ero merces tua magna nimis.*[17]

The vision of God, as described by St. Paul, has never ceased to be the object of the desires and the expectation of all the Patriarchs and Prophets, an expectation that God could not disappoint without derogating from His wisdom and His justice. "Every soul free from sin," says the Council of Florence, "is immediately admitted to heaven and sees God in His Trinity, as He is, according to the degree of his merit, one in a more perfect, another in a less perfect manner."[18]

The Holy Council adds, "This vision of God in no way comes from the forces of nature." It does not correspond to any desire or any necessity of our hearts. Outside of revelation, the human mind could not have conceived the slightest suspicion of it — "nor has it so much as dawned on man."[19] Eternal life is the highest miracle, the most sublime mystery; it is the flower in full bloom or, better still, the fruit of grace, of which the Incarnate Word has planted the seed and the root in the center of our humanity by the power of the Holy Spirit; and, so that we may attain eternal life, God had to imprint a new form in our minds, and superimpose a new faculty.

Let us add in passing that, as the vision of God is not *connatural* to man, its deprivation does not necessarily bring about sensory pain and the pain of fire. Thus, children who die without Baptism will not be admitted to the vision of God. Nevertheless, they will enjoy God to a certain extent; they will know Him with the aid of the light of their reason, and they will love Him tenderly, as the author of their being and the dispenser of all good.

The reason for this doctrine stems from the great principle that man, considered in himself and in the state of pure nature, differs from the man degraded by sin as much as he who is naked differs from him who has been stripped of his honors and prerogatives by a deserved punishment and degradation. Consequently every man with the use of understanding and freedom is predestined to eternal life, and possesses, by this fact, the capacities and means needed to reach this sublime reward. If he does not obtain it, he will feel immense grief, having, through his own fault, lost the good that should have been his lot and his crown.

But children who die without Baptism do not possess the *seed* of glory; they have never been able to apprehend its price; their minds, unenlightened by Baptism, do not possess any disposition or aptitude preparing them for the vision of supernatural things, any more than animals have the capacity to be taught by the light of reason and to grasp mathematical and speculative truths. Thus, it is inconsistent to grant that they will suffer the loss of a good to which by nature they were not destined. These children who have died without Baptism will not be separated from God completely; they will be united to Him in the sense that they will attain their natural end, and will see God, as far as it is possible to see Him, through the medium of eternal beings, to the extent that He manifests Himself in the marvels and harmonies of creation.

This is a precious doctrine, which reconciles both divine justice and divine goodness, a sweet consolation for Christian mothers who mourn their children killed in a natural accident without having been reborn by the sacrament of the Redemption!

The End of the Present World

Man will see God face-to-face, but how will this vision take place? It is of faith that we shall not see Him by representation, by an image formed in our minds. It is also of faith that we shall not rise to the knowledge of Him by the aid of reasoning, or by way of demonstration, in the manner whereby we apprehend universal and abstract truths in this world.

It is likewise certain that we shall not see Him partially and dimly like distant objects, of which we cannot discern all the features, but which we see only imperfectly and on certain sides. God will not be seen in this way. He is a single being, not made of parts. He is in the blade of grass and in the atom integrally. When we say that He is present in every sphere and in all places, our mind leads us astray: God is not in any place, but all spheres and places are in Him. He does not live in any time, but His eternity consists of an indivisible instant, in which all time is contained. So we shall see Him as He is in His simplicity, in His threefold personality, and in the same way as we see the face of a man in this world, *sicuti est facie ad faciem.*

This vision will operate by an immediate impression of the divine essence in the soul with the aid of a supernatural light called *the light of glory*. Suarez defines it thus: "a created quality and a supernatural virtue of the intellect, infused into the soul, which will give it the aptitude and the power to see God." This light of glory will transform man, says St. Dionysius; it will deify him by imprinting in him the seal and likeness of celestial beauty, and make him the image of the Father; it will expand and augment the soul's capacity for knowledge to such an extent that it will become able to apprehend immense and boundless good. Just as, by means of the light of the sun, the eye can see the variety of tangible things and, so to speak, comprehend the whole extent of the universe; just as, aided by the light of reason, it knows the reason for its own existence, and the intellectual truths; so, immersed in the light of glory, it will have infinity as its domain, and, in a sense, will comprehend God Himself.

Scripture teaches us that the light of glory is the light of God: *In lumine tuo videbimus lumen.*[20] By it, our souls will be so immersed in the light of the divine presence that we may say, with St. Augustine, that, in a sense, they will no longer know through their own knowledge, but from the very knowledge of God, and that they will no longer see with their so weak and limited eyes, but with the very eyes of God: *Erit intellectui plenitudo lucis.*

The transports that the divine vision will arouse in the elect will make their hearts superabound in the most unutterable joys; it will be a flood of delights and raptures, life in its inexhaustible richness and the very source of all good and all life. It will be, as St. Augustine goes on to say, like a gift from God of His own Heart, so that we may love and rejoice with all the energy of the love and joys of God Himself: *Erit voluntati plenitudo pacis.*

Eternal life, says St. Paul, is like a weight, like being overwhelmed with all delights, all exhilarations, and all transports: "an eternal weight of glory," *aeternum gloriae pondus;*[21] a weight that, by reviving man rather than annihilating him, will inexhaustibly renew his youth and vigor. It is a source, forever fertile, where the soul will drink substance and life in abundance. It is a marriage, in which the soul will clasp its Creator in an eternal embrace without ever feeling any diminution of the rapture it felt on that day when, for the first time, it was united to Him and pressed Him to its bosom.

Even so, the elect who see God will not comprehend Him; for the Lateran Council teaches, "God is incomprehensible to all created beings." We shall see God as He is, some more, others less, according to our dispositions and merits. Nevertheless, we could not teach theologically that the Immaculate Virgin herself, who sees God more clearly and perfectly than all the angels and all the saints together, can attain an adequate vision and knowledge of God. God is infinite, and all that can be said is that the creature sees Him; sees Him as He is (*sicuti est*), entire (*in integro*); and yet does not see Him, in the sense that what he succeeds in discovering of His perfections is nothing compared with what the eternal Being Himself contemplates, in the splendor of His Word and in union with the Holy Spirit.

If we might be permitted to use a crude and incomplete image — for it must be remembered that every comparison taken from tangible things loses all proportion and analogy when it is applied to the realm of uncreated life — we would say that, in comparison with God, the elect are like a traveler standing on the banks of the ocean. The traveler knows that it is the ocean, he sees with his own eyes the ocean, which stretches out and unfolds in the immensity, and he says, "I have seen the ocean." Nevertheless there are reefs and distant islands he does not discern, and his gaze has not encompassed all the riverbanks and all the contours of the ocean. Accordingly, contemplation of God will not mean immobility but, above all, activity, an ever-ascending progression, where movement and repose will be bound together in ineffable harmony.

In order the better to understand this, let us imagine a scholar who has been given wings by nature; he would have the power of traversing all the regions of the stars and the firmament; he would be enabled to explore all the hidden marvels in the countless groups of constellations, and this scholar would go from one sphere to another, from one planet to the next. As he advanced further into the immensity, he would meet one surprise after another, thrill upon thrill, seeing richer spectacles appear ceaselessly, opening up vaster and more radiant horizons to his gaze. However, a moment would come when he reached the limits.

But infinity has no limits, no bottom or shore. The happy mariners of that fortunate abode will never cry, like Christopher Columbus: *Land! Land!* They will say: *God, God always. God yet more* . . . Forever there will be new perfections they will seek to gain; forever more pure and more intoxicating delights they will aspire to taste. They will go from glory to glory, from joy to joy; for, as St. Gregory of Nyssa says, "The infinite Good has no limits, the desire which He arouses is immeasurable."[22]

☞

The vision and the knowledge of God are sufficient for the complete and perfect happiness of man; the knowledge he will have of contingent beings, and of visible, eternal nature is the accompaniment and accidental part of his happiness.

St. Thomas explains this truth to us with his incomparable vigor of reasoning:

All knowledge by which the created spirit is perfected is ordained to the knowledge of God as its end. Hence it follows that he who sees the essence of God has his spirit raised to the highest perfection, and does not become more perfect by seeing objects that are not God; unless, however, the objects contribute to make him see God more fully. On the same subject, St. Augustine says, in Book V of his *Confessions*, "Unhappy is the man who knows all created things and is ignorant of You, O Supreme Truth. Happy, on the other hand, is he who knows You, even if he should know nothing of any created thing. He who knows both You and every being in the universe is not thereby happier; but he is happy, solely because he knows You."[23]

Nevertheless, the sight of the divine essence will not absorb the saints so much as to make them forget the external marvels of the visible world, or prevent their relationship with the other elect. In this life, when we concentrate one of our faculties upon an object, our other faculties are left weak and inactive; but the vision of God, far from paralyzing the exercise of our intellectual and sensitive powers, will increase a hundredfold their energy and penetration. Thus God-made-man saw clearly the divine essence, and yet conversed familiarly with men, sat at their table and freely adopted all the habits of ordinary life. The angels, confirmed in grace, enjoy perfect bliss, and unceasingly see the face of their Father, who is in heaven. Nevertheless, they dispose and coordinate the material elements, preside over the movement of the stars, and are not distracted from the presence of God when they lend us their assistance during our pilgrimage, or when they enlighten us with their inspirations.

Furthermore, it is of faith that there is no perceptible space of time between the moment of death and that of the fulfillment of the judgment, and the very second when the just soul is freed from the ties of his body, he is admitted into the heavenly reward, just as, at the same moment, the damned soul is led to the place of his eternal torments.

Imagine now a man whose inward eye, carefully purified by divine grace, has never let itself be sullied by the poisoned breath of any passion. This man may have been only an illiterate, uneducated villager, for whom the humble instruction he received obediently from the Church sufficed. He closes his corporeal eyes upon the murky light of this earth, and, like a captive who, on coming out of the dark kingdom of shadows, saw, for the first time the golden rays of the daylight star, this man, freed from the ties of his body, is inundated in a strange, dazzling light; he is laid on the threshold of all science and every splendor. All those imperfect images which prevented him from contemplating the truth openly are consumed in the fire of the divine light. The holy obscurities of faith vanish: heaven, nature, and God are enigmas no longer for this king of glory.

In the twinkling of an eye, he comprehends both the entirety and every detail of this palace of creation, which is now his inheritance and domain; with a single glance, he takes in its immensity. He fathoms the properties, secrets, and innermost forces of the elements; with a single turn of his thoughts, he visits those huge globes in the firmament, which are so distant that they escape our knowledge and calculations. The tree of knowledge displays the rich collection of its fruits before him; he feeds and quenches his thirst from this ever-luxuriant fountain. He no longer feels any thirst for knowledge, and for him there is no more night, no more doubt, no more curiosity or searching.

Oh! With what envy will the wise men of this world, who spend their time devising futile theories and forget God for the sake of indulging in speculation and useless research, then regard the just man who loved God and set his heart on true wisdom!

The smallest reflection of his knowledge will throw into the shade all the discoveries and all the conquests of humanity since the beginning of time.

In this life we would succumb beneath such an abundant flow of light; the harmony of our constitution would be destroyed and our vital functions suspended.

Yet this knowledge of created being is less than a drop of water in comparison with a science of a superior order. The spirits of the elect enter into contact with the world of spirits; they see the beauty of the blessed souls, illuminated by the divine likeness, adorned with charity and its attendant virtues, as with a nuptial robe; they see the cherubim, inflamed with their ardent love, the principalities and the dominations with their strength, and the seraphim, arrayed with immaterial wings with which they veil themselves in the presence of the majesty of the Lamb; unaided by sounds and audible words, they engage in ineffable conversation with them. Their luminous, subtle, and impassible bodies offer no obstacle to the activity of the intellect and the exercise of their faculties.[24]

Then we shall understand You, hidden mystery of the Incarnation; and we shall see clearly how the divine nature, substantially united to human nature in the person of the Word, has crowned the latter with the fullness of its prerogatives and splendors, and exalted Him above all the angels and hierarchies. Then, O Virgin Mary, your august Motherhood will no longer be incomprehensible to us, and, together with the choirs of angels, we shall proclaim you blessed, and render thanks for the treasures of sanctification of your Immaculate Heart.

How sweet it will be to contemplate at a single glance all the marvels of the Most High God in the realm of nature as well as in the order of grace and glory. Then will it be that the elect, in their raptures, will unite in song and cry out in chorus, "How wonderful Thou art in Thy works, O my God! Now the universe has become a temple, where the excellence and sublimity of Thy Name are traced out in imposing and indelible characters. Blessing, honor, wisdom, and strength to our God, forever and ever!"

❧

Heaven is the repose of man's intellect, the repose of his will and affections. We shall love God, we said, with that love which

He has for Himself. Yet, what often frightens us in this life, what makes us reject heaven with a sort of repugnance and anguish, is that we imagine that in that abode, all the natural attachments of our heart will be, as it were, annihilated and invincibly extinguished by the conquering exuberance of the love in which we shall be enflamed for the Creator.

Oh! The whole of Christianity protests against this error. How could the religion of Jesus Christ, which condemns so severely our thanklessness, selfishness, and insensitivity, set the extinction of all noble and lawful friendships as the condition of our heavenly rewards? How could the natural love of husband and wife, father and son, to which God obliges us in this life, be excluded from the constituents of our eternal crown? Will that Church of heaven, wherein all our feelings will be purified and all our natural tendencies and aspirations will be raised to the most superhuman degree of perfection, be founded upon the ruin of all the ties of the heart, all our memories and family relationships? God forbid!

What we teach as certain is that in heaven *we shall see and recognize one another.* Such is the testimony and the constant voice of tradition. In Africa, St. Cyprian, who was born in heathendom and, after his conversion, raised to the See of Carthage, feeling that he was destined to die a martyr, exhorted the faithful to face death undaunted like him, and spoke to them of it as a gift and a blessing from heaven.

"Let us then hasten," he said, "and run to see our fatherland, and greet our brethren, for we are awaited by a large number of people who are dear to us; we are desired by a multitude of relatives, brothers, and children, who, assured henceforth of their immortality, are still solicitous for our salvation. Let us go to see them, let us go to embrace them . . . And what joy for all of us, for them and for me!"

The End of the Present World

Among the Greeks at Constantinople, St. Theodore of Studium, an illustrious confessor of the Faith, often consoled bereaved families. He wrote to a father whose sons were all dead, "Your children are not lost, but remain safe and sound for you, and as soon as you have reached the end of this temporal life, you will see them again, full of joy and gladness." He wrote to a man who had just lost his wife, "You have sent a most worthy spouse before you, into the presence of God. What should you seek now? You should try to meet her again in heaven, at the time desired by Providence . . .

"Without doubt, in heaven the spouses who have come from earth will themselves be like angels, and will no longer aspire to the delights of the senses.[25] However, they will taste the ever-pure pleasures of the spirit, and, as they were one in flesh during their earthly exile, so in glory they will form one single heart and soul, in the delights of another union that will have no end."

In heaven, we shall *see* and *recognize* one another; and in heaven, we shall *love* one another.

It is true that, in this happy abode, faith will disappear amidst the splendor of the great realities; the inhabitants of the celestial Jerusalem, in possession of their final end, will no longer need to be sustained by the wings of hope. But *charity*, in its full unfolding, will shine forth like a great queen, in its power and in all its perfection. All the objects and causes that captivate our hearts and arouse love in this world will act with an intensity a thousand times greater, and without encountering any obstacle, on the hearts of the elect. Thus, in this life, our hearts are fascinated by beauty, by outstanding qualities of mind and heart; the intensity of the feeling that urges us to unite ourselves with a beloved one lessens when we discover his defects and faults.

In heaven, however, we shall find our friends spotless, and their features will be more radiant than the clearest sky; they will be endowed with a gracefulness and charm that will attract our hearts forcibly and forever. In this life, love is still the consequence of gratitude, and our hearts glow at the memory of benefits and services rendered. It is only in heaven that we shall recognize the extent and the cost of the graces of every kind that our benefactors have showered upon us.

Then the child will read all the treasures of grace, solicitude, and tenderness enclosed in the heart of his mother. He will know that, next to God, it was the tears, prayers, and sighs of that mother which brought about his salvation. "O mother," he will exclaim, "I used to love you because you gave me an earthly life, and provided for my food and my childhood needs; now I love you a thousand times more tenderly, because of the eternal life I have received, and without which the first would have been a fatal gift, a source of calamities and torture for me."

O new and happy Monicas, how great your triumphs and joys will be, when you see yourselves surrounded by a whole circle of children whose glory you have secured after having brought them into existence! Then, Christian fathers, your sacrifices, courage, and heroic constancy in strengthening your sons by profitable examples, and in rearing them by noble, laborious training, will no longer be unknown. Then, O friend, they will learn of your efforts, your pious strategies to detach a friend from vice and irreligion, and to catch, by innocent allurements, a soul, the object of your holy yearning. Then we shall bless you, we shall rekindle the vividness of our memories with outpourings of love; we shall redeem the debt of our hearts in eternal thanksgiving.

Lastly, the love aroused in our hearts by the memory of favors received, or the congenial attraction of natural qualities, is usually sustained and renewed by familiarity and the mutual exchange of impressions and thoughts. How, then, shall I describe the ineffable exchanges in which the elect will open their hearts to one another, that fraternal, intimate conversation in which, at every moment, in their celestial language they will convey to each other the captivating emotions of their hearts?

In this life, when we hear the conversation of superior minds that have been matured and trained by experience and deep reflection, we lose the sense of time under the spell and fascination of their words. We sit in front of the fire during the long winter evenings, with the snow falling and the wind blowing and roaring, and listen expectantly and with rapt, unflagging attention to the seaman back from distant shores, or the warrior who tells us about the perils of a long siege and the thousand pictures of death he encountered amidst the dangers of war.

How much greater will be our fascination, as we sit at the great hearth of our heavenly Father, listening while our brothers tell us the story of their seductive and manifold temptations and of the assaults waged by hell over which they triumphed. We shall not tire of hearing about those victories won in the sight of God alone, more glorious than those of conquerors; those battles waged in silence against the failings of the flesh and the turmoil of one's own thoughts. We shall admire their efforts and their heroic generosity. We shall know about the twists and turns and uncertainties whereby the grace of the Spirit of God, through a strong but gentle impulse, led them to the harbor of repose, and turned even their deviations and falls to account, in the edification of their incorruptible crown. Ah! These will be inexhaustible subjects of conversation, which will never lose their interest and charm.[26]

It is true that the glory and happiness of the elect will be apportioned according to their merits, and that they will differ in beauty and greatness as the stars in the sky are themselves different in size and brightness.[27] Nevertheless, union, peace, and harmony will not reign any less in this countless array, in which the lesser ranks cooperate with the highest in the repose and harmony of all.

The elect will form but one heart among themselves. Their one link will no longer be force or self-interest, but charity. Forming a single body, whose head is Jesus Christ, and having become living stones of the one building, they will all share in the conquest with the same joy and the same love. Each will be rich in the richness of all; each will thrill in the happiness of all. Just as the creation of a new sun would double the fires that burn the air, so each new sun in the City of God will increase the measure of our own bliss, with all its happiness and glory.

Again, just as mirrors, placed opposite one another, are not impoverished by the mutual reflection of their rays, but, rather, the images are multiplied and each of the mirrors reflects, in its own focal point, the light and the objects portrayed in the focal points of all — so, in the same way, each of the elect will reflect the rays of his brightness upon all the others. The apostle will reflect upon the angel the grace of preaching he received, and the angel will reflect upon the apostle his knowledge and the treasures of his keener insights. The prophet will reflect the grace of his visions upon the martyr, and the martyr will crown the prophet with his palms and trophies. The immaculate beauty and grace of the virgin will be reflected on the faces of the penitent and the hermit ravaged and wasted by fasts and macerations, and the converted sinner will manifest more strikingly the merit and prerogatives of innocence preserved in its integrity.

There will no longer be any place for rivalry or envy. Each of the elect will receive the complement of his personal good from the good of his brethren. We shall read their souls as clearly as our own. On this point, St. Augustine exclaims, "O happy heaven, where there will be as many paradises as citizens, where glory will come to us by as many channels as there are hearts to show us their concern and affection, where we shall possess as many kingdoms as there are monarchs sharing in our rewards. *Quot socii, tot gaudia!*"

⁓

Such are the joys of heaven. Let us say that they are pure joys. In heaven, sin is forever excluded. The elect are no longer capable of committing the least shadow of a fault or imperfection. In Holy Scripture, eternal life is called indefectible, incorruptible — *aeterna, immarcessibilis, incorruptibile*. These terms would be incorrect if the saints could fall from grace, and this prospect alone would suffice to diminish their happiness.

In our mortal condition it seldom happens that our purest and holiest joys do not contain a mixture of conceit and selfish satisfaction. The soul that feels happy withdraws into itself for its greater enjoyment: it experiences a keener and more concentrated sense of life; to a greater or lesser extent, it seeks relaxation from the thought of God, by which alone it ought to be possessed and filled. For this reason the saints felt a kind of anxiety and unease amidst prosperity. They knew that, in this life, the most honorable pleasures and the sweetest and most lawful joys have always something debilitating and corrupting for the Christian soul.

However, in heaven, the bliss of glory, far from rendering souls more human, elevates them and makes them more spiritual. Their awareness of happiness is not distinct from their awareness of God. The harmonies that charm their ears, the lights that bathe their eyes, the aromas their enchanted nostrils inhale are naught but the power of God rendering itself perceptible to their senses. And the effect of this multifarious delight is not to induce them, by reflection, to withdraw into excessive preoccupation with themselves and the baser perfection of their nature, but, rather, to inspire them to soar upward with inexhaustible energy and lose themselves in the ever-closer embrace of God, who imbues them with His fullness through all their senses and penetrates every pore of their being. On their lips the cry of joy blends with the cry of adoration and gratitude. They do not say, like the carnal disciples, "It is good for us to be here: *bonum est hic nos esse*"; but they exclaim, "Holy, holy, holy is God Almighty."

Surprisingly, heaven is somehow the opposite of earth! Here below, man is restored and bathed anew in dignity and moral value through suffering and sacrifice. In heaven, it is the reverse: he is perfected and deified by the flood of delights wherein he is immersed.

The joys of heaven are joys that are pure and lasting. Imagine a man on earth like Solomon, whose every wish was satisfied. He has fortune, youth, and health; his heart finds contentment and repose in the presence and company of visible creatures whom he loves. All manner of fascinations combine to complete this man's happiness. Yet there are times when his soul is plunged in sorrow and struck by fear. He says to himself, "My happiness is ephemeral. Each day that passes removes a piece of it, and soon it will be no more."

In heaven, happiness is stable, since the elect, confirmed in glory, are beyond all fear. The ages will succeed one another without diminishing their happiness, and without a single line creasing their brows. The certainty of eternally possessing the benefits they hold dear multiplies their sweetness a hundredfold. What a source of jubilation when, after thousands of centuries have elapsed, they reflect upon the day in the distant past when they made their triumphant ascent, and say, "Nothing is finished yet; I reign today, today I am in possession of my happiness, and I shall possess it as long as God remains God — forever and ever!"

The End of the Present World

The joys of heaven are lasting; they are not subject to any succession. The elect in heaven are no longer prisoners of time. Their new life does not slip by in measurable hours. For them there is no more past or future; but, living the life of God, they are fixed in a perpetual present.

On this earth our joys are successive: the pleasures and impressions that we felt yesterday are not those that we feel today. Happiness comes only *drop by drop*. It is not given to any man to gather together a day's joys in an instant, much less those of a lifetime. In heaven, however, God does not portion Himself out: He commits Himself completely, in the immutable, indivisible simplicity of His essence.

From the first moment of their incorporation into the divine life, the bliss of the saints is perfect and consummated. As the future does not diminish it in any way, so they do not long for anything from the past. Illuminated by the infinite clarity of the Word of God, they see the events that will be accomplished in a thousand years as clearly as those that were fulfilled a thousand centuries ago. Every moment, says St. Augustine, they experience, as it were, a feeling of infinite joy. Every moment, as far as it is permitted to created beings, they absorb the power of divine virtue. Every moment, eternity makes them feel the accumulated weight of its intoxications, its delights, and its glories. *Deus totus simul delectat, Deus erit memoriae plenitudo aeternitatis.*

One day, St. Augustine was describing the marvels of the city of God to his people of Hippo. He did so with a voice charged with emotion, with that golden eloquence, nurtured at the fount of Scripture, which made it seem that an angel was speaking, not an inhabitant of the earth. The assembled people were deeply moved and captivated, and felt as if transported to those feasts of eternity of which such a striking picture was being drawn for them, having a kind of vision of that day when the Lord would adorn the brows of the faithful with an imperishable laurel. Suddenly, their emotion was so great that they broke into groans and cries of wonder, and tears flowed from every eye. The respect due to the majesty of the sacred precincts and the silence imposed by the presence of the speaker were forgotten, and each one invoked the day when, far from all affliction, he would drink abundantly of the waters of truth and life. Each trembled lest, overcome by his frailty or led astray by seductions, he might be deprived of the blessed vision. From all sides of the holy place rang out the words: "O beautiful heaven, when shall I see you? Shall I be so senseless as to prefer the pleasures and fortune of a day to you? Who would not consent to purchase you at the price of the heaviest sacrifices and labors?"

Interrupted by these exclamations and sighs, and surprised at the effect produced by his words, Augustine was no less moved than the multitude. He wanted to proceed, to continue with the portrait of the heavenly Jerusalem he had begun; but the sobbing of his listeners and of his own emotion stifled his voice; and his tears, mingling with those of his people, formed, as it were, a torrent of mourning for the sorrows of exile and the remoteness of the beloved fatherland.

O holy Pontiff, how I yearn to have the pathos of your voice on my lips! O golden age of the early Church, when the lure of invisible goods and the promises of the future life exerted such a lively impression upon souls — who will bring you back to us again? If our words have not the power to open the fount of tears, may the hope and the memory of you, O city of God, at least raise up our desires; may they restrain our gross aspirations and act as a counterweight to them and to the pull of the thousand inferior desires that corrupt us!

Ah! We love power and glory; we would like to be present and give orders everywhere. Why, then, turn away from the nobility of our destiny and abandon the immortal empire God prepares for us? We love pleasure and joy; we recognize that life is unbearable if affections and joys do not mitigate its misfortunes and bitterness. Why, then, spurn the only real happiness, and desire that the source of all pleasure and joy dry up for us along with the present life?

Let men whose every hope is directed toward the things of the earth seek from nature the unlimited donation of its gifts; let them seek their pleasures and glories in the indefinite perfecting of material things; let them consider themselves happy because a thousand hands are at work to serve them, and a thousand machines and instruments are in operation to interpret and fulfill their ideas and whims.

"These goods diminish," says St. Gregory the Great, "these objects lose their illusion and become contemptible, when we consider the nature and immensity of the rewards that are promised us. Earthly goods, measured against the bliss above, no longer seem an advantage, but rather a burden and a painful tyranny. Temporal life, in comparison with eternal life, deserves not to be called life, but death."[28] On the other hand, to live in the heavenly city, mingled with the choirs of angels, to be surrounded by a light that is not itself circumscribed, and to possess a spiritual, incorruptible flesh, is not infirmity, but royalty and abundance of life.

Ah, if our mind is stirred at the thought of so much richness and magnificence, and aspires to fly toward those places where happiness has no bounds, let us remember that great rewards are acquired only by great combats, and that no one shall be crowned who has not fought the good fight.[29]

Let us, then, rejoice with the prophet at the things that have been said to us: I shall go into the house of the Lord;[30] but may our hearts not become attached to the snare of tangible things, and may our feet be always standing in the expectation of your heavenly courts, O Jerusalem. Jerusalem, you who are built as a city, when shall we witness your stately ceremonies, when shall we be reunited to that cornerstone, which is the foundation, the strength, and the mortar of our building?

Already countless tribes, legions of apostles, prophets, martyrs, and virgins, just men of every state and rank, have crossed the court of your domain. How desirable their fate is, for they are freed from our temptations, our troubles, and our miseries! Seated on thrones they have themselves erected, they have built upon truth and justice. Faithful and devoted to their Master unto death, they have deserved to share with Him the inheritance of the house of David. This is the sole ambition that we are permitted. Everything that is not Jerusalem is unfit for us. Let us ask only for the goods and the peace it contains. Let us think only of heaven, let us seek only heaven, let us store up only for heaven, and let us live only for heaven.[31]

A few moments longer, and all that must end will be no more; a few more efforts, and we shall be at the close; a few more combats, and we shall attain the crown; a few more sacrifices, and we shall be in Jerusalem, where love is always new, and where there will be no other sacrifice but praise and joy. Amen.

⌒

Notes

[1] 1 Pet. 2:5.

[2] Rev. 21:2-3; 22:1-5; 4:2-5, 10-11; 7:9-10, 12, 14, 16-17.

[3] 1 Cor. 2:9.

[4] *De spiritu et anima.*

The End of the Present World

[5] Rom. 6:23.

[6] Cf. Ps. 33:9.

[7] Gen. 2:2.

[8] Cf. St. Athanasius, *On the Incarnation:* "God became man so that man might become God."

[9] St. Thomas Aquinas, *Summa Theologica*, I, Q. 12, a. 4.

[10] *Nihil est in intellectu quod sit in sensu.*

[11] Cf. Rom. 1:20.

[12] Cf. 1 Cor.13:12: "Now we see indistinctly, as in a mirror . . ."

[13] Cf. John 1:18; 1 John 4:12.

[15] 1 Tim. 6:16.

[16] Cf. John 14:21.

[17] Cf. Gen. 15:1: "Fear not, Abram! I am your shield; I will make your reward very great."

[18] *Ex decreto unionis.*

[19] Cf. 1 Cor. 2:9.

[20] Cf. Ps. 36:10: "In Your light we see light."

[21] 2 Cor. 4:17: "The present burden of our trial is light enough, and earns for us an eternal weight of glory beyond all comparison."

[22] *De Vita Monastica.*

[23] St. Thomas Aquinas, *Summa Theologica*, Supp., Q. 92, a. 3.

[24] Pure spirits have a language that, although not audible or corporeal, is nonetheless quite intelligible; it occurs when an act of their will directs their thought toward him to whom they wish to make it known. Thus, they can speak to one without speaking to others, and without being heard or understood by all. Angelic language seems to be quite simply transmission of a thought, by an act of will, toward some other spirit, who then alone has knowledge of it.

[25] Matt. 22:30.

[26] Will the damnation of a multitude of souls, who were at one time united to the elect by friendship or blood, not cloud the joys of their bliss? Or else must we say that the souls, consumed with charity, will hate the reprobate with an everlasting hatred? Let us listen to the doctrine of St. Thomas on this point: "It is possible," he says, "to

rejoice at a thing in two ways: to rejoice at the thing absolutely and inasmuch as it is considered in itself. Now, the elect will not rejoice at the sufferings of the damned in that way. But it is also possible to rejoice at the same thing by reason of its accompanying circumstances. From this point of view the elect will rejoice at the pains of the reprobate, in consideration of the order and effects of God's justice in them; and, at the same time, they will rejoice at having themselves been spared the punishments of hell" (*Summa Theologica*, Supp., Q. 94, a. 3). Furthermore, is not God's love infinitely perfect? He, too, then, should be unhappy at the sight of the damned. So, is the knowledge that the demons will be eternally unhappy something that can be expected to dampen the joy of a St. Paul, a St. John, or a St. Theresa?

[27] Cf. 1 Cor. 15:41: "The sun has a splendor of its own, so has the moon, and the stars have theirs. Even among the stars, one differs from another in brightness."

[28] *Homilia 37 in Evangelia.*

[29] Cf. 2 Tim. 2:5.

[30] Cf. Ps. 122:1: "I rejoiced because they said to me, 'We will go up to the house of the Lord.' "

[31] Cf. Ps. 122.

Christian Sacrifice,
the Means of Redemption

Caro mea vere est cibus,
et sanguis meus vere est potus.

❧

For my flesh is real food;
and my blood is real drink.

John 6:55

Our heart is an altar. The victim placed on this altar is our evil inclinations. The sword destined to slay this victim is the spirit of sacrifice and immolation. The sacred fire, which must burn night and day on the altar of our heart, is the love of Jesus Christ. The fruitful, invigorating breath that inspires and nourishes this sacred fire of love is the Eucharist.

The Eucharist is a sacrament of the living. As a sacrament of the living, it bestows supernatural life and sanctifying grace. Apart from this property, which it shares with the other sacraments, the Eucharist has a special virtue of its own, expressed in the words of Christ: "My flesh is real food; and my blood is real drink" — words that the Council of Trent explains thus: "All the effects that food produces materially in our bodies, the Eucharist produces spiritually in our souls."

Thus, food strengthens our bodies and, up to a given age, makes them grow; the Eucharist gives strength against temptations, and makes the soul grow in virtue and justice. The richer the material food, and the more discriminating the palate and the sense of taste, the more delicious it is; the purer the heart, and the better prepared the soul, the sweeter the Eucharist. It is through the Eucharist that the God of glory inaugurates His bliss in the midst of our misery; it is the source of all devotion, of all greatness, and of all holiness.

The Eucharist has a double foundation. It is, first of all, one of the seven sacraments of the New Law, in which Jesus Christ, present under the species of bread and wine, is offered for our adoration and offers Himself as food. It is, in addition, a sacrifice, in which the spotless Lamb renews the memory of His Passion and death and is truly immolated. As this conference is linked to the preceding ones, we shall deal with the Eucharist only insofar as it constitutes the sacrifice of the New Law.

In order, from this point of view, to set out the true nature of the eucharistic oblation, its excellence and efficacy, it is essential to define sacrifice in general, and to explain what it really is.

☞

Sacrifice is a solemn, public act, destined to honor the being of God. St. Thomas defines sacrifice as "an external, public, and solemn action, performed through the ministry of a specially selected man, with the object of offering to the Most High God something animate or material, but in such a way that this thing, destroyed and transformed, is set apart for the worship and honor of God."[1]

It follows from this definition, first, that sacrifice is the essence, the very soul, of worship, and the appropriate expression of the relationship between God and man. On this account, sacrifice is offered in the name of the whole people. It is in no way a private act that any individual can perform as he pleases; it can be offered only by men specially chosen and consecrated, either because these men have received investiture directly and immediately from God, or because the lawful leaders of religious and civil society have appointed them for this purpose. "One does not take this honor on his own initiative, but only when called by God, as Aaron was."[2] Elsewhere, St. Paul says, "Every high priest is taken from among men and made their representative before God."[3] Thus, under the law of nature, the head of the family was pontiff and king; under the Mosaic law, the tribe of Aaron alone had the right to celebrate at the altar; under the law of grace, none but validly ordained bishops and priests may celebrate and consecrate the body of Jesus Christ.

Secondly, sacrifice consists in the oblation of an external, tangible, and permanent thing. Hence, the offering that man makes to God of his desires and affections, the rites and ceremonies, such as prostrations and expiatory acts, observed in diverse religions, are called sacrifices only by analogy and extension. For sacrifice to take place, the object offered must be destroyed, or at least it must undergo a change or modification, which makes it inapt for any profane use and assigns it solely to the honor and worship of God.

It follows that this destruction or modification, which constitutes the very essence of sacrifice, could not be applied to the interior or exterior acts of man, which are of their nature accidental and transitory. It is essential that the matter of sacrifice should be something extraneous to man and subsisting in itself, for sacrifice is based upon the principle of substitution.

In ancient times, if man offered an animal in place of himself, this animal was killed; if it was flour or bread, the flour or bread were cooked and consumed; if it was a liquid, the liquid was poured out as a libation.

Thirdly, it follows from St. Thomas's definition that sacrifice has this in common with the sacrament: that, like the latter, it is an external and visible sign, intended to express and effect a sacred thing. Yet it differs from the sacrament in this sense: that the sacrament has as its immediate effect the sanctification of man and the transmission of certain graces or supernatural aptitudes, following a given order, whereas sacrifice has as its immediate object the honor due to the Divine Majesty, and the acknowledgment of His infinite sovereignty.

The End of the Present World

Man, formed of a body and soul, is bound to honor God by rendering Him homage for all his external goods. Thus, at all times and in all places, men have felt unable to render God a more expressive and forceful sign of their adoration and gratitude than by destroying or modifying, for the sake of His glory, one of the rarest and most useful objects in their lives. They have constantly had recourse to this means in order to show the Most High God that they were subject to His power, and that they recognized Him as the absolute Author of life and death.

For this reason it was ordained in the Old Testament that the sacrificing priest should extend and cross his hands over the victim before striking it. The purpose of this ceremony was to show that, not having the right to destroy himself, man identified himself with the victim and, insofar as it lay in his power, destroyed himself, not in reality, but by way of representation and image. Hence, he fed on the flesh of the victim in order to express the wish that the sacrifice might become inherent and in some way embodied in him; for as St. Thomas says, "Exterior sacrifice is the sign of interior sacrifice."

From these considerations it follows that sacrifice, taken in itself, includes a community of adoration and worship, and can be offered only to the one, supreme God.

It is a fact worthy of note that, in the days of paganism and among idolatrous peoples, the devils have constantly shown an appetite for sacrifices, convinced that by having such honors paid to them they were conferring upon themselves, by this very fact, the rank and honors due to the true God. "For it is not the smell of burning corpses but the divine honors associated with them that makes the demons rejoice."[4]

Without sacrifice, man cannot honor God as he ought; there is no more powerful means of obtaining His mercy, mitigating His justice, and giving prayer its full efficacy.

The Eucharist is a perfect sacrifice

In the Old Law, sacrifices had only an imperfect, figurative value. Indeed, what could the offering of rams and heifers have been worth, in the sight of the Master of all things? And even had the Most High God deigned to accept sacrifices so unworthy of His glory, what hands would have been pure enough to offer them to Him? That is why the prophet said, "Sacrifice and oblation you wished not"; and elsewhere, "You are not pleased with sacrifices; should I offer a holocaust, you would not accept it."[5]

Thus, once the sacrifice of the Cross — that oblation, infinite in itself and more than superabundant in its application and its effects — had been offered on Calvary, blood-sacrifices immediately ceased over the whole surface of the earth. They are not found either among the Jews or the Mohammedans. They are no longer practiced, except by peoples beyond the pale of civilization and history. A priest who appeared in our times with a knife in his hand and exuding the smell of immolated meats would provoke laughter and disgust.

$\approx$

The Eucharist is a perfect sacrifice. In it are manifested strikingly all the attributes of God: His wisdom, His omnipotence, and His mercy. The Eucharist is salutary in its fruits: for how could every virtue not spring forth from the wounds of the Man-God, and from the chalice of His blood? It is worthy of the sovereign majesty: it is, in fact, the very person of the Word, who annihilates Himself in order to give to His Father a glory proportionate to His sovereign perfection. The Eucharist fulfills all the conditions necessary for a perfect, consummated sacrifice.

There is, first, a principal priest, who is Jesus Christ; the secondary priest is the minister specially consecrated for this purpose. There is a victim offered, who is, again, none other than Jesus

Christ, hidden under the species of bread and wine. There is the Most High God, to whom this victim is offered. In truth, the oblation is offered equally to Jesus Christ, not only as God, but also as man. Jesus Christ is a victim, offered and immolated, according to the words of St. Andrew: "I sacrifice the Immaculate Lamb on the altar each day."

In the sacrifice there is a *subject*, for whose benefit the victim is offered; this subject is the Church and the faithful, *qui pro vobis et pro multis effundetur*. As St. Thomas observes, the excellence of the sacrifice is superior to that of the sacrament. The sacrament benefits only the person to whom it is administered; the sacrifice is salutary to all.

Lastly, at Mass there is an altar. The sacrificial act and the sense of the mystery are efficaciously expressed by the offering, the consecration, and the consumption of the sacred species. Let us add that it is part of the excellence and dignity of the sacrifice that man offers to God the best of what he has. Abel offered his first-fruits; the Patriarchs, spotless lambs and heifers. Now, what is better than Him by whom all things were done, and who is Himself the author and source of all good?

How ardent our piety and our transports of love and gratitude would have been if we had been present at the Passion of our Lord Jesus Christ — if, in the company of St. John and the holy women, it had been given to us to gaze upon the wounds of the Man-God and receive the first-fruits of that divine blood, offered for our redemption!

Now, the Council of Trent says that the sacrifice of the Mass has the same value as the sacrifice of the Cross: *Tantum valet sacrificium missae, quantum oblatio Christi in cruce*. It is the same priest who offers, the same victim who is offered, and the same immolation that is renewed: *In divino sacrificio, quod in missa peragitur, idem ille*

Christus continetur et incruente immolator, qui in ara crucis; semetipsum cruente obtulit.[6]

First, at the altar and at the Cross, it is the same priest who offers. The sacred ministers who appear clothed in priestly garments are only the delegates and ministers of Jesus Christ, the principal and eternal priest, according to the order of Melchizedek.

In other words we have, at the altar, a representative function; we assume the person of Jesus Christ, and we assume it in many ways, *multifarium et multis modis*, in our vestments, in the mysteries that we enact, and in the words that we utter.[7]

At Mass, we come out of the sacristy wearing on our shoulders that mysterious chasuble, the image of the Cross that our Lord Jesus Christ bore upon His own shoulders. The alb that covers us represents the white robe in which the Son of God was mocked at the court of Herod, but which His innocence transformed into a garment of dazzling brightness. We carry, hanging from our arms, that *maniple* of tears, intended to wipe away the sweat from our foreheads and restore us from our failings.

After bowing, we ascend the steps of the altar, as our Lord Jesus Christ climbed the steps of Golgotha. We raise our hands, when we say *Oremus* ("let us pray"), as Jesus Christ prayed, with His hands raised toward His Father. At the Canon, we speak in a low voice, like Jesus Christ, who, in the Garden of Olives, moved a stone's throw away from His disciples, in order to enter into the silence of recollection and prayer. At the Elevation, we take the Host in our hands, just as Jesus Christ, at the Last Supper, took the bread and wine into His holy and venerable hands. Then our words cease, our personality disappears, and the voice of Jesus Christ replaces that of His minister. It is no longer we who speak, no longer we who live: the body of the priest has become the very body of God. Leaning over the Host, we do not say *"This is the body of Jesus Christ, this is the blood of Jesus Christ,"* but *"This is my body, this is my blood."*

"A great mystery and a sublime dignity is that of the priest, to whom is given a power the angels do not have. Priests alone, properly ordained, have the power to celebrate and consecrate the body of Jesus Christ."[8]

At the altar, we are but mere instruments; but on the other side, our dignity is the highest that can be conceived.

Priests of the Lord [exclaimed St. John Chrysostom], the greatest things among men seem to me shorn of all glory, when I consider that which you have received. Your ministry, it is true, is performed among men; but it ranks among the celestial hierarchies, for the Paraclete is the Author of the mysteries you accomplish; you are greater than the prophet Elijah; you bear in your hands, not fire, but the Holy Ghost, beseeching Him to pour forth His graces upon all the faithful.

Priests of the Lord, there can be no doubt but that you are greater than kings. The king commands subjects; you command God. The judgments of the king affect only the things of time; your pronouncements will stand through all eternity. You have no need of the bounty and riches of the king, but the king needs your blessings and prayers. There can be no doubt that you are greater than the Thaumaturges: the Thaumaturges work miracles on the elements; you work them on souls. The Thaumaturges operate transformations in matter; you transform the bread and wine every day into the flesh and blood of Jesus Christ. There is no doubt but that, in a sense, you are greater than the Virgin Mary herself. The Virgin Mary, by her assent, brought about the Incarnation of the Word: she uttered that blessed *fiat* which made the Son of God descend into her immaculate womb. That *fiat* she pronounced only once; you pronounce it every day. Mary begot Jesus Christ to a mortal life; you beget Him to a life that lasts throughout history. Mary was obeyed by Jesus Christ in His passible state; you are obeyed by Jesus Christ impassible and glorious.

Politics, philosophy, and science have tried many times, but they have never been able to create a priest. At the time of the Great Revolution,[9] the same men who had defied reason and attempted to replace the Sunday rest by the legal rest of the *decadi* also tried to create a humanitarian priesthood, a priesthood divested of every luster and trace of divinity.[10] An official delegate of the civil power clothed himself in a white robe; he girded the sash of three colors around his loins, and moved up to the foot of an altar, dedicated to nature, to offer a bunch of flowers, the symbol of patriotism and hope; he succumbed beneath the weight of ridicule and scorn; he did not have the seal of God, that divine ray, that cast of features, something indefinable, which God alone can give to man, and which no royal appointment or any kind of lay selection will ever succeed in bestowing upon him.

It is a noteworthy fact that wherever the eucharistic sacrifice disappears there is no priest. The Protestants have found this. The day when they drove Christ from the tabernacles, where He lies in sacrifice and in goodness, their priests vanished immediately; they had thenceforth only ministers, teachers of morality, police officers in the department of religious affairs, and, as Count de Maistre has wittily said, men clad in black, mounting the pulpit every Sunday, to make decorous speeches.

Such is the reason for the unrelenting hatred of the wicked toward the priest. It is written in the book of Revelation, "Then the dragon stood before the woman about to give birth, ready to devour her child when it should be born."[11] Now, the man who delivers Jesus Christ is the priest — *parturiente linguâ*, in the beautiful expression of St. Ambrose. The sure means of suppressing Jesus Christ as far as possible, and of utterly destroying His reign here below, is to get rid of the priest, or at the very least empty his heart of faith, innocence, and the Christian virtues.

Lately, speaking of the priest, one of the leaders of contemporary impiety said, "Let us not put him to death — he would acquire new strength in blood; martyrdom would be for him the seed of a new fecundity and a superhuman strength. Let us suffocate him in filth."

But the priest cannot be vanquished. In the face of the words spewed out of blasphemous mouths that call down death and pile up great ruins, the priest conveys on his lips two words of life and eternity: a word of eternity that, each day, brings the living Word of God down upon the altar; a word of eternity that makes Him come down into souls, where He dwells, together with justice and the supernatural works of life.

At the altar, as on the Cross, there is only one priest; for the priesthood with which we are invested is nothing more than a sharing in that of Christ. Moreover, there is only one victim.

In the ancient sacrifices, the victim appeared disgraced and close to death. It was bound with chains and adorned in funeral wrappings. It was called "sacred," and this term meant both that the victim was dedicated to God and, by contrast, that it was at the same time accursed and abhorred. In this sense, it became responsible for all the iniquities of the people and, in a certain sense, was made to bear them. Hence it is that the [French] word *sacré* is used in popular speech as a term both of praise and blessing and, at the same time, as a term of curse and blasphemy.

Jesus Christ, inaccessible to our senses, and in His glorious state, is subject neither to death nor to any change; consequently He can no longer make Himself a victim. Yet it is of the essence of sacrifice that the victim should be visible, and that it should be destroyed or changed; and it was once customary that man should be able to feed on it, in order to share in the sanctification it had received.[12] However, Jesus Christ could not offer Himself on the altar with His natural features and in His human form, and, for this reason, the Jews, interpreting the divine words in a gross, carnal sense, said, "How can He give us His flesh to eat?"[13]

So Christ found means of offering Himself in a completely new and incomprehensible manner. He established His eternal priesthood, not according to the order of Aaron, but according to the order of Melchizedek. Just as this mysterious character went to meet the victorious Abraham in order to offer him bread and wine, so Jesus Christ chose bread and wine, not only as the matter, but as the symbol of His new sacrifice. So Jesus Christ does not appear on the altar in His own form and species [appearance], but under the species of bread and wine. "The Sacrifice of the Mass is composed of two elements," says St. Augustine: "the visible appearances of the substance destroyed, and Jesus Christ, really present in the integrity of His flesh and blood."

Just as in the ancient sacrifices, one part of the victim was destroyed and the other part reserved for the use of men, so at the altar what is destroyed is the material substance of the bread, while what is retained are the accidents, the form of the bread, its fragrance, color, and taste — all the nonsubstantial qualities of the bread, which remain visible and stable. [And just as the substance of the bread literally becomes Jesus Christ, so] Jesus Christ, subsisting beneath the mystic veil of the remaining accidents, becomes *bread Himself* in accordance with the words "I am the bread of life."[14]

⤢

By an incomprehensible marvel of His power and love, He makes Himself *edible,* capable of being changed into our sub-stance, and He is truly our heavenly bread and our daily food. Not less wonderful is the fact that Christ, reduced to the state of a vic-tim, should find the means of instructing us, and of offering us, in His eucharistic life, the example of all the virtues.

In His sacramental life, Jesus Christ shows us a higher, and al-together new, degree of wisdom, a wisdom that values and relishes only what concerns the glory of God and His service, the salvation and sanctification of souls. The spirit that animates Jesus Christ in His sacramental state is a spirit detached from all our human and natural views, far removed from our ways of worldly prudence, which we deem to be far-seeing, because by them we are able so to direct our resources as to accede to honors, manage our fortune, and remove the obstacles to our gross, self-seeking ends.

The virtues Christ sets before us are solid virtues that do not consist of mere desires but are revealed efficaciously and by their fruits.

Thus, He gives us admirable examples of humility. Wholly present in each Host, He becomes, as it were, a speck of dust, re-duced to the dimensions of a grain of sand[15] in order to confound our vanity and our ambitions and the thirst that men have to put themselves forward. He does not reserve to Himself any means of protecting His dignity, I don't mean against our profanations, but against our forgetfulness, our negligence, and our surprises. He gives us a heroic example of patience. He endures abandonment, loneliness, and disdain. He does not complain of our coldness and indifference. He keeps silent, never betraying His indignation, during centuries of impiety and folly, when sacrilegious hands snatched Him out of His tabernacles and cast Him away, like some foul refuse. He teaches us charity; He begs, intercedes, and bends; He restrains the wrath of His Father by showing Him the scars of His wounds; and, to appease Him, He offers up the sacrifice that commemorates the death He underwent for us.

He teaches us poverty, and gives admirable examples of the detachment that we should have in our dealings with creatures. In His eucharistic life Jesus Christ does not hold onto any created object. Whether He is enshrined in a monstrance of precious stones, enclosed in a rich luminary, or placed in a wooden tabernacle or on bare boards, Jesus Christ offers no resistance, and never complains. He is indifferent to all our refinements and splendors: if He accepts our adornments and the homage of our precious objects, it is out of graciousness, and for the sake of acquiescing in the outpourings of our piety. In this way He teaches us to despise all refinements and splendors; to remain indifferent to the goods of the earth, and to accept with the same equanimity the fame of honors or obscurity, abundance or scarcity.

Finally, He gives us examples of chastity. In the Eucharist Jesus Christ is really and substantially present, but He subsists in the sacramental state, not under His own appearance, but under the appearances of bread and wine. In this respect, and inasmuch as He dwells beneath invisible veils, His senses are incapable of receiving impressions. Our sweet odors do not flatter Him, our symphonies do not entrance Him, and our tangible objects do not enamor Him. He shows us thereby what purity should govern our affections. He wants us, like Himself, to be of flesh, without that flesh being subject to any rebellion; to open our eyes, but without bringing them to rest upon any creature merely out of pleasure and attraction; to breathe in sweet odors, but without ever feeling drawn to any but those of divine love.

What else can we say? Reigning in the highest heavens, Jesus Christ has found how to annihilate Himself each day, and deliver Himself into the hands of His minister as a servant and captive. Possessing an immortal life, Jesus Christ has found how to undergo the onset of death and decomposition; and the new life that He receives in the sacrament, He loses each time the Hosts deteriorate and decompose. Subsisting on our altars for nineteen centuries, He descends upon them every day and every moment, at some point or another on the earth, renews the oblation of His Passion and death.

If we paid heed to these teachings, what an admirable life we would lead! Ignorant, illiterate people, with their eyes fixed on this frail Host and their ears attentive to that inner voice which rings out into the depths of the soul, have performed heroic deeds; for their own sanctification and that of others, they have derived the most penetrating insights and acquired more treasures and knowledge than if they had read all the writings of the Doctors and the saints.

We ourselves, with the aid of the same examples, would become paragons of grace. Truly, our lives are filled with marvels, but will not these marvels one day bring our condemnation? Jesus Christ, on the altar, invites us to offer ourselves as living, holy victims, pleasing to God.[16] He teaches us thereby to humble ourselves in the face of praise, to endure persecution as if we were impassible, and to persevere unshaken in our commitments.

$$\sim$$

At the altar, as on the Cross, there is the same priest and the same victim; there is also the same immolation.

The Mass re-presents the manner of Christ's sacrifice

"At the altar," says St. John Chrysostom, "there is a sword." And it is we priests who carry that sword, not in our hands, but on our lips. In point of fact, the immolation does not take place physically, but *mystically* and by representation. Yet this representation is so vivid and efficacious, that it is equivalent to the reality itself.

According to St. Thomas, Suarez, and the great theologians, it is not the Offertory, nor the Communion, but the Consecration that constitutes the essence of the Sacrifice.

Indeed, as Monsignor Rosset remarks, Christ did not undergo some ordinary death. He was not carried off by illness, His bones were not torn apart, nor did He meet His end by drowning; but He gave His life on the Cross by the shedding and loss of His blood. For this reason the Mass, instituted as the memorial of His Sacrifice, must represent His death in the manner in which it was consummated. This can be so only if the body of Christ, by virtue of the sacramental words, is offered on the altar separately from His blood, and His blood in the chalice offered separately from his sacred body.

Hence, if the bread alone were consecrated there would indeed be a representation of the death of Christ but not of His death such as He suffered it. If the wine alone were consecrated, the fact that Christ hung on the Cross deprived of the totality of His blood would not be clearly and formally expressed.

Thus, when the priest says, "*This is my body,*" the body alone is called down upon the altar, and, if the blood, soul, and divinity come at the same time, it is, as the theologians say, by *pure concomitance,* because Jesus Christ, risen from the dead, cannot now die.[17] If Jesus Christ were not in a supernatural and glorious state, the body would be separated from the blood, through the power of the sacramental words. When the priest says, "*This is my blood,*" the blood alone is called down upon the altar, and, if it were not indissolubly and eternally united to the body, it would stream down as formerly, on the Cross.

The words, "*This is my body, this is my blood*" are the sword that probes deep into the very division of soul and spirit. If separation does not actually occur, the reason is not because the sword lacks power, but because it is paralyzed by the state of impassibility with which the glorious body of the Savior is endowed.

Monsignor Rosset further remarks that the perfect accomplishment of the sacrifice in no way requires the actual immolation of the victim. It is sufficient that the sacrificial act should be, of its nature, destructive of the thing offered. The Church places among the martyrs St. John the Evangelist, who was cast into boiling oil, and other saints who received wounds or underwent tortures of their nature liable to cause death, even though, owing to a miracle, their death did not take place. In the Old Law, when the sacrificing priest had dealt the victim a mortal wound, the sacrifice was perfect, and the victim was deemed immolated even if it were miraculously saved.

On the Cross and at the altar, Jesus Christ offers His Father the same death. On the Cross, He offers His present death; at the altar, His past and consummated death.

On the Cross, He offers Himself as a sacrifice of redemption; at the altar, as a sacrifice deriving from that infinite source of grace which He once poured out on Calvary — on the Cross, in the state of a suffering man; at the altar, in the state of a supernatural, mystical man. As a matter of fact, in order that the sacrifice may be performed, the visible minister must intervene; but his action is accessory, which does not in the least diminish the dignity and price of the sacrifice. This is shown by the fact that the words used by the minister are the same ones that Jesus Christ spoke at the Last Supper.

Christ's merits are distributed through the Mass

At the altar, we are not Christ in reality, but we are mystically, and we speak in His person: we say and do what Jesus Christ said and did, *hoc facite in meam commemorationem*.[18] We have the same power; for, as St. Gregory the Great says, what faithful Christian would doubt that, "at the moment of immolation and at the word of the priest, the heavens truly open, and the choirs of angels accompany Jesus Christ in this mystery"?[19] At this moment the eternal Father fixes His eyes on the offering. He does not in the least consider the person celebrating, but sees only His divine Son. He accepts His offering as supremely propitious and fitting, even if it be offered by the most unworthy and most sullied hands.

❦

The Sacrifice of the Mass is supremely propitiatory for the living and for the dead. It is fully sufficient to obtain for us an abundance of grace from above and to satisfy all our needs. Infinite in value and dignity, it is nevertheless limited in its effects and application, for the reason that, those whom the sacrifice profits — namely, the priest, the faithful, and the Church, however holy she may be — have only a finite merit and dignity. They are capable of gaining new graces, of attaining a higher degree of perfection, and, in spite of their efforts, it will never be possible for them to exhaust all the fruits deriving from such an oblation. The sacrifice of the Mass is equivalent to that of the Cross; but the sacrifice of the Cross, infinite as it is in value, is unable to bestow an indefinite multitude of merits and satisfactions, to the point where no more can be added.

When He instituted His sacrifice, Jesus Christ fixed the sum and measure of grace that would accrue to those for whom it was applied. Hence it follows that several Masses are more profitable than one only, and that a Mass said especially for the intention of this or that departed soul is more beneficial to him, and contributes more efficaciously to his deliverance, than a Mass celebrated for all Christians in general.

The sacrifice is offered in honor of the martyrs and saints who are in heaven. We ask God that they may be more and more glorified by the faithful of the Church Militant, and that the intercession and homage we render them may obtain for them an increase in accidental joy.

The sacrifice benefits the living, in order to obtain for them the grace of God, and repentance and remission of the punishments due to their sins.

Of all intercessory acts, sacrifice is the most propitiatory for the dead. Prayer, almsgiving, and works of charity contribute to the deliverance or relief of the dead only by reason of the fervor and disposition of the person offering them. They are works that, in theological language, obtain benefit *ex opere operantis*,[20] but the sacrifice of the Mass is independent of the merits or demerits of the person who offers it. It is efficacious directly, and by the mere virtue of its institution, *ex opere operato*. It is a remedy the more precious because, with regard to the souls in purgatory, the Church possesses no other that has an infallible and certain effect.

The Church cannot make the faithful departed share in her sacraments, for a sacrament is an external sign, perceptible to the senses, that sanctifies only through the intermediary of the body. Consequently, separated souls, deprived of their senses and their earthly wrapping, are no longer capable of receiving its fruits.

The Sacrifice of the Mass is thus the sole means that the Church possesses of applying to the dead the merits of the Passion and blood of Jesus Christ in all their efficacy. This is the teaching of the Church and the Council of Trent: speaking of the effects of the sacrifice, they do not distinguish between the living and the dead — which is tantamount to saying that the same power that the sacrifice possesses of drawing God's mercy upon those living on earth serves also to soften the rigors of justice with regard to the dead.

The altar can still be seen in Rome where Gregory the Great said Mass, and where Jesus Christ appeared to inform him that every time he celebrated, he obtained the deliverance of one soul from purgatory.

St. Augustine, in book 12, chapter 22 of *The City of God*, speaking of those who have departed this life, divides them into two categories: the *moderately good* and the *moderately bad*. The *moderately good* are those whose lives have been sullied only by venial faults and slight imperfections. Sacrifice easily redeems these from their punishment and leads to their swift deliverance. The *moderately bad* are those who have lived constantly in sin, whose lives were sullied by iniquity, but who nevertheless before death obtained pardon for their mortal sins. Sacrifice seldom shortens their punishment to any significant extent or secures their prompt deliverance: nonetheless, it is of great benefit to them, because it mitigates the intensity of their flames and diminishes the severity of their torments.

It is not uncommon for departed souls to appear to the living: time and again, God has permitted these manifestations, either to awaken the living from their omissions and torpor, or in order that abandoned souls might obtain a swifter relief.

The most trustworthy of these visions are that of Louis the Debonair, emperor and king, the son of Charlemagne, who, after thirty-three years of torments, appeared to his son, Louis I; that of Pope Benedict VII, who occupied the Chair of St. Peter for twelve years and, quite a long time after his death, appeared to the bishop of Lapree, who had been his friend; and that of a sister of St.

Thomas Aquinas, whom the Doctor had directed, and who appeared to him to tell him of her departure from this world and her entry into the place of atonement. All these souls, who returned for a moment to earth by an exceptional permission of God, had no intention of satisfying the curiosity of the persons to whom they appeared by disclosing to them the secrets of the next life; but urged them to fast, weep, and pray, and asked for Masses to be offered for their intentions, in order to obtain relief for them and hasten their deliverance.

The Sacrifice of the Mass is profitable, not only for the soul, but also for the body — "*ut sit ad salutem animae et corporis.*"

The Sacrifice of the Mass, says Tertullian, contributes pre-eminently to the peace of the Church. It obtains good and wise governments for peoples. It is beneficial to offer it for soldiers, for those who sail upon the sea, for the sick, and, in general, for all those who are beset by sorrow and anguish or are bereft of the goods and advantages of this life. The Sacrifice of the Mass, says St. John Chrysostom, should be offered for harvests, and for the preservation of the fruits of the earth.

St. Augustine, in chapter 22 of *The City of God*, relates that in his time there was a house haunted by devils, and that as soon as Mass had been said in it, the evil spirits disappeared. St. Gregory the Great, in his *Dialogues*, quotes the story of a man captured by pirates. He was taken to a distant land and thrown into a dark cell. For a long time afterward his wife and friends did not know what had happened to him and, despite their enquiries, were unable to find any trace of him. Released at length from captivity, he related that, on certain days, when he groaned in prison, his fetters broke loose from his feet and hands and fell off by themselves.

His wife and friends compared occasions and times, and ascertained that this marvel had occurred each time they had had the Holy Sacrifice celebrated for the salvation of his soul.

St. Antoninus, Archbishop of Florence, relates that two youths used to lead dissolute lives and give themselves up to licentiousness of every kind. One feast day they went into the country, ostensibly on a hunting trip.

One of these young men, out of a lingering regard for religion, had heard Mass in the morning, before his departure. In the evening, having indulged in debauchery and shameful, drunken revelry, the two young men prepared to return home. Scarcely had they begun their journey, when, all of a sudden, the sky became dark, flashes of lightning streaked the clouds, and a storm broke out with mingled thunderclaps and horrible wailing. Amidst this confusion of unleashed elements, a voice, the voice of God's justice, resounded unceasingly in the air, crying, "Strike! Strike!"

The young man who had not attended Mass was struck by a thunderbolt, which killed him instantaneously. The same voice continued to be heard, saying incessantly, "Strike! Strike!" The other young man, bewildered and terror-stricken, began to run, seeking to flee death and the vengeance of God that he felt approaching. But another voice was heard in the sky. It was that of Mercy, calling out, "Oh, no! Do not strike; for this morning he heard the words of salvation and life that are spoken at the altar: 'And the Word was made flesh and dwelt among us . . . full of grace and truth.'"

Alas, people no longer have even an inkling of the immense remedies and blessings they possess in Jesus Christ. They have no faith except in their physical strength and activity. They look upon themselves as tools and machines, and have no regard for one another except in terms of the level and rate of their salary.

Proudly and disdainfully, they say: Those who eat every day should work every day. Sunday, with its blessings, its Mass, and its futile ceremonies, is simply the great tide of industry held up in its course for twenty-four hours; the workman's wages reduced by a seventh; destitution in the workshop; bread and clothing taken away from the child and from the wife of the tradesman and the indigent.

St. Paul gives them his answer: Men of little faith, is the kingdom of God food and drink? Has He who clothes the lily of the fields, and gives the birds of the air their nourishment, ever disappointed those who serve Him at the feast of His providence?

St. John Chrysostom tells us that our Lord Jesus Christ shows Himself at the altar as on the throne of His clemency, His hands full of bounty and grace. He is surrounded by a multitude of angels, standing in an attitude of deep respect; and, through the medium of these celestial spirits, He bestows upon men all that promotes the good of soul and body. Who would dare, then, to affirm that this divine blood, shed every day upon our altars, had less power and efficacy than the sweat of man, rainfall, and dew from the sky to fructify our meadows and increase our industry? Where do we find prosperous families and strong, developed races, except among those who go up to the altar and help to ensure the abundance of those fruits, by the fervor of their invocations and the power of their cooperation?

In his treatise on Communion and sacrifice, Father Rodriguez relates that a farmer used to set aside half an hour of his time every day to attend Mass. This farmer lived very comfortably, his lands sheltered from the inclemency of the weather; his fields seemed to be the best cultivated and the most fertile. No hostile influence or poisoned germs harmed his trees and vines. Every year his barns were filled with copious fruits. His friends and neighbors were struck with admiration, unable to find an explanation for the marvelous fact of such strange perfection.

One day the farmer took one of them to the church, at the time when the Holy Sacrifice was being celebrated. "This is my talisman and my treasure," he said. "Here is the great source of spiritual and temporal blessings. Everyone is free to go in. On that altar, where Jesus Christ comes down every day, He is pleased to fulfill, for the sake of those who visit and venerate Him, the maxim which He spoke of old: 'Seek first the kingdom of God and His justice, and all else shall be given you besides.' "[21]

The Sacrifice of the Mass — if we applied its fruits to ourselves — would most certainly protect us from great calamities and serve our temporal interests more than our discoveries, industrial advances, and all the learning of our agricultural experts ever will. It would promptly destroy, by its own power, the vine-mildew, phylloxera, all those mysterious diseases that poison our vines, fruits, and even the tubercle the poor man uses to relieve his hunger. It would make us enjoy, even in this world, that compensatory abundance promised by the Gospel; a foretaste of heaven, abounding in the crown of bounteousness to come.

Solomon, speaking of the figurative and imperfect sacrifices of the Old Law, said, "Should a hostile sky hold back its dew and rain, we shall come to this holy Temple, Lord, to offer You our wishes, and You shall cause streams of milk and honey to run through our fields. Should sickness strike us, or wars decimate us, we shall still come to this holy Temple, and You shall stop these scourges that destroy the human race."

Ah, what would become of the world, saddened by so many misfortunes and scandals, if, at a time when hostile politicians conspire against Jesus Christ, or when a foul, licentious press by its blasphemies unceasingly calls down the wrath and malediction of

God upon mankind — if at such a time as this the voice of Jesus Christ, as He descended each day upon the altar, did not ascend toward His Father, to present to Him petitions appealing for mercy rather than justice!

And when I think that this Sacrifice is performed every minute of the day, and that the sun in its orbit around the world does not cease for a moment, at some point or other of the earth, to cast its rays upon the spotless Host, I feel my heart swell and my hopes grow, and I can no longer comprehend our fears, our uncertainties, and our rebelliousness.

Daniel, announcing the precursory signs of God's justice and the fall of kingdoms, and pointing out the great catastrophes that will wipe out from the face of the earth Jerusalem, and the great cities that were drunk, like that deicide town, with the wine of adultery and fornication, tells us, "You will recognize that the great calamities are near, *when you see the abomination of desolation in the holy place, and when the perpetual sacrifice shall have ceased.*" At the time of the final desolation, there will be a time when the un-bloody Sacrifice will no longer be celebrated over the whole sur-face of the earth. There will then be no mediator between the justice of God and man. The crimes and blasphemies will no lon-ger have any counterbalance. That will be the moment when the just Judge will appear in His glory, and the heavens will be folded up like a tent that has no more travelers to shelter.

☞

We have not yet reached that supreme period. To be con-vinced of this we need only consider the treasures of virtuous liv-ing, the marvels of dedication and heroism, which unceasingly reveal the picture of a watchful God who immolates Himself night and day.

We must surrender ourselves to Jesus on the altar

Ah, how many priests, filled with divine fervor as they leave the altar, have torn themselves away from the arms of a tearful family and hastened into distant lands, to replace one of their brethren who had been devoured by animals or by horrific cannibals!

How many virgins, voluntary captives, like St. Teresa, behind the dark gates of a cloister, have momentarily felt their hearts troubled by bitter desolations; have caught themselves, unawares, casting a regretful look upon the world and its pleasures, which they had left behind! Fortunately, the sanctuary was a few steps away from the cell in which they were subjected to those violent combats, and the thought of the divine Hermit, for nineteen centuries a prisoner of love, at once rekindled the fire of their devotion. They exclaimed, "Rather death than abandon Him!"

How many men, in a position to defend themselves, have kept silent in the face of an insult, and, instead of drawing the sword, have humbly turned the other cheek! Had these men, these "knights of ignominy," not one drop of noble blood in their veins? Were they cowards? Ah, the memory of their God, abandoned and annihilated on the altar, swallowing without complaint every ingratitude and outrage, made them trample underfoot the opinion and false judgments of men, and they exclaimed: *Quis ut Deus?* Who is like God?

This saying, *Quis ut Deus?* was the war-cry uttered in heaven at the very beginning of time. Lucifer, the most dazzling and radiant archangel, and today the basest and most horrible of devils, raised the standard of the first revolt. Among the spirits whose leader he was, he sought to hold a *plebiscite* against God, aspiring to raise himself above the clouds of heaven, and become like to the Most High. There was then a great battle, in which truth and justice triumphed.[22] The archangel Michael drew attention to the excellence and dignity of the Most High God. He reminded the good angels of the beneficence of Him who had created them, the gifts and prerogatives with which He had endowed their nature, and he kept them in fidelity and submission by saying to them, "*Quis ut Deus?* Who is like God?"

We cannot, like the archangel Michael, make the Eternal One visible on His throne; but we have in our midst the Lamb, dead and immolated from the very beginning.[23] We have the spectacle of that incomprehensible, infinite love which, in order to draw us to Him with greater gentleness and intensity, reduces itself each day to the tiny dimensions of a host, one inch in diameter.

Modern society today, in the face of heaven and earth, has proclaimed the most audacious boast ever conceived by human pride; it declares that it will exclude God from laws and institutions, creating a social order and felicity completely independent of Him; and, confronted with this satanic design, it is our duty to protest loudly, saying, with the archangel, *Quis ut Deus?*

The time has come to conclude and sum up.

The Church teaches that Jesus Christ truly dwells upon our altars, that the substance of the bread and wine is changed into the substance of His adorable flesh and blood, and that in this state He immolates Himself to His Father, for the sins of the world. However, in order that the sublime mystery of our altars may produce an effect [upon our lives], the faithful must be rightly disposed. It cannot purify a soul that is attached to its disorderly ways, nor restore to goodness a heart obdurate in evil. The Real Presence and sacrifice detach man from the life of the senses, and make him live a spiritual life; at the same time they show us the Supreme Benefactor, ever living in this valley of misery to soften our bitterness, appease our sufferings, dry up our tears, erase our injustices, and heal our wounds. Ah, if we bring forth our raptures in harmonious unison, if we surround our worship with all the magnificence

We must surrender ourselves to Jesus on the altar

of the arts, if we seek from nature the most precious things that she has to embellish our altars, and if our basilicas have shown the world new marvels and splendors, who can be surprised? The King of heaven and earth, our Savior and our God, dwells among us in person.

You, then, feeble and faint-hearted souls, who feel your faith faltering and weakening, shaken by the effrontery and arrogant clamor of the wicked, turn your eyes for a moment upon the Christian world, where, in spite of ingenious, mendacious conspiracies, Jesus Christ continues to be loved and adored. See those crowds who fill our churches at the times of the major solemnities, kneeling humbly and invoking Jesus Christ with the unshakable conviction that their prayer will reach heaven. See the dying, as they press His blessed picture to their lips so as to fortify themselves against the anguish and the fears of their final agony. See those sorrowful countenances, bowing down at the steps of His lonely altars and straightening up again, beaming with an indescribable joy. See those sinners, stricken with remorse, beating their breasts and departing, trusting that they have regained pardon. Such is the infallible voice of mankind; the striking testimony of popular faith; the profound cry of public conscience, which can be diminished for a day but which all the threats of the mighty and the artifices of atheistic science will never succeed in stifling.

Napoleon, on the rock of his exile, said to one of his comrades in arms, "I understand men, and I tell you that Jesus Christ was not a man." He openly confessed the presence of Jesus Christ in His sacramental life, himself asking to receive the last Viaticum of the dying; and when, by this noble act, he had solemnly professed the faith of his childhood, he added to the same comrade in arms, "I am happy, general, to have fulfilled my duty, and I wish you the same fortune when you die."

The End of the Present World

Let us be victims with Jesus Christ. Since He sacrifices Himself on the altar, let us give Him in return the fullness of our being. By giving Him our minds, we shall enlighten them with His understanding; by giving Him our hearts, we shall cure them of their weakness and inconstancy; by giving Him our whole being, we shall ensure our glory and indefectibility.[24]

◌

Notes

1   From Suarez, *Quaestio* LXXXIII.

2   Heb. 5:4.

3   Heb. 5:1.

4   St. Augustine, *City of God*.

5   Ps. 40:7; 51:18.

6   Council of Trent.

7   At the altar, the priest who offers is Jesus Christ. It does not follow that the officiating priests are merely mechanical, inferior agents; they offer authentically, by themselves, not as instruments, but as *instrumental causes*.

8   Thomas à Kempis, *Imitation of Christ*.

9   The French Revolution of 1789.

10 The French Revolution replaced the Gregorian calendar with the *decadi* calendar to reinforce the separation of the state from the Church.

11 Rev. 12:4.

12 It should be noted that consumption of the victim is not absolutely essential to the reality and perfection of the sacrifice. Thus, Communion is a complementary and integral part of the sacrifice of the altar, but not its essence. In the Old Testament, the holocaust was a true sacrifice and, indeed, the most perfect. It was of its essence that man did *not* feed on it.

13 John 6:52.

[14] John 6:51: "I myself am the living bread."

[15] When we say that Christ is reduced to the dimensions of a grain of sand, or a Host one inch in diameter, we must not misunderstand these expressions. We are speaking metaphorically, in respect to ourselves, and relatively, in respect to what is perceived by our senses. In actual fact, Jesus Christ is present in His entirety, in each particle of the Host visible to the eye or tangible to the senses. There is absolutely nothing changed with regard to the intrinsic quantity and proportions of His body.

[16] Cf. Rom. 12:1.

[17] Rom. 6:9.

[18] Luke 22:19; 1 Cor. 11:24: "Do this in remembrance of me."

[19] St. Gregory the Great, *Dialogues*.

[20] A sacrament or any religious rite is said to work *ex opere operantis* when its efficacy is not certain or absolute but depends, mainly or partly, upon the merits and the degree of holiness of the person who performs it. A liturgical rite or a sacrament is said to work *ex opere operato* when its efficacy is certain and absolute, independent of the minister who confers it or of the subject who receives it, and acts directly, by virtue of its institution. Hence, the Sacrifice of the Mass, and all the sacraments of the New Law, work *ex opere operato*. The sacrifices and sacraments of the Old Law, as well as the sacramentals used by the Church, such as prayers, Signs of the Cross, and sprinkling with holy water, have an effect only *ex opere operantis*.

[21] Cf. Matt. 6:33.

[22] Cf. Rev. 12:7.

[23] Cf. Rev. 13:8.

[24] In a picturesque town in Switzerland, surrounded by green, wooded mountains, irrigated by an abundance of clear water, the author of this conference was walking one day in the company of a Protestant minister. The latter acknowledged that he accepted the Real Presence, and could not imagine how Calvin could have denied it; but he refused to accept the truth of the Sacrifice of the Mass, on the grounds that, as the sacrifice of the Cross was, of its nature, superabundant and infinite, all other sacrifices became, by this very fact, useless and superfluous. The person to whom he addressed this opinion asked his interlocutor to consider the waterfalls that flowed down from the

rocks, and the limpid streams that gushed from the hills or wound in and out through the meadow. "You see those springs," he remarked to the minister. "They, too, are perfect and plentiful. Will you, then, assert that it was useless to build aqueducts, and provide taps, in order to bring the water inside the town?" The minister, who was a man of great learning and good faith, perceived the allusion and said immediately, "I understand." The Mass is, in fact, an application, not an addition to the Sacrifice of the Cross; it is the means and the channel whereby the infinite power of the sacrifice of Calvary, accomplished once only, flows down upon the Church and the faithful.

The Mystery of Suffering in Its Relationship with the Future Life

Homo natus de muliere,
brevi vivens tempore, repletus multis miseriis.

☞

Man, born of woman,
is short-lived and full of trouble.

Job 14:1

There is a law that is inevitable, mysterious, universal, and inexplicable to science.

It is the law of suffering.

This law, promulgated on the day when sin entered the world, is set out in three sentences that, in their sad universality, embrace the evils and all the misfortunes that afflict the human race: "By the sweat of your brow shall you earn your bread," the man was told. "In pain shall you bring forth children," the woman was told. In the dust, you will feel the sickness and germs of this decomposition that will be consummated in the tomb.

From the day when this threefold sentence was thundered forth, pain became a great law of mankind. Like an immense river, it has carried its bitter waters through the course of the ages for two thousand years. All mortal beings — to a greater or lesser degree, indeed, but all, without exception — have drunk deep therein.

All that has life, the apostle Paul says, is condemned to weep and groan: "Yes, we know that all creation groans and is in agony even until now."[1] The disinherited race of Adam, like a man gravely ill, turns over and over on its bed of grief and anguish. Notwithstanding its desperate efforts, and despite its industry and the extent of its conquests, it has not ceased for a moment to suffer; up until now it has been unable to overcome poverty, illness, and death.

The End of the Present World

Before Christ, mankind bore the appearance of a tortured *criminal*, smitten, says Isaiah, from head to foot, and without a single part of his body left sound. To free it from the inexorable law that had weighed it down since its fall, nothing less was necessary than a doctor from heaven. The sick man could be cured only by the application of a higher, divine remedy.

Without doubt, Jesus Christ could have abolished pain at a single stroke, and, by virtue of the infinite grace of the Redemption, restored man to the state of complete, unmixed bliss that he enjoyed in the paradise of innocence. He did not so wish. He judged that, for some, suffering would be a source of merit, a gain, a source of glory, and a means of renewal and triumph; that, for the greater number, it would be a necessary expiation. He therefore maintained suffering, but purified, ennobled, and transfigured it by taking it upon Himself. He became the man of sorrows, *virum dolorum*,[2] in the strict and absolute sense of these words.

Jesus Christ could have appeared among us, radiant with joy and encompassed by divine splendor, amidst the glitter and pomp of His sovereign majesty. He deemed it more worthy of His glory and more profitable to the salvation of men, to show Himself to them girt with a diadem of thorns, clothed in purple and stained with blood, His face bruised, the gaping grimace of death on His lips, bearing the bloody unction of the nails imprinted on His hands and feet.

In uniting Himself closely with suffering, Jesus Christ assuredly did not smooth all its severity and all its pangs; but He removed part of its bitterness, corrected and destroyed its poison. He made the chalice of His Blood fruitful. Like the brazen serpent set up by Moses in the desert, He implanted Himself in the center of the world as an inexhaustible instrument of mercy, life, and health. Owing to this transformation, His divine wounds, like fountains ever gushing, remain eternally open to all straying and fallen souls who are eager to escape from their coarse, sensual aspirations, wanting to immerse themselves anew in the joys of sacrifice and the honor of purity.

Who would not admire here the depth of the counsels of infinite Wisdom! Man had become lost in the paradise of bliss; he will rise again amidst the sorrows of Calvary. He had refused to go to God by the way of happiness; Jesus Christ will open a better and surer way for him — that of the Cross. "Heaven and earth were separated; the Cross has brought them together." In the Cross is salvation; in the Cross is strength and joy of mind; in it is to be found the complement of virtue and the profusion of all holiness.[3]

The cross, before Jesus Christ let Himself be nailed to it, was a mark of infamy, an instrument of malediction and disgrace; but when, resigned and inflamed with love, He had lain down upon that tree of woe like the spouse upon his marriage bed, the cross was washed of the ignominy with which it had been sullied; it became the starting-point of glorious renovations, the emblem of royalty and greatness, the prize of genius and gallantry, the fruitful stimulus of heroic battles, the source of the most indescribable joys and of the surest and truest consolations.

"O sweet Cross," exclaimed St. Andrew, "adorned with the limbs of the Lord, long desired Cross, tenderly loved, sought after unceasingly, take me in your arms back to my divine Master, so that He who, through you, has redeemed me may, through you, vouchsafe to receive me."[4]

So it is that the rugged splendors of Calvary infinitely surpass all the delights and raptures of Tabor, and that, following their leader Stephen, countless generations of martyrs and saints have relished more sweetness in the hail of stones that were cast at them than they would have tasted in showers of perfume and roses.

Such is the exalted, magnificent doctrine we shall treat in this last conference, enlarging on it and harmonizing it.

Let the philosopher, guided only by natural reason, complain in his trials; let him take his sufferings as an excuse for blaspheming heaven and Providence, or, wrapping himself in the mantle of stoic disdain, let him exclaim, "Suffering, I spurn you, and you are but a useless word."

We Christians, however, guided by a higher light, raise our eyes toward the celestial future, of which the tribulations of this life are the preparation and pledge. Has not our Master told us that suffering is the antechamber through which we must pass in order to enter the kingdom of glory?[5] Let us accept it, as proof of the tender beneficence of this God, who makes us share in His sorrows and agony only to render us worthy of the eternal crown He is preparing for us.

In order to cover the general lines of our subject, let us study suffering from the three aspects of nature, grace, and glory.

From the point of view of nature, suffering is a principle of dignity and moral strength for man. From the point of view of grace, it is the principle of our incorporation into the divine life of Jesus Christ. From the point of view of glory, it is a principle and source of hope.

Before speaking of the advantages of pain and the marvelous benefits it brings to the soul, it is appropriate to recall its meaning in philosophy.

St. Thomas defines pain as evil that repels[6] — that is, the obstacle which obstructs the exercise of the powers of the soul, or the free development of corporeal and sensitive life. Pain is an impression that affects the soul and causes it repugnance, either when the mind cannot attain the truth that is its object, or when the will is frustrated in the good it pursues. Whether pain has its seat in the mind or in the body, it is an impression abhorrent to the creature who feels it; to an extent, it deforms him and causes a deterioration and a kind of diminution in him.

In the mind, an evil or obstacle is called sadness, regret, or anguish; in the body, it is called debility, pain, or sickness. Whatever may be the nature or the countless forms pain may assume, it is, in essence, a vexation, a conflict, a lack of balance and harmony, in the intellectual faculties or in the sensory organs of the body. In short, pain is an impediment that runs counter to the normal course of life, just as joy is a mode of consonance that promotes its full expansion.

The pagan philosophers, aided solely by the light of reason, had a certain understanding of the advantages and rewards of suffering.

They regarded it as the best of schools, where man could train himself in the laborious and difficult study of himself, and prepare himself to fulfill, one day, the great tasks of human life.

"Woe to the child of fortune," they would say, "reared amidst the lure of luxury and softness, the man upon whom the world has constantly smiled, and who has never been thwarted or hindered in his desires." If, among men intoxicated and corrupted by prosperity, there is a lingering trace of tenderness, if there is human compassion in them, and if the heart of a man still beats in their breast, it will be merely for the sake of their selfishness and the satisfaction of their disordered passions. "Woe to the peoples, when such men succeed in taking hold of the scepter of public power. Like Tiberius and Nero, they will be the scourges of the human race. The whole earth will come before their eyes like a prey reserved for the satisfaction of their colossal pride and their most extravagant and brutish appetites."

Those sages further added:

What mortal has ever looked at suffering, with its severe and somber countenance, or squared up to it, without soon blessing it as a sweet gift from heaven? Just as the hardest metals soften and melt under the effect of fire, so it is that suffering transforms noble souls. It arouses in them a virtue that moves, restores, supernaturalizes, and soothes them.

Take, for instance, the poor man who has long suffered indigence and unhappiness. If he attains wealth, he will use it with wisdom and moderation. He has learned through hard experience how much it costs to be poor, to eat a seldom-found loaf of bread, and to live on earth wandering, sick, and ignored.

Look at the statesman, the mighty and respected prince. If, before being raised to the throne, he has endured the anguish and bitterness of exile, if he has drunk to the full the cup of ingratitude and opprobrious conduct, he will not let himself be dazzled as much as another man by the grandeur and glitter of his sovereignty. He will willingly cast a respectful and compassionate eye upon an obscure subject fallen into disgrace. He knows that nobility of thought and loftiness of soul can lie hidden under rags no less than under the dignity of kingship; he calls to mind that he, too, has long lived in banishment, a fugitive unknown and defamed.

Or look at the priest: when, by the melancholy of his eyes, the premature deterioration of his features, and the smile of resignation on his lips, people conclude that suffering has often visited his soul, he is held in greater respect and affection. Those who are forsaken will lean their grief-stricken souls more trustingly upon his, in the belief that remedy and consolation are bound to flow from his soul in a more paternal and merciful manner.

Lastly, is this man, tried by long and bloody misfortunes, an obscure, forsaken creature? Far from despising him, we see in his pain a glorious purification of his life. A secret feeling tells us that such a man is a privileged being, carefully prepared by the divine hand for a destiny more glorious than that of time. In him we admire a nobility more splendid than that of blood, the nobility of suffering unflinchingly borne.

I do not know whether everyone thinks so, but the soul that has suffered long and greatly seems less attached to the earth. His changed and chastened disposition makes him seem more angelic than human. This man and that woman have lived amid the joys of life, without ever having felt or tasted them. Does not such a state imprint an immortal sublimity upon them? Does not an inner voice tell us that these souls possess a closer and deeper vision of the mysteries of heaven; that their heart is a sanctuary which sends forth a more expansive fragrance of faith, hope, and love?

In the East, there are certain aromatic woods that are crushed and mashed so as to make the fragrant liquor, mingled with their sap, spring out. In the same way, divine goodness tramples and crushes man in the winepress of affliction, in order to chastise in him a flesh that has served as an abode for early disorders, to set him free from all dregs of corruption, and so that he may become the mysterious vessel from which will flow the inexhaustible source of all virtue.

The End of the Present World

One thing is certain: there has never been, and never will be, moral sublimity, heroic holiness, or virtue worthy of the name that does not have its principle or draw its growth and strength in suffering freely accepted or dauntlessly undergone.

How is it that our will is often wavering and undecided, that our life is strewn with such strange fluctuations and such unhappy fickleness, that we are dejected by insignificant things, that an inconsiderate word said to us, or a change in the serenity of the sky, is enough to make us go from the height of joy to the depths of gloom? The cause of these fluctuations and changes is simply the repugnance and instinctive horror we feel toward suffering.

By the assiduous care we take to refuse the slightest hardship and the least injury, and to keep away from us anything that seems even in the smallest degree demanding, we create for ourselves a state of abject bondage. Our heart falls under the sway of as many tyrants as there are impressions, each of which in turn grips us in its influence. No virtue can subsist in such fickle souls, no high position is compatible with a character that drifts along with every current and turn of fortune.

Thus, the man in this state turns aside from his stern duties and becomes a slave to the most futile fantasies. Forgetting that human life is a reality and not fiction, he seeks diversion in frivolous amusements, squanders his best years in pleasures and idleness and boredom, and consumes fruitlessly the talent that God had entrusted to him. In this enfeebling frame of mind, a man need only come before him with threatening words and the power to interfere with his repose, interests, or pleasures, and that man will at once be his master, will have full power to subject him either to a degrading bondage or to unspeakable tortures.

How far removed from the inexhaustible pettiness of these flabby, effeminate souls is the firm, high-minded attitude of him who, by dint of doing battle with suffering, has become, as it were, insensitive to its wounds and blows! How fine it is to see him serene and majestic amidst storms and the agitation of passions, fulfilling the words of the wise man: "Whatsoever shall befall the just man, it shall not make him sad."[7]

Calmly he hears the noise of revolutions, and sees republics and dynasties pass; it is as if the scene of men's vain and conflicting interests lay in the nether regions beneath his feet. No disturbance on this earth moves him, because he has learned to see events in the infinite wisdom that governs all things by its providence, and which permits evil only in order to draw good from it by a striking manifestation. He carries within himself a kind of sanctuary of peace and happiness. Mankind and the elements combined are powerless to offend or harm him. Is he sent into exile? He will reply with a great bishop: For me, the whole earth is my native land and my exile. Is he stripped of his goods? He has learned how to possess them without permitting them to enthrall his heart. Is he put to death? Death, for him, is the transfiguration to a better life, emancipation from his sufferings.

Such was the serenity and heroic constancy of St. John Chrysostom, banished by Eudoxia, Empress of Constantinople:

When I was fleeing the town, I did not feel my misfortune at all, and I was interiorly inundated with the most indescribable consolations. If the Empress sends me into exile — I said to myself — I shall consider that the earth and all that it contains is the Lord's. If she has me thrown into the sea, I shall remember Jonah. If she orders me to be stoned, I shall be the companion of St. Stephen. If she has me beheaded, I shall have the glory of John the Baptist. If she strips me of what I possess, I shall reflect that I came forth naked from the bowels of the earth, and must return to it naked and stripped of everything.

Count de Maistre relates the story of a girl who was the wonder of the city of St. Petersburg. Suffering had transfigured her, and had made the light of supernatural, anticipated glory shine out in her bearing and features. She was consumed by a cancer that was eating away her head. Her nose and eyes had disappeared already. The disease was moving across her virginal brow like a fire that consumes a palace. The whole city was amazed at the sweetness of her voice and her angelic resignation, and hastened to wonder at the delightful spectacle. When someone expressed compassion for the sufferings of the girl, she replied, "I do not suffer as much as you think, for God grants me the grace of often thinking of Him."

One day, to people who asked her what prayers she would offer to God when she was in heaven, she replied, "I shall ask Him to grant you the grace to love Him as I love Him myself."

The pagans had already perceived this reflection and this halo of beauty and greatness that suffering leaves on the creature's brow.

One day, the prince of their philosophers set himself this daunting problem: if the Divinity ever deigned to descend upon earth, under what image would it be fitting for Him to appear? Plato walked about for a long time, silent and meditative, passing over, one by one, all the figures of human history in review. The most dazzling countenances, those of potentates, did not seem pure enough to him.

Finally, he imagined a man who was master of his affections, whose least thoughts were irreproachable; he was pleased to picture him as being a stranger to all strife, responding to the cruelest treatment with the gentleness of goodness, calm and serene amidst the outburst of insults and fury of a riotous multitude, radiant even on the infamous gibbet, where the incomprehensibility of virtue would have been mounted.

Plato considered that, if mankind ever succeeded in producing such a figure, it would have achieved its highest endeavor, and that the earth would have no finer spectacle for which to envy heaven; and, with the enthusiasm and solemnity of a wise man affirming one of those great truths which the human ear has never heard, Plato exclaimed, "If the Divinity were ever to deign to become visible to men, there would be only one image worthy of It: that of the just man suffering."

≈

Has Jesus Christ made complete and absolute satisfaction for our sins? Did He take upon Himself, not only the eternal punishment, but also the temporal punishment due to them?

St. Thomas replies in the affirmative, and gives as evidence the constant practice of the Church, which does not impose any penance upon the faithful reborn by Baptism, and the universal tradition that, once man has been enveloped in the image of Jesus Christ by the water of Baptism, he dies entirely to his former vices, has no further punishment or atonement to undergo on this earth, and, if he died after being regenerated by the sacrament, would be admitted immediately to the vision of God, without passing through the flames of purgatory.

But, for the unfortunate transgressors of baptismal innocence, guilty of serious faults after the supreme grace of the first sacrament, redemption is not transmitted in this privileged form and in this full and superabundant measure. After Baptism, when divine mercy descends upon us, it is always accompanied by a measure of justice. We are still assured of the infinite merits and fruit of

Christ's sufferings, but on condition that we obtain them by personal cooperation and by energetic and violent efforts.

In a word, penance, as Tertullian calls it, is a *laborious baptism*. In this sacrament, destined to regenerate the soul that is dead a second time owing to sin, the blood and tears of Jesus Christ are no longer shed in order to spare our own, but instead to render them fruitful and proportionate to the scanty virtue of our amends, and to the immensity of the debts incurred by our crimes.

It follows that there are only two paths leading to eternal life: innocence and penance.

Penance is a law of *proportion*. St. Paul tersely sets out the principle that determines its intensity and degree in these words: "Just as formerly you enslaved your bodies to impurity and licentiousness for their degradation, make them now the servants of justice for their sanctification."[8] Reparation is sufficient insofar as it equals the disorder contained in the fault. The state of the sinful man in his relations with creatures is not that of the man who has never rendered himself guilty of any offense. The person who has been unfortunate enough to let himself be misled by the voice of the tempter and, adhering to the gross attractions of creatures, has preferred their deceptive and limited beauty to the beauty of the Creator — such a person is bound, at the cost of the most indescribable, heart-rending efforts, to tear himself away from the occasions of sin that have led him astray, and from the people who have charmed and enticed him. Making his way back through the slimy waters of the torrent that dragged him along, he must rigorously punish the heart, imagination, or senses that had rebelled against reason and the law of God, just as he would punish an intractable servant or some rebellious slaves.

The fundamental principle of penance consists in the fact that, for one who has fallen a second time, there is only one means of reintegration: the courageous and voluntary acceptance of a measure of pain equal to the measure of pleasure and sweetness relished amidst iniquity and crime. Hence it follows, in accordance with the profound observation of St. Ignatius Loyola, that penance by no means consists in the renunciation of all excess, or in the reduction of that which is useless and superfluous. To eliminate unnecessary things is the virtue of *temperance*, not the virtue of penance. Penance takes place only when man cuts out what is agreeable, and deprives himself of part of what is useful or necessary.[9]

Nonetheless, the mystery is still not resolved. There are on earth souls exempt from all trace of sin and imperfection. Leaving aside the Most Holy Virgin, conceived without sin, and St. John the Baptist, sanctified in the womb of his mother, a multitude of other saints have led quite celestial lives here on earth, closely united to God, without any coarse desire or any trace of the senses ever darkening the beauty and radiant splendor of their souls. Yet they have assumed a larger share of this immense legacy of pain bequeathed to our sorrowful humanity.

Hence, suffering has a higher and more universal cause than expiation. This cause is the consequence of one of the most profound and incomprehensible mysteries of our Faith, in which the whole economy of Christianity is summed up and on which we seldom ponder: the mystery of the incorporation of our life in the divine life of Jesus Christ.

It can be said that, in a certain sense, Jesus Christ in heaven is not complete. On the throne where, since His glorious Ascension, He has reigned, seated at the right hand of His Father, there is still not the *totality*, but a mere *beginning of Jesus Christ*. "Jesus Christ is the same *yesterday, today, and forever*."[10] Jesus Christ and the universality of the faithful form but one body and one spirit.[11] This Mystical Body of Christ, which is the same as the Church, is built up gradually; it expands and grows by incorporating the elect, whose minds are open to the light of the faith and whose hearts are open to the unction of charity. Jesus Christ will not attain His perfect development, He will not reach the fullness of His years and *the maturity of man*, until the angel of the Lord shall have marked the seal of the living God upon the forehead of the last of the predestinate. Until that day the mystery of the Ascension will continue; it endures and increases each time a soul cooperates efficaciously with this divine structure and, emerging from a pure life, super-adds itself to form the celestial city, and "super-constructs" itself, as a living stone, in the eternal basilica of the saints.

Now, the mystical and collective body of Jesus Christ is modeled upon His individual body.

To bring about our redemption, Jesus Christ had no need to pass through a period of thirty-three years' duration. Scarcely after having been conceived He could have leapt forth from his mother's womb in dazzling splendor, and gone to astonish heaven by His triumphant and unexpected entry. He did not wish this.

To enter the sanctuary of His glory, the shortest and easiest way was not the one that most attracted His heart. He preferred to ascend to heaven by the bloody stages of His ignominies and searing pains. He desired that the whole of eternity and the omnipotence of His radiance should spring from the very scars of His wounds; and, so that there should not be a single part in the whole of His body that did not shed its special ray of beauty, He desired to give it over completely to pain and, from head to foot, to feel its cruel, murderous assaults.

What was accomplished in Jesus Christ individually must be continued in His collective, or mystical, body. Such is the law of indestructible solidarity, established between the head and the members. It would scarcely be fitting if the latter were to soar up into glory without passing through the transformations endured by the head. It cannot be granted that Jesus Christ wanted to open up two differing paths leading to heaven, one for Himself, rough and excruciating, the other for His followers, comfortable and strewn with roses and pleasures.

The apostle Paul teaches us that the Body of Jesus Christ is closely bound together in all its parts; all disparate elements are incompatible with its composition;[12] it is sublimely arranged, and unites in its structure that harmony and perfection which, one day, will produce an incomparable reflection of the sovereign glory and majesty.

Now, says St. Bernard, would it not be an unnatural medley, a strange, incongruous contrast, if a head crowned with thorns were joined to an exquisite limb, or a flesh scourged with lashes to a flesh reared in luxury and softness? *Pudeat sub capite spinato membrum esse delicatum.*

Ah, the sufferings and afflictions that break our hearts and draw harrowing cries from us, even to the point of making us shed tears of blood, are far from leaving Jesus Christ indifferent. No one has had more experience of them than He, or felt them more keenly; for He suffered their effects, and, in the Garden of Olives, as Isaiah says, personally bore our infirmities and carried our sorrows.[13]

However, would not a natural sense of pity that led Him to abolish suffering and dry up the source of our groans at every turn be, on His part, an illogicality, an act of blind, insensate tenderness? Could Jesus Christ derogate from the plan of His wisdom, abolishing the duties inherent in the nobility of our origin and in the glorious prerogatives bestowed upon us by Baptism?

As subjects and members of a divine head, our first duty is to follow our Master in all His ways and undergo all the vicissitudes He Himself endured. In order to deserve to be glorified with Him one day, it is imperative that, on this earth, we should suffer with Him: "But if we are children, we are heirs as well: heirs of God, heirs with Christ, if only we suffer with Him so as to be glorified with Him."[14] Just as, at the end of our lives, we shall begin to share in the Ascension of Jesus Christ, so conversely, in accordance with the mind of the apostle Paul, we must complete in ourselves, as long as our pilgrimage lasts, that which is lacking in the sufferings and anguish of His Passion: "In my own flesh I fill up what is lacking in the sufferings of Christ for the sake of His body, the Church."[15]

Indeed, the Passion of Jesus Christ did not end at Golgotha. At Golgotha, Christ endured pain in all its intensity. His pain was immense, as harsh as the waters of the ocean; it exceeded all measure, all comparison, all expression. But He did not endure pain in all its aspects and in all its forms. He was pierced by nails, but He was not burned over a slow fire. He saw His disciples flee, frightened by the scandal of the Cross; He did not experience that other kind of pain, less sharp perhaps, but more extensive and filled with groans and tears, of a mother who sees death tear a beloved child from her arms. He felt real pain, caused by the sins and malice of men, but He did not feel the imaginary and fanciful sorrows of a rebellious soul, which feeds on myths, and looks forward with delirious fervor to a future it is unable to attain, and cannot find contentment in duty and the austere practice of virtue.

Jesus Christ felt the disturbance and repentance due for *our* sins; He was not smitten with the remorse and disturbance that overwhelm the sinner as he recalls his *own* personal iniquities. All these kinds of pain, which Jesus Christ did not suffer in His own person, He must complete in His members. The sorrowful Passion of the Savior must be consummated in all ages and places. For, just as later, in heaven, Jesus Christ will be all and in all through His bliss and glory, so, in this world below until the end of time, He must be all and in all through his afflictions and agonies: "Christ is everything in all of you."[16]

These considerations explain the ardent thirst for suffering that consumed the saints, and the indescribable delights that made them thrill with joy at the stake and on the rack, when their flesh was being burned and their bones dislocated. The love of the cross, with which they felt inflamed, made them break forth in incomprehensible strains of joy.

St. Teresa, numb with cold, tormented by rheumatism, and overwhelmed by fatigue and austerities, yet transfixed in the inmost depths of her soul with the sword of the Seraphim, would exclaim, amidst her languor and distraction, "*Aut pati, aut mori* — either suffer or die."

St. Ignatius of Antioch, sentenced to be thrown to the wild beasts, was on his way to Rome to take part in the festive games ordered by the emperor Trajan. On the journey he was surrounded by soldiers, savage beasts with human faces, who roared about him like tigers and leopards. Amidst their vociferous clamor, and escorted by friends and disciples who pressed forward to receive his final greetings and injunctions from his own lips, he majestically raised his head, already shining with a celestial, superhuman glory, and, seized with a holy transport, full of hope in God, uttered words hitherto unknown to the human tongue:

May the fury of the beasts be my joy . . . Be not moved by a false compassion for me. If you act against me in this way, I shall be the first to excite the animals and urge them to devour me. Forgive me, my sons; I know what is good for me. I am now beginning to be a worthy disciple of Jesus Christ, and no longer seek visible things, so that I may the more swiftly and surely find Jesus Christ . . . Yes, come fire, cross, and beast, come the severing of my limbs and the breaking of my body.

And, on hearing the roar of the lions, he cried out, "I am the grain of Jesus Christ, I want to be ground by the teeth of the animals so that I may be served as pure bread at Christ's table."

⇝

To understand the sentiments that inspired the holy bishop and to grasp the meaning of the strange words that came forth from his lips, we must recall that Jesus Christ, in the Gospel, compares the Church and heaven to a granary, and the elect to a grain of wheat.

This similitude is the source of a whole doctrine and a lofty moral. The grain of wheat does not attain its complete perfection until it undergoes a threefold death, the *effect* of which is to raise it to a threefold dignity and threefold life.

Thus, as autumn draws to its close, the farmer plows the grain of wheat into the furrow; the grain dissolves and decomposes under the effect of the humidity, mingles with other sap, and disappears, so much so that, to the casual observer, it seems irretrievably lost; but, at the first rays of the spring sunshine, the grain that seemed forever extinct draws fecundity from its apparent death, and is reborn in the form of a rejuvenated, renewed ear of corn.

Yet this is not the final point in the perfection of this grain of wheat. It is called to a still more marvelous transfiguration, to attain which it must undergo a second death, by being placed beneath the millstone, crushed, and ground into powder. From this, bread will be made, and it will become the food and flesh of man, sharing in the dignity of his intellectual life.

Lastly, for this grain of wheat, there remains one dignity and perfection above all others. It will be placed upon the altar; the priest will pronounce over it the sacramental words of consecration; this time it will be utterly annihilated, right to the root of its substance; no trace or shadow of its original essence will remain; but, in exchange, this inert bread will cease to be base matter, and become the God whom the angels adore.

Thus it is only by undergoing a threefold death that man shakes off the coarse trappings of material nature that darken his vision and corrupt him, and emerges from the transitory and finite into the eternal and infinite.

In order to raise himself to the height of perfection and restore the faded image of God in him, it is necessary for him to die to his senses, his spirit, and his own judgments, and, finally, to immolate himself in his heart and die to his own affections.

Jesus Christ is the father of the family, and the great celestial harvester. From heaven, where He is seated, He sees the good seed on earth dissolve and perish in the fire of affliction. Far from feeling sorrow, His divine heart quivers and breaks out in transports of joy and benediction, exclaiming, "This is my wheat; it is being purified and transformed; it will be worthy to enter into my fullness; and then the most ardent desire of my heart will be fulfilled.

"O Father, all those whom Thou hast given to me are become *one* with me; they have been joined to my life by a union as intimate, an affinity as wonderful, as those which, from all the ears of corn ground under the same stone, form one bread, one single substance, *unus panis, unum corpus.*"[17]

Such is the magnificent result of suffering, which makes us die — for a moment — to ourselves, only to make us live a divine life in Jesus Christ that buries us in a dark and mournful shroud, only to cast into the depth of our being the seed of immortality and introduce us gently, by way of anticipation, into the state of glory and resurrection.

⁜

In order to alleviate our ills and lessen our trials in this valley of disappointments and misery, the merciful Savior desired to give us a sure pledge of His tenderness, and to offer us a guarantee of the heavenly bliss He is preparing for us. This guarantee, this real testimony of the Beatific Vision, which made the souls of the saints sigh with joy, is not the brilliant successes of this world, or temporal glory or happiness, but *trials and suffering.*

The saints did not aspire to any other goods, and wanted no other wages for their labors. If they met one of their friends they would say, "Come, brother. Our dwelling-place is in the hollow of rocks, where we sleep on wet ground and where there is no bed; we feed on wild herbs, and for our refreshment we have but the water of the springs; around our dwellings we hear the roars of wild beasts, which are, however, less fearsome than inhuman tyrants and barbarians, whose hatred and implacable ferocity pursue us unremittingly; but come without fear: there are indescribable joys and consolations, for there is indescribable suffering."

At first sight, language of this kind conflicts with reason, and upsets all our human judgments.

Yet the saints, living on these lofty heights of faith, saw the events of the present world and the destinies of mankind from a different point of view, and a different perspective. They judged the things of time by their relationship with those of eternity, and they understood the profound meaning of one of the most sublime sayings of Scripture: *Trial produces hope.*[18]

Without trial there is no hope.

Let us take the case of a man whose every desire on this earth is satisfied; he will be lulled to sleep amidst this fatal prosperity; he will seek no other life; thoughts of heaven will be powerless to detach him from the slime of material and tangible things; but, should an affront to honor or a cruel affliction press its sharp, painful barbs into that man, then, like a liquor compressed into a narrow vessel, his heart, annihilated and crushed beneath the weight of the misfortune, will at once seek a way out for itself; and not finding a single object to which it can turn for support or which assures it of relief, it breaks free from the ephemeral bonds of space and time, and casts its longing gaze upon the mountains of infinite mercy, whence flows all refreshment, light, and relief.

The patriarch Job, in his moving story, reveals to us the profound economy of suffering, and describes the abundant founts of joy wherein souls can drink deep amidst the most heart-rending sorrows.

Job had flocks and countless sheep; and these flocks were decimated by epidemics and plagues. Job had magnificent, sumptuous houses; and these houses were consumed by fire from heaven. He had children who were his pride and joy, united to one another by the most tender affection; and one day, while they were seated at a fraternal repast, they lost their lives, pitifully crushed beneath falling ruins. He had friends; and these, instead of comforting him, considered that he had been struck by the hand of heaven for some mysterious and unknown crime. He had a wife; and his wife, filled with disgust and horror, shunned the infection of his sores. Finally, he had a God, to whom he offered sacrifice seven times a day; and God withdrew from him the dew of heavenly consolation and seemed to have utterly abandoned him.

Certainly, never before had such a violent profusion of pain fallen upon the head of a victim.

At one moment despair seemed to overcome the soul of Job, and his whole strength appeared as if shackled.

> Life has become an unbearable burden for me [he exclaimed] . . . Perish the day on which I was born, the night when they said, "The child is a boy!" May that day be covered in darkness; may it not be counted among the months, nor be reckoned in the days of the year; may it remain enveloped in a fog and an endless gloom! . . . Why did I come forth from my mother's womb and not die before seeing the light of day? . . . Why was I rocked on the knee, and why did I feed at the breasts? Shall the fewness of my days be ended shortly? Is it worthy of your power to have an affection for a mere shadow? Suffer me, therefore, that I may lament my sorrow a little before I go, and return no more to a land that is dark and covered with the mist of death.[19]

Suddenly, Job ceased to complain, a transformation came over his person, his face lit up, his countenance and gaze became clear and radiant; the hymn of hope sprang from his lips, like a torrent of joy and peace. How lovely it is to see this Job, who had previously said to the worms, "My mother and my sister," and to rottenness, "Thou art my father," when, seated on his dunghill, like a conquering hero, he cries out, in the elation and enthusiasm of his faith, "*I know that my Redeemer lives, and that one day I shall see Him with my own eyes, and not those of another.*"[20]

Never had human lips given voice to a canticle more eloquent and divine. Does not this prime example of the sorely tried, crushed, and annihilated just man, reduced to the ultimate degree of moral and material want, gain compensation, in the twinkling of an eye, for all that he has suffered? He leaps to his feet and puts himself beyond the senses, beyond human nature and anything that human reason has dared to conceive. His prophetic gaze encompasses the span of the ages, and he knows intuitively the day when he will shake off the dust from his coffin – an intuition written in unshakable certainty, engraved in the depths of his heart: "*I know that my Redeemer lives, and that one day I shall see Him with my own eyes, and not those of another.*"

How right the admirable patriarch was, at the end of his beautiful canticle, to cry out again, "Oh, would that my words were written down! Would that they were inscribed in a record: that with an iron chisel and with lead they were cut in the rock forever!"[21] — probably so that they might be read by the generations to come, and fill with the same consolations the immense family of the distressed whose only nourishment is bitter bread and tears.

"*I know that my Redeemer lives.*" Oh, which of us has ever uttered those words of Job with lively faith without at once feeling their effects? Have not these words brought the dawn of calm amidst the deepest mourning?

Have they not filled our inmost soul with a higher, unknown joy, just when a tear of blood was slipping from our eyelids? Roaming about, bereft of everything, laid low in the wake of triumphant rapacity, we found in the inexhaustible fount of our woes reasons for love and trust. Far from becoming downcast and giving vent to impatience and grumbling, we blessed God, dimly perceiving the infinite depths of His mercy in the secrets of His justice.

If the Lord, we would say, gives happiness to His friends, what does He reserve for His servants? If, in His distribution of the good and the bad, He tips the scales in favor of those who offend and blaspheme Him, the reason is that, for His friends, all the wealth and all the empires of the world seem to Him too insignificant a present. Let us, then, rejoice in our tribulations, and let us measure our future greatness by our present affliction and by the severity of our trial.

In his homily on the bad rich man and on the poor Lazarus, St. John Chrysostom reveals to us the sublime philosophy of suffering. Paraphrasing the passage in St. Luke where the rich man, tormented with pain, beseeches Abraham to permit Lazarus to bring him a little drop of water on the tip of his finger to refresh his parched, burning tongue, he comments upon the words of Abraham as he says to the bad rich man, "My child, remember that you were well off in your lifetime, while Lazarus was in misery. Now he has found consolation here, but you have found torment. And that is not all. Between you and us there is fixed a great abyss, so that those who might wish to cross from here to you cannot do so, nor can anyone cross from your side to us."[22] From this reply of Abraham, St. John Chrysostom draws an admirable teaching.

The bad rich man, says Abraham, had received *good things in his life*. In what way? The great commentator explains it thus: the bad rich man, amidst his great wickedness and depravity, had, in this world, done only very little good acts. In the present life, no one can be absolutely bad; at times the most wicked malefactors comply with the moral law on certain points; amidst their dissipation, they maintain some remnants of natural virtue. As inhuman as they are, and slaves of their cupidity, nevertheless there are rare and exceptional circumstances when they consent to be just, merciful, and impartial.

Now, God, reserving to Himself the task of punishing them rigorously one day on account of their crimes, and, on the other hand, desiring, for the honor of His justice, to leave no good work unrewarded, however small and imperfect it may be, often, in this world, showers pleasures and temporal goods upon the wicked and ungodly. He grants them, as to the bad rich man, a dazzling, sumptuous life: exquisite and abundant food, soft carpets, a large number of flatterers and parasites, the glitter and pomp of all desirable pleasures. *Thus, the bad rich man had received his good things.*

Lazarus, by contrast, endowed with all the heavenly gifts and having attained the height of perfection by his heroic patience, had probably fallen through weakness into some slight faults. We may suppose that, at the sight of the ostentatious wealth of the man whose crumbs and surplus he had begged in vain, his heart had felt momentarily embittered and revolted. Perhaps his faith and trust had faltered and, to some extent, weakened.

Now, God, who intended to place Lazarus among His elect and crown him through all eternity, and who, on the other hand, will take the just to Himself only when they have been completely purified of every fault, desired in His hidden designs that Lazarus should undergo long and difficult trials during his earthly career, and sent him sores, sickness, poverty, abandonment, and contempt. Thus, when Lazarus reached the end of his life, he had paid his debt to justice; *he had received his woes.*

The bad rich man and the poor man each received their due from the divine Remunerator: the rich man — sensual pleasures, honors, and wealth in this life, but, in return, endless and unsparing punishments; the poor man — extreme trials and tribulations in this life, but, in compensation and at the end of the trial, unmixed and unchangeable happiness.

Thus it is that order and equality will one day be eternally restored, and that the conduct and hidden designs of Divine Providence will find their complete justification on the day of judgment.

Let these salutary considerations be engraved upon our minds, and then life's adversities will never succeed in disheartening us. Far from breaking out into complaints and grumbling against the harshness of God when His paternal hand strikes us, we shall bless

Him at all times, gratefully receiving the afflictions of the body and the cruel sorrows of the mind as the surest sign of His preference and tenderness.[23] *Quem enim diligit Dominus, castigat.*[24] Did not this thought open to the saints the source of the firmest and most exhilarating consolations?

If we recalled the course of life, we would readily acknowledge that it was on the occasion of desolations and great anguish that our heart felt most deeply moved by the action of God and that we seemed to come closer to heaven.

So, the world has forsaken us: we have seen our close friends — those who ate our bread and sat at our table — turn away to avoid meeting us, but immediately, the Lord, like a tender mother, clasped us more lovingly in His arms: *Dominus autem assumpsit me.*[25]

Gloomy death has taken away from you a son, whom, like the mother of Tobias, you called "the apple of our eyes, the staff of our old age, the comfort of our life";[26] or, still young, you are driven to separate yourself from the world, to mourn your premature widowhood. Yet, have you not obtained supernatural and glorious visions? Have your eyes not had a sort of glimpse of the heavenly future? In the light of divine contemplation you have perceived those dear, lamented beings, enjoying repose in a better world. In your inmost soul, you have heard them say: *We are happy, and we await you.*

This pain, by crushing us in its grip, tears us away from the love of present things; it is the sword that cuts through the clouds, and half-opens other prospects for us, by raising us up to higher hopes. In the fire of tribulation, all the wealth and all the goods for which we yearned so ardently appear as they really are, and become in our eyes mere smoke and empty shadows. Human life seems to us nothing more than a *moment* in the words of St. Paul. But that moment is a fruitful bud; fertilized by our tears, it will be changed into an immeasurable weight of glory.[27]

Oh, let us, finally, cease to accuse the Creator of harshness and injustice. If God puts us to the test and removes what we hold dear, if He makes the bitter dregs of disappointments and every heart-rending pain trickle down upon us, it is by no means, the apostle Paul assures us, in order to rob us, but in order the sooner and the more strikingly to re-clothe us in immortality, as in an outer garment.

Let us take the case of a great artist who wants to make a statue. Beneath his hand he has a piece of coarse, shapeless marble; he takes up his chisel, strikes vigorously and mercilessly and makes the stone split into fragments, until the idea that inspires him is reflected in the lines of the statue and pours out that grace and majesty which will be the admiration of the world.

God does the same: holding in His paternal hand the chisel of mortification, He cuts into the quick of our affections. He lets Himself be moved neither by our groans nor by our cries. Mercilessly, He cuts off those links, those friends, that health or reputation, which were as living parts of ourselves. In the fire of pain, He absorbs the attachments, the secret and invisible links that draw us into love of perishable, earthly things. He melts them down, violently eliminating all that remains in us of dross, human alloy, and sensual affections, in order that our souls, thus spiritualized, may become like a well-prepared canvas, on which the rays of divine goodness will, one day, succeed in leaving their imprint: "that what is mortal may be absorbed by life."[28]

Before being subjected to this purification, man resembles tainted, murky sand; cast into the crucible of suffering, he becomes refined, and is now a limpid, transparent crystal, where the substantial glory of God, no longer encountering any obstacle, can flow freely, like a river without bed or banks: then God will be all and in all things. Just as the images of the sun, of palaces, and of trees are reflected, with their shapes and sharpness of outline, in the mirror of a clear river, so the perfections of the divine attributes will be reflected on all the elect without losing their immutable indivisibility. We shall be enveloped in the radiant light of the divine life; it will then be the end, the consummation, the age when time has run its course, the reign of stability and repose, the happy reign to which creatures look forward, and for which they call with such groaning, like a mother in labor who calls to be delivered, and expresses her suffering in plaintive cries and long, painful sighs.[29]

Such was the hope of the incomparable mother of the Maccabees. She had seen the tender bodies of her six young children being torn apart and mangled before her eyes by the sword of an inhuman tyrant. She stood, bathed in their blood, amidst their mutilated and scattered limbs. Yet in spirit she entered the tabernacles of eternal joy and the abode of calm and sweet transports. All the horror that this fearful sight aroused in her, all the grief and cruel pangs inflicted upon her maternal heart, faded before the radiance of her hope, and she encouraged the youngest son, saying, "Son, have pity on me, who carried you in the womb for nine months, nursed you for three years, brought you up, educated and supported you to your present age. I beg you, child, to look at the heavens and the earth and see all that is in them; then you will know that God did not make them out of existing things; and in the same way the human race came into existence. Do not be afraid of this executioner, but be worthy of your brothers and accept death, so that in the time of mercy I may receive you again with them."[30]

＠

Let us conclude with a final point.

In the time of the Emperor Theodosius, there was a woman in the East whom the fires of youth and the taste of pleasure, along with the perils of poverty, had plunged into the disorders of a life of corruption and licentiousness.

This woman's name was Mary. She was converted sincerely to God, and the Church has crowned her and raised her to the honors of the altar under the name of St. Mary of Egypt.

She betook herself one day to Jerusalem, for the great solemnities of the feast of the Exaltation of the Holy Cross. Suddenly she thought she heard a voice, coming from the banks of the Jordan and the depths of the wilderness, call out to her: *Come over to us, and you will find innocence and repose.*

Without waiting, although the day was beginning to decline, she hastened to run to the place indicated; but the water was deep, the land around the river abandoned and deserted, and the voice, becoming more insistent, called out unceasingly, in a ringing tone: *Come over to us, and you will find innocence and repose.*

While she wandered about here and there, consumed with anxiety and fretting in expectation, she saw, coming toward her on the shore, a man of the desert, one of those great hermits, with a face transfigured by penance and the voice and gaze of a wonder-worker.

He cast his cloak upon the river, and beckoned to the Egyptian woman to stand on it.

Then in the distance, beneath the clear light of the moon, one might have seen the resplendent courtesan walking dry shod over the water, fleeing what she had loved, and departing in silence, far from the noise of men, to throw her soul upon God, immersed in the ecstatic joys of prayer and in the chaste and austere delights of penance and immolation.

She lived for many years in the desert, visited by angels, immersed in the transports of divine contemplation and drinking deeply of the foretastes of paradise.

The End of the Present World

Then, one Good Friday, far from the sight of men, on the banks of a steep, wild torrent, attended solely by God and His angels, she died. We may believe that her final blessing, and the prayer of her agony, were for the hermit who led her into the wilderness and, in making her love suffering, opened her soul to the treasures of peace and cleared the way for her along the path of everlasting bliss.

May we, too, gentle reader, deserve a similar favor from you. In offering these conferences for your meditation, we have no other purpose than to turn souls away from the limited concerns of time, and raise them up to the thought and desire of the good to come. These modest pages, which we submit to your indulgence, are but the ration of deliverance, a compass intended to guide our lives through the numerous perils of this world — in short, a skiff that may help us reach the shores of heaven.

This book is a mere reminiscence and feeble echo of our apostolate. However, just as, when autumn is ending and the trees shed their fading leaves and become bare, it often happens that a lingering passerby gathers up these disregarded leaves in spring in order to build a bed or put together a shelter for himself, so, likewise, it often happens that the seed which has not taken root in the field of the head of the household is later blown away by the gusts and whirlwinds of the storm, beyond deserts and oceans, and, after a period of many years, raises up forests and ripens crops. Similarly, these studies on our last ends may have the power to lift souls up to meditate upon the things to come, or, at the very least, our feeble words will be for some sluggish Christians a seed blessed by God, which will bear fruit when the time of the harvest has come. How fortunate if they should have the power to help us through the stormy and uncertain course of our pilgrimage, and enable us more surely to reach the eternal meeting-place which awaits us, one day, in the Heart of Christ!

If we dared flatter you with this hope, gentle reader, we would bid you goodbye — until we meet again! The time is near when the hour of the final departure will strike, when the celestial Spouse, whom we have loved and served, will say to us: *Cross, come to me and enter into bliss and eternal repose!*

⌒

Notes

[1] Rom. 8:22.

[2] Cf. Isa. 53:3.

[3] "In the Cross is salvation; in the Cross is life; in the Cross is protection against our enemies; in the Cross is infusion of heavenly sweetness; in the Cross is strength of mind; in the Cross is joy of spirit; in the Cross is excellence of virtue; in the Cross is perfection of holiness. There is no salvation of soul, nor hope of eternal life, save in the Cross" (Thomas à Kempis, *Imitation of Christ*).

[4] Roman Breviary, *lectio* for the feast of St. Andrew.

[5] Cf. Luke 24:26.

[6] St. Thomas Aquinas, *Summa Theologica*, II, Q. 25, a. 6.

[7] Cf. Prov.12:21 in the Douay-Rheims edition of the Bible. Horace expressed the same thought in the well-known line, *Si fractus labatur orbis, impavidum ferient ruinae:* "If the whole world disintegrated, the fragments would strike him unperturbed."

[8] Rom. 6:19.

[9] If you do not do penance, our Lord has said, you will all perish. It is of the nature of penance to be proportionate to the fault. If amends are not made spontaneously in this world, they will be made without fail in the next. The Church does indeed offer us the merits of the saints and indulgences as repayment for the debts we have contracted; but indulgences imply penance. They are a substitution and a means of reversibility. Just as in the social body, by virtue of the solidarity that unites the various members, one subject may discharge another of part or the whole of his penalty by himself undergoing the punishment deserved, so the Church, which has assiduously gathered in her

treasuries the blood of Jesus Christ and the satisfaction offered by the saints, applies them to us, by means of conditions easy to fulfill, in order to come to our aid in our weakness during this life and to spare us cruel torments after death; but this doctrine, which is none other than that one man is able *morally to represent* another man, exemplifies even more forcefully the truth that there is no remission of sins but by blood.

[10] Heb. 13:8.

[11] Eph. 4:4.

[12] Cf. Eph. 4:16: "Through Him the whole body grows, and with the proper functioning of the members joined firmly together by each supporting ligament, builds itself up in love."

[13] Isa. 53:4.

[14] Rom. 8:17.

[15] Col. 1:24.

[16] Col. 3:11.

[17] "One bread, one body." Cf. 1 Cor. 10:17: "Because the loaf of bread is one, we, many though we are, are one body, for we all partake of the one loaf."

[18] Rom. 5:3-4: "But not only that — we even boast of our afflictions! We know that affliction makes for endurance, and endurance for tested virtue, and tested virtue for hope."

[19] Cf. Job 3.

[20] Cf. Job 19:25, 27.

[21] Job 19:23-24.

[22] Luke 16:23-26.

[23] St. Ambrose held that a life free of trials was a certain sign of divine malediction, and said, "I should not wish to live for a single night under the roof of a man who has never suffered." Another saint said, "Why attach any importance to afflictions? Temporal life is but a transition. A whole lifetime of pain in this world is of no more consequence than an uncomfortable night in a bad hostelry."

[24] Heb.12:6: "For whom the Lord loves, He disciplines; He scourges every son He receives."

25 Cf. Ps. 27:10: "Though my father and mother forsake me, yet will the Lord receive me."

26 Tob. 10:4.

27 2 Cor. 4:17: "The present burden of our trial is light enough, and earns for us an eternal weight of glory beyond all comparison."

28 Cf. 2 Corinthians 5:4: "While we live in our present tent we groan; we are weighed down because we do not wish to be stripped naked but rather to have the heavenly dwelling envelop us, so that what is mortal may be absorbed by life."

29 Rom. 8:22: "Yes, we know that all creation groans and is in agony even until now."

30 2 Macc. 7:27-29.

Charles-Marie-Antoine Arminjon

Charles-Marie-Antoine Arminjon was born in 1824 in Chambéry, France. In 1842, he entered the Jesuit novitiate at Melan, near Sallanches. He was ordained a priest in 1849 and was assigned by his superiors to the task of preaching.

He left the Jesuits in 1859, with the full approval of the Society, became a professor at the major seminary of Chambéry, was appointed honorary canon of Chambéry and Aosta, then "apostolic missionary" by a decree from Rome in 1863.

Soon afterward, he left his post at the major seminary of Chambéry to devote himself entirely to his preaching. Hundreds of letters from bishops, archbishops, and cardinals, preserved by his family, show the esteem in which he was held. Every diocese in France received him in turn, many of them several times. He preached innumerable retreats and Lenten and Advent sermons, which, correspondents say, had a profound influence on his time.

He was a friend of Cardinal Lavigerie and, at his request, preached at Algiers, and of Cardinal Mermilliod, Bishop of Geneva, whom he assisted in the stimulus which that great prelate gave to the Church of Geneva in very difficult times.

He was also renowned for his conversational talent. He had many guests during the summer in his house at Apremont, near

The End of the Present World

Chambéry, and his courteous and frequent hospitality was attested by numerous letters from his visitors.

He possessed a singularly powerful personality, many facets of which are still spoken of in Savoy.

He died in 1885 in Chambéry.

In the last days of his life, a friend who was surprised to find that he was so much afraid of purgatory — "after such widespread services" — asked him, "What have you to reproach yourself with?" "Ah, vainglory!" he replied somewhat mournfully.

Sophia Institute

Sophia Institute is a nonprofit institution that seeks to nurture the spiritual, moral, and cultural life of souls and to spread the Gospel of Christ in conformity with the authentic teachings of the Roman Catholic Church.

Sophia Institute Press fulfills this mission by offering translations, reprints, and new publications that afford readers a rich source of the enduring wisdom of mankind.

Sophia Institute also operates two popular online Catholic resources: CrisisMagazine.com and CatholicExchange.com.

Crisis Magazine provides insightful cultural analysis that arms readers with the arguments necessary for navigating the ideological and theological minefields of the day. *Catholic Exchange* provides world news from a Catholic perspective as well as daily devotionals and articles that will help you to grow in holiness and live a life consistent with the teachings of the Church.

In 2013, Sophia Institute launched Sophia Institute for Teachers to renew and rebuild Catholic culture through service to Catholic education. With the goal of nurturing the spiritual, moral, and cultural life of souls, and an abiding respect for the role and work of teachers, we strive to provide materials and programs that are at once enlightening to the mind and ennobling to the heart; faithful and complete, as well as useful and practical.

Sophia Institute gratefully recognizes the Solidarity Association for preserving and encouraging the growth of our apostolate over the course of many years. Without their generous and timely support, this book would not be in your hands.

www.SophiaInstitute.com
www.CatholicExchange.com
www.CrisisMagazine.com
www.SophiaInstituteforTeachers.org

Sophia Institute Press® is a registered trademark of Sophia Institute.
Sophia Institute is a tax-exempt institution as defined by the
Internal Revenue Code, Section 501(c)(3). Tax I.D. 22-2548708.